Anthony Crosland

Kevin Jefferys

Published in Great Britain 2000
by Politico's Publishing
8 Artillery Row
Westminster
London
SW1P 1RZ

Tel 020 7931 0090
Fax 020 7828 8111
Email publishing@politicos.co.uk
Website http://www.politicos.co.uk/publishing

First published by Richard Cohen Books 1999

First published in paperback 2000

A catalogue record of this book is available from the British Library.

ISBN 1 902301 71 4

Printed and bound in Great Britain

Contents

Illustrations

Preface and Acknowledgements

Why write a life of Tony Crosland? This is not an 'official' or authorised biography. Early on in my research for the book, Crosland's widow, Susan Crosland, wrote to say that she had nothing to add to her account of her late husband's life and career, published five years after his death, but that she was not opposed to 'free enterprise'. This biography is therefore the product of 'free enterprise', and is based primarily on the collection of Crosland papers at the London School of Economics, on published diaries and newspaper material, on Crosland's own extensive writings, and on the recollections of many of his friends, colleagues – and critics. My own interest, as a historian specialising in post-war politics, was prompted initially by the forcefulness and clarity with which Crosland appeared to set out the case for socialism as equality. This was reinforced, increasingly as the project went on, by the belief that some of the most interesting figures in British politics – with due respect to Prime Ministers such as Clement Attlee and John Major – are those who never quite reach the top of the 'greasy pole'.

In preparing a work of this sort, there are inevitably numerous people and institutions whose assistance should be acknowledged. For willingness in sharing with me their memories of Crosland – whether in taped interviews, telephone conversations or correspondence – I am grateful to the following: Dougie Atkins, Professor Wilfred Beckerman, the Rt Hon. Tony Benn MP, Major Neil Boys, Dr David Butler, Sir Michael Butler, the late Sir Alec Cairncross, Lord Callaghan, John Cole, Dr Alex Comfort, the Rt Hon. Edmund Dell, the late Lord Donaldson, Bruce Douglas-Mann, Gwyneth Dunwoody MP, General Sir Anthony Farrar-Hockley, the Rt Hon. Michael Foot, Lord Gladwin, Professor A. H. Halsey, Lord Hattersley, Lord Healey, Anthony Howard, the late Lord Howell, Lord Jenkins of Hillhead, Lord Jenkins of Putney, Dick Leonard, Professor David Marquand, Lord Merlyn-Rees, Bob Mitchell, the Rt Hon. Gordon Oakes, Sir Angus Ogilvy, Lord Owen, Christopher

Price, Lord Rodgers, Ted Rowlands MP, Lord Shore, Lord Taverne, Alan Watkins, Baroness Williams, and the late Lord Wyatt.

Thanks must go to archivists and library assistants at the following institutions: the Bodleian Library, Oxford; the BBC Written Archives Centre, Reading; Churchill College, Cambridge; the Brotherton Library, Leeds University; the London School of Economics; the National Museum of Labour History, Manchester; the National Newspaper Library, Colindale; Nuffield College, Oxford; and the Public Record Office, Kew.

The project was fortunate in receiving financial assistance from two funding bodies. The Nuffield Foundation made possible the employment of a part-time research assistant in 1996, and during 1997-8 the British Academy funded a period of research leave which greatly facilitated the completion of the typescript.

I am very grateful for the help I received on the project from Simon Rippingale, and from his successor as research assistant, Nick Patch. Both proved to be extremely efficient and good-natured in tracking down material on Crosland; without their help, the task would have been altogether more daunting. Among colleagues and fellow historians in the academic world, I would like to thank Harry Bennett, Martin Francis, Robert Hole, Rodney Lowe, Kenneth Morgan, Neil Riddell, Nick Smart and Richard Williams.

A special word of thanks must go to Dick Leonard, for suggesting amendments and allowing me to see an advance copy of his edited collection *Crosland and New Labour*; to Peter Hennessy for reading the text; to Ruth Winstone as editor; and to Richard Cohen and the staff at Metro Books for taking on and backing the project. My greatest debt, however, is to my wife Sue, who has been an unfailing source of support, encouragement and guidance throughout. As is customary, while thanking all the above for their help, it should be added that any responsibility for errors or questionable judgements in what follows rests with me alone.

Kevin Jefferys
January 1999

For permission to use copyright material, the author and publishers would like to thank: Tony Benn MP, the British Library of Political and Economic Science (Dalton diaries), Lord Callaghan, Susan Crosland, Gwyneth Dunwoody MP, Michael Foot (Crossman diaries), Lord Hattersley, David Higham Associates Ltd (Crosland's published and unpublished work), Anthony Howard, Lord Jenkins, Lord Owen, Professor Ben Pimlott and Baroness Williams.

The author and publishers are grateful to the following for permission to reproduce photographs: private collection of Susan Crosland (photo numbers 1,2,3); private collection of Lord Jenkins of Hillhead (4); Olga Davenport (5); International News Photos (6); Zoltan Glass (7); *Evening World* (8); Keystone (9); Neil Libbert, *Observer* (10); L. Parton, County Hall, Grimsby (11); *Evening Standard* (12); *Daily Express* (13); *Sunday Times* (14); Hulton Getty (15); *Daily Mail* (16); Central Press (17). Thanks also to Telegraph Group Ltd and Express Newspapers for permission to reproduce cartoons.

Introduction

Anthony Crosland was one of the foremost figures in the post-war Labour Party. His socialism took shape in his days as a student at Oxford in the late 1930s and while he was in uniform during the Second World War. In 1950 he became Labour MP for South Gloucestershire, and in 1956 he published the book upon which his reputation was primarily based, *The Future of Socialism*. This was the most important product of the 'revisionist' thinking in Labour ranks during the 1950s; indeed for many it remains the finest work produced on the centre-left of British politics since the war. Crosland lost his South Gloucestershire seat in 1955, but four years later he returned to parliament as MP for Grimsby, the constituency he represented for the rest of his life. After the unexpected death of his friend and patron, the party leader Hugh Gaitskell, Crosland held a series of middle-ranking posts in the Labour administrations of the 1960s and 1970s. Following the resignation of Harold Wilson in 1976, he was appointed Foreign Secretary by the new Prime Minister, James Callaghan. It was widely anticipated that he would go on to hold the post that he had long coveted – that of Chancellor of the Exchequer. Some commentators speculated that his forceful personality might help carry him eventually to the leadership of the party, but at the height of his powers Crosland died suddenly after a severe stroke in February 1977, aged only 58.

Since his death, there have broadly speaking been three categories of writing about Tony Crosland. Each of these gives important insights into his life and career, though my starting point is that each also has its limitations, and that as a result scope remains for a fresh effort to understand Crosland's full significance as a politician and intellectual. The first category comprises those who are generally sympathetic to the case for revisionism as developed in *The Future of Socialism* and in later works such as *The Conservative Enemy* (1962) and *Socialism Now* (1974). Some of his friends and colleagues have argued that Crosland's legacy was a positive one: even after his death, his unique brand of 'radical humanitarianism', his commitment to equality and liberty, continued to offer to the world of British politics 'the seeds of a rich harvest'.[1] Several political scientists and economists have also underlined what they regard as the unrivalled seriousness of Crosland's efforts to understand and influence the development of post-war British society.[2] Aside from a sympathetic tone, these two interpretations – whether by friends or writers from the academic world – are united by their focus on Crosland's major written works. As a result, we get little sense of the unfolding of his life, or of his complex, multi-layered personality. Inevitably, as one reviewer has observed, he often emerges as a kind of 'machine for the production of ideas, not as a human being, with ambitions to pursue and rivals to discomfit, buffeted and disorientated by changing circumstances'.[3]

A second category of writing on Crosland is more critical of his legacy. All political careers, Enoch Powell once said, end in tragedy, and this maxim has been applied by other contemporaries who worked with or were at some stage close to Crosland. John Vaizey, for example, places him alongside other leading post-war politicians whose talents were never fulfilled, such as Gaitskell, Iain Macleod and Edward Boyle. They were all, Vaizey argues, part of a generation that helped to shape modern social democracy, but which failed to tackle the fundamental economic and social problems of the age. The unexpected deaths of all four while relatively young was symbolic of 'the tragedy of a generation of high ideals and poor results'.[4] This line of thinking was much influenced by the difficulties confronting Jim Callaghan's government after 1976, culminating in Labour's crushing defeat at the hands of Mrs Thatcher in 1979. The harshest con-clusions were reached by some of those whose disillusionment with Labour was such that they helped to form the breakaway Social Democratic Party (SDP) in the early 1980s. One, David Marquand, writes that Crosland ended his career with his 'project in ruins', his tragedy being to reach the top at a time when the assumptions on which his thinking was based – rapid economic growth, redistri-bution of wealth, high taxation and social spending – were becoming untenable. When the IMF crisis of 1976 arose, Crosland was intellectually defenceless, claims Marquand. 'Croslandism', like the broader 'Labourism' of Callaghan, had come 'to the end of its tether'.[5]

The personal tragedy of a life cut short has been vividly described in the third category of writing – the biography *Tony Crosland*, written by his second wife and published in 1982. Susan Crosland's book, hitherto the only full-length study of her husband, has been described as a dazzling account of his character and as a 'loving memorial'. Without falling into self-indulgence or hagiography, she paints an 'intimate, affectionate portrait', so that by the time she movingly recounts the final days of his life, 'one really feels one knows her Tony'.[6] The biography has also been lauded for providing a window on the workings of the Wilson and Callaghan governments, and a snap-shot of the pressures of ministerial life. But for all its merits Mrs Crosland's book had its critics. The emphasis is heavily weighted towards Crosland's later career; his books and ideas are only briefly summarised; and key set-piece events such as the IMF crisis are not located within the broader context of Labour politics and the crisis facing Callaghan's government. Nor has much attempt been made to analyse her husband's legacy or to look at him through the eyes of those within Labour's ranks who disagreed with him, whether on the Bevanite/Bennite left or the Jenkinsite right. The result, it has been suggested, is a compelling personal memoir, but 'the substance of Crosland's career is only hinted at, the serious issues it raises never faced'.[7]

This new biography aims to remedy some of the shortcomings of earlier work. It attempts to strike a balance between Crosland's political ideas, and the context in which they developed, and the highs and lows of a political career in which there were many 'ambitions to pursue and rivals to discomfit'. It hopes to distinguish 'Croslandism' from 'revisionism' and 'social democracy', terms which are often used interchangeably, and also to give due weight to the various phases of Crosland's life: from his flamboyant early years and protracted rise in Labour politics, through to his contribution as a minister after 1964, culminating in his short spell at the Foreign Office.

Crosland described himself as a 'political animal', and while the focus here is on his public work, the chapters dealing with his early life in particular seek to integrate the twists and turns of his career with an account of his colourful private life. But Crosland's significance can only be properly understood against the backdrop of evolving and contentious debates in Labour ranks over revisionism versus fundamentalist socialism; over attitudes towards Europe; and over management of the economy. This biography tries to tackle the 'serious issues' which Crosland's career raises. What was his legacy?

Did he die a disappointed man, with his 'project in ruins', or should Croslandism be credited with important and lasting successes?

Many judgements on Crosland's career were made in the period of Labour turmoil during and after 1979. Twenty years on, with Thatcherism come and gone, and with 'New Labour' in power under Tony Blair, it is easier to assess Crosland's place as a historical figure, without the immediate din of battle that accompanied the resurgence of the Labour left on the one hand and the formation of the SDP on the other. Unlike the majority of previous studies, this book is written by someone who never knew Crosland. It is therefore, inevitably, a more detached account. I can only know Crosland through the eyes of his friends, rivals and contemporaries, including Gaitskell, Wilson, Callaghan and other crucial figures such as Hugh Dalton, Roy Jenkins and Tony Benn. To his admirers he was a man of immense presence and attraction, blessed in his early life with looks which left some men and women 'glazed with servile adoration'. To his detractors, as Ben Pimlott has written, he was arrogant, languid and self-indulgent.[8] If Crosland appears as a sympathetic figure and his voice comes across the loudest, this does not mean that the author has set out to be uncritical or unfair to those with whom Crosland worked, by downplaying 'supporting actors' to the advantage of the central character. But the likes of Gaitskell, Wilson and Callaghan, Dalton, Jenkins and Benn have their own chroniclers and advocates; this is Crosland's story.

1

Highgate and Oxford, 1918–40

What made Anthony Crosland a socialist? At first sight, his comfortable middle-class background makes this a difficult question to answer. Several key figures in the history of the Labour Party as it emerged in the first half of the twentieth century came from affluent backgrounds; but they were the exceptions in a movement founded to further the interests of the industrial working class. Crosland's father Joseph, born in Lancashire during the 1870s, won a scholarship from Manchester Grammar School to Trinity College, Oxford and went on to become a leading civil servant at the War Office in Whitehall. His mother Jessie was the daughter of F. E. Raven, governor of the Royal Naval College at Greenwich. After receiving an MA from Bedford College in London, she became a lecturer at Westfield College and wrote extensively on French medieval literature, publishing her first book in 1907. The Croslands' first child, Richard, died at the age of four, and it was not until much later, at the end of the First World War, that another son was born. Jessie was sent away by her doctor, from the family home in London to Sussex, and Charles Anthony Raven Crosland was born on 29 August 1918 at St Leonards-on-Sea. The family enjoyed a standard of living characteristic of the professional middle classes between the wars, occupying at first a large semi-detached house in the expanding suburb of Golders Green. Young Anthony and his two elder sisters were attended to by nannies, a cook and a couple of female servants who lived at the top of the three-storey house, which also had a tennis court in the garden.

As Labour developed from a pressure group into a serious national political force, forming short-lived governments in 1924 and 1929, its small but influential band of middle-class adherents increased, drawn towards the left by a mixture of idealism and ambition. Tony Crosland's identification with the party of the workers can be partly understood in these terms; but it was also strongly affected by one overriding feature of his home life. On both sides, his family had for several generations belonged to the Plymouth Brethren, a fervent nonconformist sect which emerged in Dublin during the 1820s in reaction to the alleged failings of the established church. By the time the first permanent settlement was established in Plymouth, the Brethren was splintering into smaller groups, usually termed either Open or Exclusive, according to the degree to which they permitted fellowship among those regarded as doctrinally unsound. What characterised all Brethren was a simplicity of religious practice. There was no formal organisation – ordained ministry was regarded as a pernicious influence – and no prescribed set of rituals. Instead the Brethren would meet in homes or local halls, where any man with the gift for 'searching the scriptures' could expound upon the meaning of biblical passages.

Along with this approach to religion went a distinctive lifestyle. Crosland's parents, who had met through the Exclusive Brethren, lived by clear if unwritten guidelines. On Sundays the reading of newspapers was forbidden and mornings and evenings were taken up with prayer and instruction meetings which the children were always expected to attend. Crosland's father, a tall, impeccably dressed man, would allow drink in moderation at home but not smoking. Cinema was permitted, though not theatre-going or listening to the wireless; when the latter was allowed much later, the set was usually covered on Sundays, sometimes with a Bible placed on top. Pleasure for its own sake was eschewed. Love of others was to be resisted, for it was felt that surrender to physical and emotional pleasures might militate against the working of the Holy Spirit.[1] By the time of his adolescence Anthony Crosland was beginning to react against the confines of this upbringing. Indeed many of those who came to know him later emphasised how his personality and especially his strong hedonist streak was shaped by rebellion against his background.

Yet it would be wrong to overlook how much he assimilated from these early years. The ultra-individualism of the Brethren, a willingness to speak one's mind without fear or favour, the puritanical work ethic, and an intense dislike of formality and ritual – all this was to be characteristic of Crosland in later life, along with his mother's concern for rigorous scholarship and his father's interest in public affairs. Above all, he inherited from his parents the Brethren conviction that all were equal in God's eyes. It was this which led Joseph Crosland to turn down a knighthood, fearing that it would set him too much apart from other Brethren. An ingrained egalitarianism, however much this seemed at odds with the family's material circumstances, was a potent force from an early age, and stayed with Crosland despite new political experiences and influences.

One of these formative influences was school. Crosland's parents doted on their son and were distraught when, aged four, he, like his brother, became seriously ill. A year of Anthony's childhood was spent at a Swiss sanatorium, after which he returned restored to health as a noisy five-year-old. Concern to have the boy close at hand may have influenced the decision to educate him locally at Highgate, an independent school catering mostly for children from middle-class families in north London. The school originated in the sixteenth century, and had struggled for many years serving poor scholars in what was then a country district until given a new lease of life in the nineteenth century. In the early years of the twentieth century its formidable headmaster, Dr J. A. C. Johnston, built upon the school's reputation in classics by leading the way in the development of science and technology. The number of boys rose from about 500 before the First World War to over 650 by the time Crosland arrived at the age of twelve, holding a Senior Foundation Scholarship, in January 1931. Johnston was an alarming figure who would sweep through the school, his gown billowing, 'like a ship in full sail'. While many of the boys were in awe, fellow staff were less impressed, resenting Johnston's autocratic style and suspecting that he was expanding the school for financial advantage, enjoying a reputation as the best paid headmaster in the country.[2]

As a weekly boarder, Crosland was able to spend weekends with his parents, who in the early 1930s moved from Golders Green to a more spacious property in Sheldon Avenue, Highgate. Before long there were some tell-tale signs of adolescent rebellion. Crosland brought home one of his school-friends, Alan Neale, the son of a local shopkeeper, and the boys were caught with cigarettes, much to the annoyance of Joseph Crosland, who around this time suffered a minor stroke.[3] At school, recalled Neale – who in later life became a prominent civil servant – Crosland became a rebel, occasionally leading other boys into trouble.

The headmaster was known for taking an unusual attitude towards the sexual education of his charges, and had once written to parents informing them that it was school policy for masters to use a few well-chosen words to give 'the kind of instruction which boys are otherwise apt to acquire in imperfect and unfortunate ways,

3

sometimes from polluted sources'.[4] A dim view was taken of some of Crosland's exploits. He was occasionally beaten and a letter sent to Mr Crosland complaining about his erring son. On Sundays, during the family routine of visits to meeting houses in Highgate, the erring son would frequently be found sitting apart with other older boys who were reluctant to take part in proceedings, entertaining themselves by making up rude verses to the hymns.

These were difficult years for a teenager growing tall, with darkening hair, and struggling with new emotions. He was close to his parents but, as he became more independent, he found it difficult to follow them down the same devotional path. Instead of engaging in open conflict, he began to channel his energies in new directions. Almost as a substitute for the faith he could not bring himself to believe in, Crosland turned with fervour to the world of politics. His father was open about his own Liberal sympathies but, in accordance with Brethren tradition, did not cast a vote at elections. In the belief that there was little point in discussing politics without voting, Crosland rapidly developed pronounced views of his own, joining the Left Book Club and avidly reading its growing stream of publications.

His sympathy for left-wing ideas was influenced not only by his Brethren upbringing but also by the depression of the 1930s, which saw mass unemployment accompanied by searing poverty for thousands of working-class families. Crosland later dated his introduction to politics to a time when, in his teens, he stayed with miners in the depressed areas of South Wales, working alongside some of the unemployed men on their allotments. Though not on the scale of George Orwell's journeyings in *The Road to Wigan Pier*, it was nevertheless an important experience for an impressionable adolescent, and Crosland proudly kept a piece of coal on the mantelpiece at home for some time afterwards.[5]

In the late summer of 1935, just after Crosland's seventeenth birthday, Joseph Crosland, having recently retired from the civil service at the age of sixty, had a further massive stroke and died. For the three children this was a devastating blow; for Anthony Crosland it might well explain how he was influenced by more than one 'father figure' in his early career. His mother requested that he become a day-pupil so that he would be near at hand, and for some months he would often retreat to his room to read monthly volumes from the Left Book Club and listen to a radio which had been smuggled into the house. As a sixth-former he did, however, develop an increasingly high profile at Highgate. He was a strong athlete and won the school mile championship, in a time of just over five minutes; he became head of his house and excelled in debate at the Sixth Form Society. Several masters later remembered him as one of their most outstanding prospects, and despite his father's death it was assumed he would go on to university.

Each year a small number of boys from Highgate regularly secured places at Oxford and by the summer of 1937 Crosland had obtained his Higher School Certificate and won an open scholarship to take a four-year course in classics at Trinity, where he was to be accompanied by friends such as Alan Neale. His mother was proud that the Trinity connection would be maintained, but being ambitious for her son, she was furiously jealous that another pupil walked away with most awards on school prize-giving day.[6]

While the curriculum at Highgate was much concerned with the ancient world, Crosland's attention was turning to the modern, and some of his sixth-form essays give an early indication of ideas he was to develop later. His dislike of formal ritual was evident when he asked provocatively what right one had to complain that fascism compelled men to wear uniform while 'we writhe under the equally oppressive tyranny which compels us to attend a dinner uncomfortably clad in the uniform of the boiled shirt?' Crosland's dislike of formal dress became obsessive, causing him particular problems when he became Foreign Secretary. His burgeoning concern for the underdog was expressed in an essay on the theme of 'Bread for the Masses, Cake for the Few'. And the strident libertarianism of his more mature writings could be detected when he wrote that man was born to live 'his individual spiritual life to the full', even if this meant defying the conventions of the day.

> Perhaps the unit which is most open to tyranny of thought is the family; it is only natural for a father to wish his sons to hold the opinions which in his view are the right ones, and for him to educate them in those opinions until they are of an age to think for themselves. But directly this age is reached, it is imperative that they do form their own conclusions without bias or prejudice; and the parent has no right to object if these conclusions happen to differ from his own . . . We may be certain that it is the duty of each of us to be eccentric in thought, and not to conform weakly to the ideas of age, class and country . . . Non-conformity must be regarded as a virtue, as a proof of a bold and independent spirit.

His teacher felt he had pushed his case for 'liberty of personality' a bit far, adding that the writer was clearly 'dissatisfied with the age'.[7]

This dissatisfaction 'with the age' became more pronounced when in the autumn of 1937 Crosland went up to Oxford. While his left-wing sympathies originated at home and at school, it was at university that these sympathies were consolidated and took root. Oxford opened up exciting new possibilities, having established itself over several generations as a nursery for aspiring politicians. In particular, the university was a training ground for would-be Labour leaders: Oxford's contribution to Labour Cabinets was to rise from 15 per cent in 1924, to 28 per cent in 1945-51 and 41 per cent in 1964-70. The three politicians who led the party successively after the Second World War – Clement Attlee, Hugh Gaitskell and Harold Wilson – were all Oxford men. Under the auspices of G. D. H. Cole, the 'godfather of inter-war Oxford socialism', a romantic figure who acted as a magnet for many young idealists, the Labour Club – reflecting developments nationally – had steadily overtaken the Liberal Party in attracting student support. By the time Crosland arrived, the Labour Club had the largest active membership of any undergraduate association, often attracting to meetings more than half its 750 members. As a leading light in the Oxford branch of the British Universities' League of Nations Society Crosland also came across prominent politicians of the day, organising talks for the likes of Ellen Wilkinson, the fiery Labour MP for Jarrow and later Minister of Education. And it was well known that a glittering political career beckoned for those who shone in debate at the Oxford Union – a collection of red-brick neo-Gothic buildings in the city centre, with its formal Westminster-style proceedings, some of which were highly publicised in national newspapers.[8]

In making the most of Oxford's promise, Crosland gravitated towards several like-minded friends who helped to influence his outlook. The Labour Club provided a congenial meeting place for undergraduates from middle-class backgrounds attracted by its detachment from the aristocratic atmosphere associated with other parts of the university. Trinity, chosen primarily because Crosland's father had been there, was dominated by upper-class 'bloods' who, as one of them confessed, were 'cliquey, extremely limited in our horizon . . . and in no way dissatisfied about it'.[9] Crosland was soon part of a small group of left-wing sympathisers, most of them scholars or products of grammar schools. One of his closest friends came to be Philip Williams, studying history at Trinity, who taught him much about the Labour movement. Throughout their time as undergraduates, the two would avidly discuss politics and their latest reading. In Crosland's case it included most of the leading socialist theoreticians of the day. He read John Strachey's work *A Programme for Progress* twice, looking for ways in which the left in Britain might challenge the entrenched authority of the Conservative-dominated National Government. In addition to the work of British writers such as Cole and Douglas Jay, he also turned for the first time in depth to the revolutionary teachings of Marx and Engels, finding much with which to agree.[10]

Though Oxford widened his horizons, it was the deepening international crisis in the late 1930s which did most to develop Crosland's socialism. For idealistic young undergraduates alarmed by the rise of fascism, communism was an attractive alternative. In the early 1930s the Oxford Union had passed a motion that the Russian experiment in socialism was a success that deserved support, and in 1935 the Communist Party was formally admitted to the Labour Club, making up for the remainder of the decade almost half of the membership, including students Denis Healey and Iris Murdoch. When Crosland arrived in 1937, Republican resistance to General Franco in Spain further enhanced sympathy inside the Labour Club for communism. Rumours of Stalin's purges in Russia were brushed aside. Denis Healey recalled that Crosland 'considered himself a Marxist, but could not nerve himself to join the Communist Party outright', despite frequent discussions on this point with Philip Williams.[11] Crosland's support for radical solutions at a time of acute crisis was not in doubt. Several years later he reminisced how he and others would frequently troop off to the Labour Club, 'pausing only to spit through the Trinity gate as we went past. We lived in a world of pamphlets, meetings, marches, demonstrations – and very exhilarating it was. Marxism . . . had the same appeal to young people as Christianity. . . . Both the unemployed at home and the Spanish Republicans abroad had an obvious emotional appeal, and the result was an attractively single-minded enthusiasm for which I today feel a very strong nostalgia.'[12]

For his first two years at Trinity, Crosland found himself, while not formally a communist, supporting many of their policy positions. In September 1938 a by-election was held in Oxford at a time when undergraduate feeling was running strongly against the Munich agreement and the policy of appeasement under Chamberlain. The Master of Balliol, A. D. Lindsay, was urged to stand as an Independent Progressive candidate in order to maximise non–Tory support in a Conservative constituency. When he agreed, under-graduate communists – with Crosland's backing – flooded a meeting of the Oxford City Labour Party and helped produce a majority compelling the official Labour candidate to stand down. Lindsay was eventually defeated by Quintin Hogg, but student enthusiasm in the campaign contributed to a much reduced majority. In the late summer of 1939 many of the communist faithful were shocked by the Stalin–Hitler pact. Crosland was among those who defended the move, even after the formal outbreak of war in September 1939, which saw Poland rapidly carved up by Germany and Russia. During a Union debate in November, he claimed that the pact had been made in self-defence, after the Poles had refused to allow Russian troops on their soil. According to a report in the *Oxford Magazine*, it was Crosland's best Union speech so far, showing himself adept at dealing with interruptions.[13] Russia's invasion of Finland over the winter came as a further shock to communist sympathisers in Britain, but when the Finnish ambassador came to Oxford to plead for aid for his country in January 1940, Crosland organised a demonstration, using a banner that read 'Hands Off Russia'.[14]

By this time he had become a well-known figure in Oxford, treasurer of the Union though defeated for the post of president by Robin Edmonds, later to become a diplomat and writer. Crosland's reputation was based on his personality as much as his politics. As a reward for winning a place at Oxford, Mrs Crosland had bought her son a second-hand sports car, which he drove to Germany in the summer of 1937, determined to see the Black Forest while the frontiers remained open. Susan Crosland writes that he experienced his first brief romance there with an American girl. But much of his adolescence had been spent in the company of boys, and Woodrow Wyatt – who became a friend and fellow Labour MP after the war – claimed in his memoirs that Crosland's 'homosexual side' was in the ascendant at Oxford.[15] As with Hugh Gaitskell, who had been at Oxford in the 1920s, homo-eroticism featured in the intense friend-ships formed at university. One of Crosland's friends expressed disappointment that Crosland was 'denying satisfaction' to a Fellow of All Souls who might be a useful political contact. Other friends claim that Crosland in his youth was attractive to both men and women and was almost certainly bisexual.[16] All were agreed that at over six feet tall he cut a dashing figure. This was confirmed by Roy Jenkins, who went up to Balliol in the autumn of 1938:

> He was a very impressive undergraduate, showing every sign of intellectual and social self-assurance. He was immensely good-looking, and even in those days rather elegant. He wore a long camel-hair overcoat, and drove a powerful low MG known as the Red Menace. I, like many of his near-contemporaries, admired him from afar and was rather intimidated. Then, one winter's evening a few months after the outbreak of war, he came to my rooms, probably on some minor point of Labour Club business, and having settled it, remained uncertainly on the threshold, talking, but neither sitting down nor departing for nearly two hours. His character was more ambivalent than I had thought, but also more engaging.[17]

Thus began one of the most important relationships in the life of both men over the next thirty years. As we shall see, it was what Jenkins calls a 'fluctuating friendship' and one which was to have significant consequences for the development of the Labour Party. In the early months of 1940 the two were continually seen together at the Union and the Labour Club. Jenkins in many ways deferred to Crosland, both on grounds of age and reputation, playfully calling him 'the great but temperamental Tony, the complex character, the difficult boy who would suddenly erect a façade of sulkiness'.[18] In alliance, they brought about a decisive shift in Oxford's under-graduate politics. In the bitterly cold winter of 1940, Crosland wrote that he found it increasingly implausible that the Red Army was fighting to liberate the Finnish people from a reactionary govern-ment. This together with the communist anti-war line in the West, became a breaking point, especially as Crosland was convinced that communist thinking exaggerated the militancy of the working class; he could see few signs of the Labour Party in Britain being out-flanked by the Communst Party even in wartime.[19] As members of the executive committee of the Labour Club, Crosland, Jenkins and Ian Durham, a mature trade-union student, began to question the orthodox line. During the Easter vacation the three dissidents decided to split the club and, 'thinking ourselves very bold', went ahead when the opportunity came up in late April.[20]

By 182 to 108, the club voted to continue outright opposition to the war, but the minority led by Crosland broke away to form their own Democratic Socialist Club, loyal to national Labour policy in backing resistance to Hitler. With G. D. H. Cole as president, Crosland became the first chairman of the new group and Jenkins – accepting his role as junior partner – the first treasurer. Within days membership was growing rapidly and eclipsing what Jenkins called the 'bunkered rump' of the old club. The Democratic Socialist Club re-affiliated directly to Labour nationally, and even received – in the form of a typically terse one-liner – support from the party leader, Attlee.[21] These events reinforced Crosland's friendship not only with Roy Jenkins but also with his parents, particularly Arthur Jenkins, the MP for Pontypool, and also Attlee's Parliamentary Private Secretary (PPS). Crosland became a regular visitor to the Pontypool home of the Jenkins family, and he developed great respect for Arthur as a Labour MP solidly rooted in the working-class life of the valleys. After the death of his own father, Crosland found something of a surrogate in Arthur Jenkins, who was soon giving him advice which Crosland might have resented coming from anyone else. Oxford, Crosland was told, was a first-rate place for a socialist, but if he wanted to be more than a 'sort of neighbour' to the movement, he would also need to gain experience of the 'real world'.[22]

During the early summer of 1940, events moved with alarming rapidity in the 'real world'. Neville Chamberlain was forced to resign and was replaced by Winston Churchill, Prime Minister of a coalition which provided seats in the Cabinet for Attlee and his senior Labour colleagues. Hitler's violation and defeat of France left Britain isolated and facing the prospect of invasion; the phoney war was over. These events made a deep impression upon Crosland and under the strong influence of Arthur Jenkins, Crosland turned more to orthodox Labour. Writing to Philip Williams, he said that 'Papa' [Jenkins] was 'practically neurotic on the subject of the Left, with a very marked anti middle-class intellectual bias'. But the impact on Crosland of, in his own words, 'Transport House propaganda' was evident in his attacks on efforts to remove Chamberlain altogether from his senior post in the coalition. To antagonise the Chamberlainite Tories, who remained numerically the strongest force in the House of Commons, would be 'pure folly'. And the idea that people would fight more willingly if the old guard was removed amounted to 'pure idealistic balls' by 'fatuous cranks'. Over the summer of 1940 Crosland began to disdain left-wing journals which attacked Labour for not pulling its weight in the coalition. Such criticism, he told Williams, was playing straight into Hitler's hands by threatening to create a sullen force of defeatists. Deeply impressed by the patriotism of George Orwell's tract 'The Lion and the Unicorn', he told his friend that he felt so strongly that he wanted to 'murder everyone who writes in the *N[ew] S[tatesman]* + *Tribune*', saying that the 'vapourings' of the Left intellectuals had 'nothing to do with practical politics'.[23]

In later life Crosland was less than honest when he claimed that in his early years it never occurred to him to find a home other than in the Labour Party. Once he had come into the Labour fold, however, he was to remain a strong party man for the rest of his life, with a depth of conviction which was later compared to Evelyn Waugh's approach to the Roman Catholic Church: he was not born to it and was inclined to take it a bit too seriously, with an exaggerated respect for humble monks and nuns.[24] So it was with Crosland. Yet his home background, combined with the twin circumstances of depression and fascism, made his brand of middle-class socialism far from an aberration. It had much to do, he said – speaking for himself as well as for others – with 'the emotional need for a God, a religion, a Heaven, for something to believe in that transcends the individual'.[25] The evolution of Crosland's politics still had some way to go, but in the late summer of 1940 he had other things on his mind. At the outbreak of war university undergraduates, unless they volunteered, were allowed to continue with their studies, but as hostilities intensified the government switched course and Crosland was called up for military service around his twenty-second birthday. It was time to get experience of the 'real world'.

2

Socialist Subaltern, 1940–43

Crosland's war started slowly. After a short period of training in the ranks, he became an officer in the Royal Welch Fusiliers, but was to see no active service until 1943. After the comforts of Oxford, military life came as a great shock. Shortly after being sent for training to Northwich in Cheshire, he wrote to tell his mother that his time was initially spent on anti-gas training and preliminary rifle drill, though his company had not yet been issued with rifles. The work was physically hard, for example twelve hours on duty as a cook-house orderly, washing up 'hundreds of filthy dishes, moving coal about and goodness knows what'. He made a special note of certain annoying features of army routine: having to ensure that his uniform was constantly tidy and ready for use, and spending an excessive amount of time standing on parade 'waiting for the next thing to happen'.[1] He was also disappointed to discover that the class system was alive and well in war-time. He was soon commenting on how 'farcical' interviews for officer material were, based as they were not on current ability but on past education and whether one was the 'right type'. This had obvious effects on the 'toiling masses – who are, of course, as securely shut out' from positions of authority as ever, whatever might be said about war-time democratisation.[2]

Crosland's sense of dislocation was compounded by his failure to team up with any kindred spirits. While he was a 'likely fellow' for a commission by virtue of his background, his natural irreverence placed him temperamentally on the side of the ranks. It was not long before he was punished for using the term comrade rather than corporal, and it greatly irked him having to salute the officers, most of whom he felt were either 'stupid disciplinarians who think you will beat Hitler by folding up overcoats in a particularly baffling way . . . or else they are just amiable old dodderers'. Few of them, he believed, had woken up to the fact that they were not back in the days of the Great War. By contrast the Londoners he met intrigued

12

him: 'Most of the company here is purely working class + I have found no one I know. These Cockneys, although rather coarse + loud voiced in the mass, are astonishingly decent + generous when taken singly + altogether I get along exceedingly well with them.'[3] But while he developed a regard for London factory workers he could hardly become 'one of them', and this added to the strain of being catapulted into an alien environment.

He told Philip Williams that he was 'gradually ferreting out the relative intelligentsia of the place' and spent time in their company at weekends. In particular he made one friend who shared his more cynical and detached view of 'stupid spit-and-polish'. It was only this, he claimed, which helped to overcome that 'awful feeling of loneliness and spiritual isolation which nearly killed me during the first few days here'.[4]

It was in order to counteract the tedium of army life that he bombarded Williams with his thoughts on coalition politics. He admitted that he had been naive about Churchill being won over to socialist policies overnight, but in line with his thinking since the spring he defended the party against left-wing charges that it had been duped and was not pulling its weight. With Ernest Bevin and Herbert Morrison in powerful positions, he felt progressive policies were at last being implemented. He was equally harsh on communist 'wishful thinkers' who claimed that people would only fight if offered radical war aims. He found that working-class Londoners were inspired by vague patriotism rather than deeply felt anti-fascism, and that they were profoundly non-political. When Crosland heard that Lord Beaverbrook had joined the war Cabinet – to him 'sensational news' – he found that no one on his camp was in the slightest bit interested. Visits to Pontypool to visit the Jenkins family, sometimes when Roy was away, advanced his acceptance of the party line. On one occasion he met Attlee. He found the Labour leader 'fantastically unimpressive' at first sight, but extremely good on detailed policies. 'Clem', he reassured Philip Williams, 'is still very much of a socialist', and was much more intelligently aware of the government's shortcomings than the 'idiots who write leading articles in the N[ew] S[tatesman]'.[5]

As the weeks went on, Crosland complained of life becoming 'incredibly boring and tedious'. If anything his contempt for the professional officers had grown, for he found them not only inept but insensitive to the feelings of civilian conscripts, so making life ten times worse than necessary and 'morale so low as to be, in my opinion, positively dangerous'. It was therefore with great relief that Crosland finally got through his interview for a commission; though he had a momentary fright when he heard that officers thought he held 'extreme political views'. At least this meant moving on, in his case to an officer training camp at Barmouth in North Wales at the end of 1940. Here his initial delight at having a comfortable bed in a seaside boarding house after months under canvas gave way to resentment that 'petty discipline' was worse than elsewhere in the army, 'since the theory still pertains that unthinking obedience . . . is the backbone of a successful Army'.[6] Crosland knew that his cynical streak found little favour among his 'earnest-minded' fellow trainees, and he admitted that he made a bad impression by failing to remove his pipe from his mouth during a mock bayonet charge. It came as a surprise to him in the new year when, halfway through his four-month course, he was graded twenty-ninth out of 105 cadets. One of his regular reports concluded he was intelligent, but inclined to be casual about his work and 'generally too critical'.[7]

Another means for Crosland to stave off boredom was to read works of political economy as avidly as possible. The writings of Lucien Laurat in particular made him more critical of the Marxist ideas he had absorbed before the war. He realised that his friend Philip Williams was now more radical than he, reversing their university roles: 'you look upon me as a hopelessly complacent Transport House stooge, while I regard you as a permanently nagging Left intellectual, carried away by catch-phrases & determined (à la N.S.) to read the worst into everything'.[8] Crosland conceded that his 'excessive loyalty' to the party was being reinforced by the apathy and ignorance about politics that he found all around him. Whereas the ranks regarded Westminster as a remote world, among officers he was amazed at how often his views earned him the label of communist. He admitted that his ideas were still evolving and that he was 'bang in the middle of the steady process of intellectual flux that started when my faith in the CP and 100% Marxism was shattered, & continued when my brief period of faith in the Left Intellectuals and 85% Marxism was shattered. Where I shall end Heaven knows – I am still moving.'[9] In the meantime, he found an outlet for his energies in writing several essays on the shortcomings of officer training, some of which appeared anonymously in journals signed by a 'Socialist Subaltern'.[10]

In the spring of 1941 Crosland was commissioned at Wrexham, the regimental home of the Royal Welch Fusiliers. He later said he joined this regiment because he liked its emblem, though writing to his mother – who had been evacuated from Highgate to north Oxford – he revealed that he wanted to be stationed somewhere in the 'west', as Arthur Jenkins knew many people in the area and 'this might easily be useful at a later date'.[11] In the first clear indication that he hoped to embark on a political career, Crosland made efforts to get to see the national agent of the Labour Party, though without any success. In Wrexham he began a two-month course in signals training, making friends with another young subaltern, David Graves – son of the writer Robert Graves – who shared a dislike for the officers in higher ranks, many of whom came from upper-middle-class backgrounds. Fortunately the commanding officer was sympathetic to Crosland, enabling him to pass his signals course. Others on the camp were not amused when he complained that the professional officers had magnificent mess facilities while subalterns were given a dingy annex despite paying the same mess rate. Crosland was promptly posted. For the remainder of 1941 and into 1942 he found himself on home defence duty in the 10th Battalion of the Fusiliers, mostly at locations in Sussex and Dorset. He continued to have brushes with higher authority over his robust views, and his brashness even came through in reports on his truck driving – 'very good, though inclined to drive too fast'.[12]

Wider events in the war inevitably influenced Crosland's political thinking. In the summer of 1941, Britain finally acquired a major ally with Hitler's invasion of the Soviet Union. Relief in Britain was such that attitudes to 'Uncle Joe' switched overnight from hostility to enthusiasm. Crosland felt that 'realists' for whom Stalin's policy was dictated by power politics had been proved 'abundantly right' by this turn of events, and added that as he feared, 'the intellectual Left has once again become quite naively pro-Russian'. He felt that many on the left failed to distinguish between the need for aid and an alliance with Russia in the short-term and the caution required towards a speedy Red Army victory that would allow Stalin to dominate mainland Europe. His distrust of the '100% Marxism'-model of the Soviet Union continued to grow as it had done since the break to form the Oxford Democratic Socialist Club. He found among some of the Welsh working-class troops based in Sussex an even greater level of political apathy than among Londoners he met in Cheshire,

15

confirming his view that Marxism made a completely unrealistic assessment of revolutionary consciousness. After reading a new biography of Engels, he was convinced that there was little to learn from the whole corpus of writings by Marx and Engels, save for a view of history as a dynamic process revolving around class change. All other theories were, 'to me, largely valueless today'. As well as hoping to enter parliament, Crosland was already entertaining thoughts of writings major works of political theory. 'I am engaged on a great revision of Marxism & will certainly emerge as the modern Bernstein', he told Philip Williams in a reference to the great German 'revisionist' of the late nineteenth century.[13]

In the early months of 1942 Crosland, like many, was downcast by a series of military humiliations for the British. With the entry of the USA into the war in late 1941, hopes had been raised that the Allied powers might begin to seize the initiative. Instead British forces suffered defeats in North Africa and the Far East, with Churchill admitting that the Japanese capture of Singapore was one of the gravest reverses in British military history. Crosland wrote that he was 'very depressed'. He was uncertain where to place the blame, saying that either the Government and the Chiefs of Staff were incompetent or that journalists 'ought to be shot' for their exaggeration of the situation. In May 1942 political news added to the gloom. Under the terms of an electoral truce, the main parties agreed not to put up candidates against each other at parliamentary by-elections. One consequence was that independent candidates, campaigning on the need for greater efficiency in the war effort, began to score notable by-election successes, especially in Conservative-held seats. For Crosland this confirmed 'our worst prognostications', namely that the Tories were losing ground electorally which Labour was not at liberty to make up. The result was a 'vague Utopian radicalism, un-canalised and anti-Party, potentially anti-democratic, Fascist, Communist or anything else'. There was little that Labour could do, he lamented, since breaking the electoral truce might only lead to a premature break-up of the coalition and an election that Churchill was certain to win. The mood of popular unrest, he suggested, would only be dispelled by military success: 'the only hope lies in a change in our fortunes of war'.[14]

His hopes were borne out with the 'turn of the tide' late in 1942, when British victory at El Alamein and Russian resistance at

Stalingrad finally saw German forces pushed on to the defensive on several fronts. By then, Crosland had made an important personal decision. His company was addressed by General 'Boy' Browning, seeking volunteers for a Parachute Brigade as part of the newly formed 1st Airborne Division. It was well known that the casualty rate for paratroops was high: aside from dangers of unreliable parachutes and the possibility of being shot in the air or attacked by civilians on landing, the German SS by repute took few airborne prisoners. In spite of this, only one officer of Crosland's company failed to volunteer; ironically he was killed on another exercise in a matter of weeks.[15] Crosland thus joined the renamed 6th Battalion Royal Welsh Parachute Regiment, and was soon writing to Philip Williams:

> After the 7th jump I am granted the triple privilege of a parachute badge on my right sleeve, 2/- a day extra danger pay, and a liability to be shot for cowardice if I ever afterwards refuse to jump. How I came to volunteer for this I am still not quite sure. This time a year ago I should have regarded any such prospect with the utmost distaste and repugnance: in fact my one aim in life was to remain as blatant a "base wallah" as possible. But a second year of Army life . . . has changed the ratio of my interests: politics have gone down to just that extent that military affairs have gone up. . . . This combination of growing interest in, and self-identification with, the Army was psychologically the determining factor, tho' mixed with many others – vanity, bravado, browned-off-ness with the infantry, a feeling of the utter absurdity of spending 3 years of one's life in khaki without even getting an interesting psychological experience for one's pains, etc, etc, etc. So there it is. So far I have no regrets, as I am still enjoying the pleasant experience of having something new and interesting to look forward to.[16]

Over the winter of 1942-3 hard training remained the order of the day. From a base on Salisbury Plain, Crosland wrote to tell his mother that he had to endure 25-mile marches, but had reached double figures with his parachute jumps. After admitting that his first had been more terrifying than he could imagine – with that 'awful 3 seconds plunging helpless through the air' before the chute opened – he felt that each successive jump became slightly more bearable, though it was never likely to become 'positively enjoyable'.[17] These private fears were not obvious to those around him. One new friend from this period, Dougie Atkins, from Barry in South Wales, noted that Crosland would often make a flippant remark – a characteristic often noted in later life – that would make the other paratroops laugh as they prepared to jump.

Once the novelty of his new challenge began to wear off, Crosland's interest in coalition politics resurfaced. He was encouraged to see the annual conference of the Trades Union Congress (TUC) continuing their ban on Communist Party delegates and constructing the type of national policy he felt essential if Labour was ever to come to power; as for the call of TUC leaders for the Allies to launch a second front, he remarked that he would try to be inspired by their 'high-minded desire for my premature decease'. By early 1943 he was also pleased by the reception given to the Beveridge Report, which he felt would boost Labour's chances of success when 'clean politics' returned at the end of the war.[18] The main distraction from intense training, however, came in the form of a relationship formed while on leave with an an eighteen-year-old girl back from school in Canada, Pat Horsfield. According to Susan Crosland, this was his first experience of falling 'overwhelmingly in love'.[19] But the chances of romance blossoming were not good. The Parachute Regiment was posted to North Africa; Tony Crosland was at last off to war.

3

On Active Service, 1943-5

In North Africa the monotony of waiting for action continued. The difference for Crosland and his colleagues was that training posed different challenges, such as surviving in the desert for long periods without much water. He told Philip Williams that he was suffering from heat and flies, and that Philip's recent reference to a minor internal ailment 'provoked a loud rumble of sympathy from my stomach, which at the moment is as mobile as a Panzer Division'.[1] The prospect of encountering real Panzer divisions came closer in the summer of 1943. On 9 July an airborne invasion of Sicily by the Allies began. Members of Crosland's regiment were on the runway ready to go when told that the first drop ahead of them had been so successful they were not needed. Two months later, Italy surrendered. As the Germans moved south to withstand Allied advances, it was decided that some of the Parachute Brigade should be used as part of a sea-borne invasion of the Italian mainland. Crosland's ship successfully made the difficult entry into the harbour at Taranto, the Italian navy's main base. His friends on an accompanying vessel were less lucky, and went down under heavy German fire. It was Crosland's first experience of the terrible realities of war. He admitted that much of his 'schoolboy enthusiasm for fighting' had been dented by 'the sight and stench of those washed up bodies, horribly and grotesquely swollen, limbs distorted, flesh decomposing: and the grim business of . . . burying them in a huge communal pit, trying hard not to be sick'.[2]

After this baptism of fire, Crosland experienced little face-to-face combat with the enemy for several months. His contact with those at home became less frequent, though he did – in defiance of the rules – keep a diary which set out his thoughts on life in Italian communities often devastated and torn between rival armies and factions. In September he recorded that he had been promoted to captain and appointed adjutant after a colleague was evacuated to North Africa. He was, he said, 'slightly shamefaced' after his various protestations about methods of promotion.[3] Crosland's main disputes were on the political front, notably when he became embroiled in a bitter controversy between the 'popular and reactionary' elements in a small town. Crosland sided with socialists who were attempting to organise a concert in the face of resistance from the local mayor: 'I was loudly cheered as a champion of the people's rights.' The next day the mayor made a formal complaint that a British captain had called him a fascist; Crosland's superior officer 'pacified the little shit and sent him away'.[4] He regarded the incident as indicative of the political implications of the Italian campaign. With fascism defeated in Italy it was ironic, he wrote, that the British Army did business with semi- or ex-fascist authorities. British and American commanders such as Eisenhower were too 'politically ignorant' to see what damage was being caused by not favouring progressive forces. 'And all the bloody little Fascists in our mess, so far from taking any interest in and encouraging our professed war aims, adopt an equally superior & domineering attitude to all Wops, Wogs, Frogs & others unlucky enough not to be born British.'[5]

In December 1943 Crosland experienced sustained close combat with the enemy for the first time. His battalion was pinned down defending a salient with Germans on two sides. He recorded in his diary the awful short gap between whistle and bomb-blast as he came under persistent shelling; the sight of a colleague with his head blown off; the immense psychological test which meant that it was not 'the physical specimens or the battle drill kings who come out best'; the enormous sense of relief among the troops as they were finally relieved by another unit.[6]

The day after returning from the front line Crosland was surprised to discover that the major in charge was removing him from his post as adjutant and making him instead an intelligence officer, with the possibility of demotion in rank from captain later, saying he didn't think Crosland was sufficiently 'regimental'. In speaking his mind and openly giving superior officers unwelcome advice, Crosland was always liable to make enemies, and he refused to swallow his medicine without protesting:

The real reason is two-fold: (a) we are temperamentally complete opposites. (b) I make no attempt to hide my disagreement with him, and in general appear too casual and lackadaisical — in other words, not enough bullshit and hypocrisy. As I don't consider this an adequate reason for reversion, I ask for an interview with the Brigadier. I tell him frankly why I think Roderick has made the change, and ask for a transfer to another Bn. He says wait until Col. Barlow comes back, and meanwhile he will guarantee that there shall be no change in rank. I agree unwillingly.[7]

Within days Crosland was embarked upon what one colleague called the 'highlight of his operational service'.[8] As an intelligence officer, his task was to discover the deployment of German troops on the route to the German HQ on top of the citadel at Monte Cassino. Together with an interpreter, he found himself crossing a succession of steep ravines and gulleys in the pitch dark, constantly fearful of running into a German patrol. This was followed by ten bitterly cold daylight hours in a small trench close to houses they believed to be German-occupied, followed by a 'nightmare' return journey, fighting against mud, raging thirst and 'the almost unconquerable impulse to sleep'.[9] Well into the new year Crosland remained in severe danger, experiencing dive-bombing by the enemy and encountering several German patrols – 'we killed two and captured two, which raised our morale not a little'. He also noted his paradoxical attitude to the enemy: hating them bitterly whilst under attack, but finding that once close up as prisoners they become 'human beings, for whom one feels sympathy'.[10] In February 1944 he described to Philip Williams the 'fruitless battle of patrols and constant shelling' amidst terrible destruction in the war zone. He said it was not physical discomfort which caused most stress; the real problem was the 'cumulative strain on the nerves' after months in the line without a break. Although his only injury so far was a scar on the cheek, 'I find I like it less and less as it goes on.'[11]

At the same time Crosland told his friend that, engaged in the fight for survival, he had become cut off from news of home and the fate of contemporaries. He had heard, however, that Roy Jenkins – working at Bletchley deciphering German codes – was suffering from jaundice, and Crosland mischievously suggested that Roy thinks 'this should entitle him not only to a wound stripe, but also the 1939-43 Star, and I believe he is making representations to this effect in the highest quarter'.[12] Crosland's source for this information was probably a recent letter from Arthur Jenkins in which he also said that the Labour Party was looking for new parliamentary candidates, especially those in the forces, and that he had given a good account to Transport House. Crosland turned out to be one of the youngest on the official list of service candidates circulated to constituency parties in anticipation of a post-war election. Aware that he had no entitlement to leave which might enable him to attend selection conferences, Crosland was unable to summon up much enthusiasm. 'Anyway', he told Williams, 'I expect to be fighting in the swamps of Burma long after the next three General Elections have been fought.'

After serving at or near the front line for a year, Crosland was sent to Egypt on a five-week course in aerial photography interpretation, with a view to improving allied location of enemy positions in Italy. The relief of being out of imminent physical danger and the architectural pleasures of Cairo were tempered by being in the company of those he despised. 'God save me from the British bourgeoisie', he wrote, with their 'imbecile myths and illusions', for example their contempt for foreigners, their dislike of Labour ('who caused the war by forcing disarmament on an unwilling country'), and their belief that all civilian workers were living a life of luxury at home. Among his circle of officers, about 60 per cent appeared to swallow these myths 'emotionally and passionately', and his own attempts to offer different views met with 'scant success'. His spirits were lifted, however, by hearing that there was a good chance of being selected as Labour candidate for Henley, which he knew was a 'hopeless Tory seat' but one which offered the prospect of political experience and a better seat later on.[13] Before long it was time to return – with mixed feelings – to his battalion in the Italian mountains. He reflected that he loved the opportunity to read and relax, but felt increasingly anxious about being away from comrades. 'My personality', he wrote, 'is dual: one wants a V.C., the other a quiet cultured life.'[14]

In August 1944, after initially being told he would not be taking part, Crosland was chosen as one of a team to be parachuted into the south of France to prevent the Germans counter-attacking against Allied forces landing by sea. On 11 August his diary spoke of his fury at the prospect of being left behind, 'mainly from vanity: the shame of never having parachuted into action, the feeling of being thought a base wallah'. Once he was included, the old training fears reasserted themselves: 'in order of terror, first of jumping, secondly of flak, third of the Germans, fourth of the fatigue & discomfort'.[15] By the end of the month Crosland was back in Italy reflecting on the most bizarre fortnight of his life, which had begun with fear and trembling and ended with 'a night of pure pleasure at liberated Cannes'. He sustained a minor injury in landing after a problem with his chute, and was met with enemy fire on the ground. Fortunately after that the operation went better than expected: within days Allied armoured cars were linking up with the paratroops. Crosland with a few others borrowed jeeps and made their way into Cannes, where they were met by wildly cheering crowds; hence his only operational parachute jump ended with 'a holiday on the Riveria'.[16] In later years it would give him great amusement to recall how his contribution to the D-Day assault had been to drop on the millionaires' playground in the south of France.[17]

Returning to Italy, from where the attack on southern France had been launched, Crosland told Philip Williams that he recently received two unwelcome letters on the same day. One told him of the engagement of 'his beloved' to a Canadian pilot; the second, from Henley Labour Party, informed him that, tired of waiting for a reply, they had chosen another candidate for the election. When on top of that he heard from 'Willy [Williams]at his gloomiest', it was not surprising that Crosland replied in some despair, saying he felt he had 'no hope' of selection for a seat while abroad, whereas other potential candidates were now managing to secure home leave. Compensation came in the form of six weeks at a base near Rome and even managing forty-eight hours in Florence, 'most of which I spent in the bath'. Only a spell at the front, he said, made him fully appreciate 'what unadulterated bliss it can be to be clean, warm + well-fed'.[18] By the beginning of 1945 Crosland was no longer in the front line. As a photographic interpreter with 6 Armoured Division his task was to provide information about landing sites, though on at least one occasion several parachutists got soaking wet after landing in rivers, and teased Crosland about his competence. One colleague recalls him at this time as relaxed and waiting for the end of the war, joining in with football matches at the Divisional HQ while trying to convert the soldiers to socialism.[19]

There were more distressing scenes to be witnessed, however, before the war came to an end. As General Alexander's army drove north in the spring of 1945, Crosland completed a journey that had taken him almost the entire length of Italy. He found himself on the Italian–Austrian border coming into contact with a bewildering array of displaced and dislocated refugees and troops: among them Chetniks, Croats, Slovenes, Cossacks, and Ukrainians. On the day before Germany surrendered he came across 35,000 Cossacks hoping to be received by the British as refugees. 'A sad never-ending procession, huge packs or cases on their backs, bent double beneath the weight. What they did for food, God knows, but if one gave them a cigarette they were so grateful it made one ashamed.'[20] By 11 May he was commenting on the 'utter chaos' in the region, with the troops left to deal with political and diplomatic problems among a mass of people on the move: civilians, German troops ordered to stay put, plus 'large and varied Quisling forces'. For the most part he felt this was done with common sense, but soon he was reporting on the 'most nauseating and cold-blooded act of war I have ever taken part in', acting upon orders (which caused great resentment among officers) to return thousands of anti–Tito fighters to Yugoslavia. The sight of one group being shepherded cheerfully into trains while being deceived about their destination haunted Crosland for years to come.

The defeat of Hitler in May 1945 was greeted by Crosland with mixed feelings. Alongside relief that the war was finally over was a sense of frustration at not having been selected for the general election in Britain that had been called for early July. With Churchill's coalition breaking up, he told his mother that the 'coming election is clearly off as far as I'm concerned'; his only distant role being to go round various units 'giving impartial (sic) lectures'.[21] During the previous year he had been invited to eleven selection conferences, but owing to difficulties in communication three-quarters of the invitations had only reached him after the date set for the selection, and the remainder with only a day or two to go. His frustration was compounded by hearing that Attlee had spoken highly of him in looking at the candidates' list. But the chance of securing home leave remained remote. Indeed despite the ending of the war in Europe, Crosland faced the prospect of waiting for up to a year to be demobilised. From the comfort of his billet in Austria, he considered various options: joining the Allied Military Government in Austria (which meant staying in uniform for up to three years), looking for a posting in the Middle East, or joining the South-East Asia campaign, where troops were needed for the continuing war against Japan. In the meantime he was assigned to a topographical department, undertaking work similar to his previous employment as a photographic interpreter.

His main satisfaction in the summer of 1945 came from hearing news of Labour's stunning election victory in Britain, which saw the party sweep to power to form its first-ever majority goverment. 'What a day!' he wrote to his mother. 'Even I, in my wildest dreams, never expected a landslide like this.'[22] Two weeks later he could still hardly take the news in, admitting to Philip Williams that he had made a 'monumental mistake' in always assuming that Labour could never win substantial middle-class support while voters associated the party with a 'largely Union policy'. What he called the 'middle-class swing-over' – with Labour capturing scores of previously solid Tory suburban and small town seats – was the most 'staggering' feature of the result. He also conceded his mistake in thinking that Attlee would not be successful in countering Churchill's charismatic appeal. Like many, including senior Labour figures, Crosland believed it would require a second post-war election for the party to come to power.

In the aftermath of the election he had further thoughts about what to do next:

> Failure to get back for the election has rather altered my plan for life. I have always rather assumed that I would go straight out of the Army into active politics. But there will not be another turn-over of candidates such as we have just seen for very many years, and thus chances of getting a reasonable seat in the near future are very remote. I am therefore tending to plan on the basis of not going into politics until early middle-age (assuming I haven't reached that happy period already).[23]

Quite what he would do instead remained in doubt for some time. Following the abrupt ending of the war against Japan, news came through that the government was to allow several thousand arts students serving in the forces to resume their studies. In September he told Williams that he had not previously thought of going back to Oxford, but as it meant 'exchanging one's last and probably barren year of Army life for a slightly less barren life at Oxford . . . this I am prepared to do if pressed, even with Trinity thrown in'.[24] For a few months uncertainty continued, and in November he was unsure if he was going home on leave or permanently. But by the end of 1945 his war finally came to an end; he was back in Oxford.

The war had clearly been a formative experience. Crosland's years in uniform reinforced his move away from orthodox communism, a process that began with the formation of the Oxford Democratic

Socialist Club back in 1940. For him Labour's stance of supporting the war effort while pressing for more progressive policies on the home front had been vindicated by the result of the 1945 election. With Attlee as Prime Minister and the government moving quickly to implement its detailed programme of social and economic reform, he had become a firm supporter of mainstream Labour and a stern critic of the fundamentalist left, whether inside or outside the party. In October 1945 he mentioned meeting Andrew Schonfield, a contemporary, whose views 'have swung much like mine during the last few years, except that he is if anything even more anti-Soviet than I am'.[25] As for his personal life, this had been put on hold by the demands of war. He wrote in his diary early in 1945 that amongst his current reading books he found the works of Trollope disappointing because, like the novels of Jane Austen, they were largely concerned with 'marriage, gossip + intrigue about marriage – to me a very tedious subject'. Friends remembered Crosland returning from the war making '*efforts de normalisation*' in terms of his sexuality. At the age of twenty-seven, he could feel that the war had robbed him of an important part of his youth; he was about to make up for lost time.[26]

4

From Oxford to Westminster, 1945–50

Tony Crosland stood out as an impressive figure on his return to post-war Oxford, where fresh-faced undergraduates sat alongside older, hardened war veterans. As well as being chairman of the Democratic Socialist Club, he became president of the Union and was also on the national executive of the Fabian Society. Having switched from classics – about which he now spoke disparagingly – to politics, philosophy and economics, he worked hard and secured first-class honours by the end of 1946. One of the few Conservatives with whom he remained on good terms throughout his life, Edward Boyle, remembered him as an excellent speaker after the war: graceful, but with top-quality intellectual content allied to a sharp cutting edge of sardonic anti-Toryism and contemptuous of 'mindless "Left" generalising'.[1] His disdain for 'Left generalising' included a firm rejection of the Marxist doctrines that seemed so attractive in the 1930s. Marx, he wrote in his diary, had been correct to interpret history in terms of a continuing struggle between classes – 'his supreme contribution to human thought'. But this had to be set against the 'childishly rigid & inflexible' approach of present-day Marxists, especially their adherence to the founding father's view of the inevitable collapse of capitalism in the face of strong evidence to the contrary.[2] Allied to this was his view that authoritarianism was inherent in communist practice, as was becoming obvious in Eastern Europe 'in the shadow of 350 Red Army divisions'.[3]

After graduation, Crosland faced the question of how to make a living. What outlet could be found for his great energy and ambition? Continuing to believe that another election was unlikely for several years, he flirted with the idea of working for the Fabian Society in London, but eventually accepted an offer from the President of Trinity to stay on in a lecturing capacity. When his post-war tutor Robert Hall left to become an adviser to the Labour government, Crosland replaced him as Trinity's Fellow in Economics.[4] In his large room off the centre courtyard, he would listen to students reading their weekly essays. His pupils remember him as a stimulating tutor, always keen to relate economic theory to the world in which the government operated. He was also unashamed in his efforts to convert even those from the most unlikely backgrounds to his way of thinking. After graduating, Angus Ogilvy wrote to offer thanks and told Crosland that he was regarded by his own family as three-quarters of the way to Moscow, so well known was his tutor for injecting 'Socialistic theories into Tory Old Etonians'.[5] Crosland's economics writing, much influenced by senior Keynesians in Whitehall such as Hall and Donald MacDougall, showed a similar concern for applying theory to practical problems. He began to publish a series of closely argued essays, mostly in left-wing journals, dealing with issues ranging from the pricing policy of the National Coal Board to the distribution of manpower and the future of public ownership, which at this time he wanted to see extended to over 50 per cent of industry 'if our society is to enjoy the degree of equality which as socialists we desire'.[6]

These early pieces of published writing, which began to establish Crosland's credentials as a serious economist, were narrowly focused in content. He was, however, also concerning himself with a broader picture. Already in the late 1940s he was beginning to outline how socialism might develop over the next generation, and in doing so he touched upon themes that were to become prominent in his best-known works. Looking ahead to Britain in 1970 and assuming opti-mistically that Labour would remain in power for many years ahead, he envisaged moves towards Scandinavian-style social democracy, marked by improved living standards, wide but not universal public ownership and a high degree of equality. As this would fulfil traditional socialist objectives, attention should turn to the broaden-ing of cultural opportunities. The ultimate socialist ideal, he believed, had little to do with nationalisation, but rather with creating a society in which people could concentrate on what they were born for – 'pleasure & enjoyment of full life'. Marx would be replaced by William Morris. And there would be no need for a Ministry of Fine Arts to organise people's leisure for them:

> Nonsense to say people can't be perfectly happy on sex, gin & Bogart – and if that is what they want under Soc., well & good. I know many cultured people who want just that (e.g. me). All that matters then will be sufficient variety of culture & enjoyment opps. . . . fight v. dullness &

uniformity & homogeneity in leisure life will then be main battle –
abolish Lord Chamberlain, abolish divorce laws, bring flagellation back
into sex, have open-air cafes open all night – lights, dancing, gaiety,
culture, & no talk of economics, politics, or the need for a new
Fabianism.[7]

Crosland found the earnestness of many within the Fabian Society a
trial, especially as he began to attend some of the regular Summer
Schools held at locations such as Dartington in Devon. The Society
offered another potential route towards a career in politics, and its
popularity was high in the aftermath of Labour's 1945 victory. But
Crosland had doubts that old-style Fabianism offered the way
forward. His ambivalent attitude towards the Society's founders,
Sidney and Beatrice Webb, was expressed in a highly revealing diary
entry. He agreed that they were admirable characters, but then went
on:

> Their considerable indifference to all forms of art or culture, their lack
> of temptation . . . towards any of the emotional or physical pleasures of
> life, the consequent priggish puritanism (B.W. on 'spooning' & on
> abortion in Russia), their inability to relax into anything for its own sake
> – all this is v. unattractive. Unlike most other critics, I personally do not
> feel any antipathy to the blue-book part of their lives: I like blue-books,
> & like research – but it all becomes v. unattractive when it is *unrelieved*
> by any recreation or alternative interest. . . . No, I shouldn't have liked
> the Webbs. I should have admired them, been fascinated by them:
> enjoyed talking shop with them: recognised that they had achieved a
> happiness & peace of mind (tho' B. W. only after gt. struggles) that was
> far beyond my powers & comprehension: recognised indeed that they
> were saintly where I was sinful. But with what a feeling of relief &
> release I should have walked out of their house![8]

This left the Webb tradition in his eyes as a useful guide in the past
but not for the future. The Webbs he believed had pointed socialism
in one permanently necessary direction (the need for efficiency and
administrative practicality) and one temporarily necessary direction
(collective action by the state to remedy economic injustices). But
any inspiration for the years ahead must come from elsewhere. In
some respects a 'complete reversal' of the Webb tradition was called
for. Before 1900, when socialists were mainly utopians, a 'good filing
system' was imperative, but in an age when fact-finding research was

well established, the Labour movement really needed some of the 'fire' of the early pioneers and 'a bit more radical individualism', especially in relation to social conventions:

> I want more, not less, 'spooning in the Parks of Recreation & Rest', more abortion, more freedom & hilarity in every way: abstinence is not a good foundation for Socialism, & the almost unnatural normality of the Webbs, & their indifference to emotional & physical pleasures, really would, if universally influential, make the Socialist State into the dull functional nightmare wh. many fear.[9]

Here then in his diary notes, which he developed in published writing, we find two key themes in Crosland's emerging political philosophy: egalitarianism and libertarianism. In the Oxford world of the late 1940s, he argued passionately for the first and went some way towards living out the second.

Crosland's days were spent engaged in rigorous academic work, consorting with friends and colleagues such as Philip Williams, who after the war secured an Oxford lectureship in Politics. But evenings were given over to riotous living: gambling, smoking, drinking whisky or gin and womanising, often in company with another friend, Raymond Carr, a Fellow of All Souls. One later profile of Crosland noted that this was the time when he really broke loose from his family background, being by turns charming and enormously rude, 'a lady-killer who realised that women were very attracted to him'.[10] His method of approach tended to be confrontational, looking for a response to his deliberate provocation, and quickly turning elsewhere if snubbed, confident that there would be other opportunities. One undergraduate remembered him as an immensely magnetic figure for the young, combining the attractions of a red beret denoting his war experience with a reputation for 'girls who left his college rooms at dawn'.[11] Another student at the time recalls how Crosland berated the minister Manny Shinwell at the Labour Club for his handling of Britain's fuel crisis early in 1947. Shinwell lost his temper and, fearing that blows would be struck, one of the most attractive women present whispered in Crosland's ear that he might accompany her out of the room. He left as quietly as a lamb.[12] It was also at this time that he first met Hilary Sarson, a seventeen-year-old from an affluent family based in Berkshire. Crosland, according to his second wife, soon 'fell in love with Hilary.

She was pretty, playful, good-natured, sexy. He was promiscuous, but sooner or later he returned to Hilary.'[13]

His life-style had obvious attractions after the hardships of war service. In later years Crosland said that from about the age of seventeen he had wanted to go into Labour politics, hoping to shape and influence policies: 'more satisfactory than writing books about them from an Oxford chair'. But at Trinity he did waver. He was once described as being 'effortlessly a don', with his careful arrangement of new books on his table, papers in piles on the floor, writing in classic small script while lounging in a chair wearing slippers and pullover. This together with his flamboyance, his 'listening glare' and his drawl made him 'a member of Hebdomadal Council, head of his house, a splendid Oxford man'.[14] He was regarded by some as the most glamorous Oxford don of his generation, and he clearly impressed political aspirants of a similar age. Jim Callaghan, one of the new intake of Labour MPs in 1945, met Crosland when delivering a speech to the Labour Club, and recalled being intrigued by his 'casual manner as he told me of his ambition to stand for Parliament'. Callaghan, who had been denied the opportunity of higher education by virtue of his more humble origins and the early death of his father, added that he was unable to see why parliament would be more worthwhile or pleasant than what he was already doing.[15] One of the students whose political ambitions Crosland encouraged was Anthony Wedgwood Benn. 'Anyone would think from your wealth of aliases', he told him, 'that you were hiding from the police.'[16]

However, he was encouraged to continue thinking about leaving the academic world for politics by his contacts with senior Labour statesmen. In 1946 Crosland attended the Durham Miners' Gala and heard speeches by Attlee ('no pyrotechnics, but an able speech') and by Aneurin Bevan, with whom he was deeply impressed. He thought that Bevan overdid class conscious radicalism in abusing the rich, but he was 'a very great man. I could listen to him by the hour.'[17] Writing to Philip Williams, Crosland admitted he was taken aback by Bevan's breadth of vision, moderation and 'essentially constructive outlook', and was persuaded that he should be the next Labour leader.[18] He was equally impressed when in 1947 he met Shinwell's successor as Minister of Fuel and Power, Hugh Gaitskell, who in later years was to be his principal political ally. But the most important contact Crosland made in the short-term was Chancellor of the Exchequer, Hugh Dalton. In the early months of Attlee's government, it was the towering and controversial figure of Dalton who did much to maintain a radical sense of purpose, pushing on the introduction of Labour's programme of economic and social reform, taunting the opposition with deliberate insults and becoming the most reviled of ministers by the Tories. 'Keep that man away from me', Churchill remarked; 'I can't stand his booming voice and shifting eyes.'[19]

After a visit to the Oxford Union early in the summer of 1946, the Chancellor said to officials: 'Make a note! Make a note! Name's Crosland! I want him here!' Soon afterwards Crosland, still at the time an undergraduate, visited Dalton at No. 11 Downing Street, and was added to his long list of young hopefuls whose careers were to be encouraged. Dalton advised Crosland to take the Trinity lectureship, saying that it would make one more socialist teacher of economics at Oxford while he kept his options open for later.[20] In 1947 the Chancellor spent his sixtieth birthday at the Berkshire home of the economist Nicholas Davenport, recovering from exhaustion caused by a sudden economic crisis. Davenport wrote in his memoirs that Dalton 'adored good-looking and gallant young men who were physically fit and strong' and had specially requested the attendance of the dashing young Fellow of Trinity, hoping to become better acquainted after their meeting of the previous summer. Crosland arrived in the Red Menace wearing his regimental beret, and was at his 'most mischievous and magnetic'. Davenport added that, as Crosland drove away, he could see in Dalton's eyes the rekindling of his love for handsome young men.[21] When Dalton resigned as Chancellor in November following a budget leak, Crosland wrote to say he was shattered and barely able to teach for the day, being haunted by the 'personal tragedy of the thing', aside from the loss to the government and the country.[22] Released from the burdens of high office, Dalton was able to spend more time than ever encouraging young protégés such as Callaghan, Healey and his favourite, Tony Crosland.

Dalton's repressed homosexuality was well known among friends, and usually took the form of teasing conversation, lightly putting his hands on an arm or expressing jealousy of any girlfriends his young charges might have. All these traits were evident in his attitude to Crosland, who revived in Dalton some of his youthful feelings for Rupert Brooke. Some of those who witnessed Dalton's growing attachment, such as Nicholas Davenport – who saw him chasing Crosland playfully round his Berkshire home, turning furiously jealous when Crosland left abruptly with a girlfriend – believed that 'Tony was greatly embarrassed by this attention'. But others, for example Dalton's friend Catherine Walston, scolded Crosland at one house-party for leading Hugh on by draping himself languidly over a sofa. Ben Pimlott, Dalton's biographer, raises the question of whether there was in Crosland, as there had been in Rupert Brooke, an 'emotional ambivalence that enabled him to respond to the affection of another, especially an older, man'.[23] Certainly, following the sudden death in April 1946 of Arthur Jenkins, a crucial influence hitherto, Dalton emerged as an alternative father figure. As Pimlott notes, they were often seen playing a type of game in which Hugh was the doting, over-attentive parent while Tony was the irrepressible, ungrateful but always forgiven son, able among other things to get away with calling Dalton a windbag to his face. On both sides the relationship satisfied deeply-felt emotional needs.[24]

Dalton's main practical contribution to furthering the cause of his young friends was to help them find parliamentary seats. In September 1948 he told Crosland he had hopes of 'fixing up you and others'.[25] The assistance was welcome, for early in 1949 Crosland remained uncertain of his prospects as an election began to loom on the horizon. He informed Tony Benn, who was also hoping to become a Labour candidate, that recent efforts had come to nothing. He had been in the running for South Hammersmith, but to no effect, and he had decided after some agonising not to take up nominations by four wards for a vacancy in Oxford. The only person still optimistic about my chances 'is dear old Hugh'.[26] For some time, however, 'dear old Hugh' had been carefully watching events in the South Gloucestershire constituency, aware that the sitting Member, J. H. Alpass, was due to retire on grounds of ill health. Dalton was active in making introductions and sending letters of encouragement; he even warned off Roy Jenkins, insisting that South Gloucester was a 'good seat for Tony'. In September 1949 Crosland secured a large majority over two union-sponsored candidates at the selection conference, beginning nervously he said but then warming to the task. The biggest round of applause, he told Dalton, came when he refused to promise any financial contribution to the forthcoming campaign. Dalton, in accepting the thanks which Crosland sincerely felt for helping him to secure the nomination, noted that 'favouritism is the secret of efficiency'. He added his view that 'if you have fair luck and don't drink too much', you would 'do damned well in politics'.[27]

The prospect of Crosland beginning a political career had therefore improved dramatically. In November 1949 Dalton told him that in conversation a Tory MP recently admitted that South Gloucestershire 'should be a cinch for you'. This was in part because of the redrawing of constituency boundaries, which favoured Labour by including in the seat the northern suburbs of Bristol, regarded as strong territory for the party.[28] In the event, Crosland's campaign did not get off to the smoothest of starts. He, like many other candidates, was taken by surprise when – for the first time in decades – the government called a winter election, to be held in February 1950. Stafford Cripps, Dalton's successor as Chancellor, insisted that voting should not be delayed until after what might be considered an electioneering budget in the spring. In January Crosland told his mother that the timing of the election was 'most awkward', coming in the middle of the Oxford term. He planned to spend three weeks in Oxford then three weeks away in the constituency, during which time it was costing him dearly in fees to ensure that his undergraduates were 'farmed out' to other tutors. It also meant he had to devote much time and energy unexpectedly soon to his election address, believing this was the only communication many voters would read. When he eventually set off on 2 February for his campaign headquarters, a hotel in Bath within easy reach of all parts of the constituency, it was in the 'most dismal possible circumstances' of driving rain that left him soaked through.[29]

Crosland's campaign diary indicates that he quickly adapted to the demands of electioneering. His initial public meetings left him with two impressions: one was that 'the bitterness of the old workers about pre-war is fantastic – an absolutely solid deep-biting hatred of the Tories, a complete mistrust of any of their promises'. His second reflection was astonishment that those who came along and made impassioned speeches about being 'workers together' bore him no ill will. 'I am continually amazed at the lack of any feeling against me . . . I obviously come from a different class.' As rumours circulated that Crosland came from a humble background, he decided to supplement his election address, in which he echoed Labour's national campaign by speaking of the choice between full employment and fair shares or the Tory alternative of deflation, decontrol and a return to the 'inequalities of an unplanned society'.[30] In addition, he put out a statement of his family history and university record so that the Tories could not claim he was seeking to distort his background. The first week of the campaign also taught him hard lessons about handling the public: hecklers he found were difficult to contend with when they expressed strong personal grievances, for example over losing their jobs. There was also the danger of over-doing things: '4 meetings in one night – v. unwise'. At one of these meetings he discovered it didn't pay to be too courteous to 'the squirearchy' who walked in halfway through; fortunately a local character took over and attacked them as a 'dying class', after which they promptly walked out again.[31]

On 15 February he addressed a crowd at Badminton, home of the Duke of Beaufort and hitherto off-bounds for any Labour candidate. With the Duke in attendance and an audience of about seventy, Crosland confidently held the attention of listeners and brushed aside any awkward points, notably a lady complaining that three fitters had been sent to repair her daughter's gas cooker. His response drew laughter from the farm workers: 'I can only suggest, Madam, that if your daughter's beauty resembles yours in any way, two were gazing at her in admiration while the other was working.' His own diary records that there were about forty Labour sympathisers 'cheering hard'. Questioning dried up before time, a sign that the meeting had been a 'howling success'.[32] From this point onwards his belief that victory was likely grew stronger.

In the run up to polling day he needled his Tory opponent by singing the 'Red Flag' within his earshot, spoke of a 'terrific' reception at his final meetings, and beat off attempts by some Tories to let his car tyres down.[33] After nearly collapsing with fatigue at the end of the contest, Crosland recovered to hear that nationally Labour had fared badly, its majority falling from over 150 to a mere six seats. But in South Gloucestershire the party won comfortably by some 6000 votes. At the age of thirty-one – young in parliamentary terms but rather later than he hoped had not the war intervened – Crosland was leaving Oxford for Westminster.

5

Entering the House of Commons, 1950–51

It was not the easiest of times to embark upon a parliamentary career. By 1950 Attlee's government had carried out much of its programme. Full employment had been maintained; nationalisation of key utility and service-sector industries had gone ahead; and a new 'welfare state' had been introduced, including the highly prized National Health Service. But the Cabinet, which contained most of the same faces as before, was conscious of the constraints suddenly imposed by a tiny majority in the House of Commons. Dalton said the election result was the worst of all possible outcomes, leaving Labour in office but 'without power or authority'; several of his colleagues doubted if the government could survive for more than six months.[1] In contrast to 1945, the party had few bold proposals to offer, and any momentum ministers sought to develop was curtailed when in July 1950 the outbreak of the Korean War led to new stresses. British support for the United Nations intervention against the communist forces of North Korea required a massive increase in defence spending, placing great pressure on the economy and foreshadowing internal party divisions of a sort largely unseen during Attlee's first term. Labour MPs were also put on their guard by frequent all-night sittings of the House; the Tories hoped to wear down the government by inflicting demoralising parliamentary defeats. At first Crosland travelled to London from his rooms in Oxford, but since he needed to be constantly in attendance at the Commons he decided to take a flat within easy reach of Westminster. Although disparaging in conversation about Trinity, it was with several backward glances that he left the academic world for a new life in politics.

With the government on the defensive, and talk of the need for another election to clear the air, it was difficult for a new backbencher to make much impression. Crosland focused his maiden speech on his obvious area of expertise – economic policy. In preparing to speak on the spring budget, Dalton offered him advice based on long experience of the House: don't put too many figures in – just enough to impress the 'conscious amateurs' – and also try to mix appreciation of the government's wisdom with helpful suggestions, in a tone combining 'determination and humility'.[2] In a fluent speech the new MP, while maintaining the tradition of refraining from criticism of the other side, was not as lenient towards his own Chancellor, Stafford Cripps. The main thrust of Crosland's forthright effort was his claim that Cripps had achieved much but – in spite of his reputation for austerity – had not sufficiently tightened fiscal policy. Parliamentary commentators were impressed and Dalton congratulated him on a 'striking personal success', one which showed his desire from the outset to be seen as someone with considered views on the economy.[3] This was his main focus during his first year in the House and in the series of articles he steadily produced. After the outbreak of the Korean War he was keen to counter the view of many newspapers that a straight choice existed between rearmament and social reform. The task of enlightened statesmanship, he claimed, was to ensure that both objectives were met while providing the necessary military support for South Korea.[4]

When he became Foreign Secretary in the 1970s it was claimed that Crosland had no real interest in overseas policy, yet in his early days in parliament he was a regular participant in debates about the development of Europe. Once again Dalton was a catalyst, inviting him to become a member of the British delegation to the Consultative Assembly of the Council of Europe, which met in Strasbourg. The Council had been created in 1949 with the aim of achieving greater unity among member states, but divisions emerged between federalists who favoured a 'United Europe' and Britain, Scandinavia and Ireland, who advocated a more cautious approach. In August 1950 tension came to a head over Britain's rejection of the Schuman Plan, designed to encourage economic integration, and there was some danger of the Council collapsing. Dalton as head of the British delegation reported to Attlee on his unhappiness with the outcome but not with the support he had received from younger colleagues. Crosland was originally invited as an economic assistant, but ended up with a 'tough assignment' on the general affairs committee as a substitute for Callaghan when the latter was called home. According to Dalton, Crosland faced some strong and crafty opponents, such as Bidault and Mollet, but did 'jolly well. He has lots of pluck and persistence and was very resourceful and quick-witted in debate. He also spoke French well. It was a great test for a young man who has never been to an international conference of this kind before. He certainly won his spurs.'[5]

Strasbourg was not all work and no play. Jim Callaghan later recalled the nightly receptions given by national delegations at which champagne flowed freely, followed by dinner at one of the city's many excellent restaurants. Dalton took upon himself the culinary education of the delegation, introducing its members to many fine dishes and Alsatian wines. At weekends Dalton would drive off with young protégés such as Crosland, Callaghan and Healey, motoring through spectacular countryside to the Vosges. Callaghan, over six years older than Crosland, was the senior of the trio, a tough-minded political loner and already a junior minister for three years. Healey, an equally no-nonsense figure, was not yet an MP like Crosland, but had built up powerful contacts as head of Labour's International Department since 1946. Dalton was particularly struck by one trip he led to Le Donon in the Vosges in mid-August, taking with him 'the three coming men of the Labour Party' and describing a wonderful weekend, 'seasoned with wit and wisdom, walking and wine'.[6] For the three younger men, each with other interests back in England, these were pleasant interludes in their busy schedules, but for Dalton – in the twilight of his career – they were more special, and reflected the amount of energy he was investing in seeing his young charges succeed. In his diary soon afterwards he said he was 'thinking of Tony, with all his youth and beauty and gaiety and charm and social success and good brains . . . & with his feet on the road of political success now, if he survives to middle age. . . . I am more fond and proud of that young man than I can put into words. I think of him . . . as something between a beloved only son and a gay and adorable younger brother.'[7]

Crosland was disturbed by the intensity of these sentiments, and a few weeks later he provoked the older man by questioning him about what impact Freudian theories of repression had upon his life. Dalton responded with a long introspective letter apologising for 'fussing' too much since Crosland became an MP. He also included several references to what he believed to be his young friend's own state of mind. It was evident, Dalton said, that Crosland was finding the House of Commons 'disappointing, boring and narrowing'. He referred to Crosland telling him that aside from those he already knew, such as Roy Jenkins – who entered the House at a by-election in 1948 – he had met only one person, John Freeman, whom he wished to call a friend. He was also of the opinion that if he had stayed in Oxford, he would have had a 'more comfortable and intellectually satisfactory life'. Dalton urged Crosland to take a more positive view of recent events: he reassured him that he had done well in Strasbourg, and said he was aware of the pleasures that had been received from good food and drink and night life – 'you are such an artist, and so quick on the ball, on all that side of life's playing field'. It could well be the case, Dalton concluded, that the government was unlikely to last a full term and would lose the next election, but if Crosland held his seat, he would find himself well placed to get a foot on the ministerial ladder when Labour next returned to power. With Jim Callaghan likely to be in the forefront of the younger generation with a place in the Cabinet, Crosland might become a junior minister or perhaps even have a department of non-Cabinet rank: 'you'll find politics much more fun then!'[8]

Dalton's overbearing personality was such that Crosland was finding it difficult to step out of his shadow. In spite of his pledge not to 'fuss' so much, Dalton was soon offering Crosland fresh advice on political and personal issues, some of it unwelcome. With talk in the air of Crosland becoming engaged to Hilary Sarson, Dalton suggested he take another three years before starting on the 'monogamic monotony' of marriage. 'I now think you may go right to the top. So you want somebody extra good . . . and you needn't feel remorse much – or long. For you'll have given them all great fun while it lasted.'[9] Crosland was more appreciative of the help Dalton gave him in preparing to review a new biography of J. M. Keynes. Although not 'a comrade', Dalton told him, his key works such as *The General Theory of Employment, Interest and Money* were 'all up our street'.[10] Crosland's review elaborated on this by emphasising a crucial point in his own thinking: that the great contribution of Keynes had been to provide the techniques by which full employment had become sustainable in post-war Britain. What failed to get into the review were his thoughts on the private life of Keynes and his social circle: 'How did Apostles + later Bloomsbury succeed in getting through such an extraordinary amount of creative work plus serious discussion? No sex? And no really frivolous drunken evenings? In my post-war world at Oxford, I think we accomplished (just!) a comparable amount of work: but we certainly didn't have the constant long evenings on serious argument – they went on sex + parties.'[11]

In the spring of 1951 the government's prospects were blighted by a major row between ministers. After the resignation of Cripps through ill-health, the Chancellorship had gone to Hugh Gaitskell, at forty-four one of the youngest holders of the post in the twentieth century. Gaitskell's rapid promotion was resented in certain quarters of the party, not least by Aneurin Bevan, who after his success in establishing the NHS believed he merited promotion to a more senior post. Aside from personal rivalry between two potential successors to Attlee as party leader, Gaitskell and Bevan were soon at loggerheads over policy. In particular, the new Chancellor insisted that increases in the defence budget – made necessary by the Korean War – could only be met by making economies on domestic spending, including the NHS. With the Prime Minister absent in hospital during critical discussions, the Cabinet overwhelmingly backed Gaitskell in proposing new health charges as part of his budget in April. Two weeks later Bevan, having warned of the consequences of breaching the principle of a free health service, resigned from the government, followed by two other ministers, Harold Wilson and John Freeman. For Crosland, as for many others, it was a time to choose. He was amongst those who had been impressed by Gaitskell's economic expertise and administrative competence. On the other hand, he was an admirer of Bevan. After meeting Crosland on 10 April, Dalton wrote in his diary that 'he is very pro-Nye, but he is against him on this'.[12]

Crosland decided on which side to come down in the debate after consulting with two fellow MPs, Roy Jenkins and Woodrow Wyatt, who between them had earlier hatched a plan – subsequently abandoned – to resume their soldiering careers in Korea.[13] Although saddened by events which he felt undermined any chance of the government surviving for long, Crosland threw himself into the fray. Most MPs, he told Dalton, were 'frightful cowards, watching which way the cat would jump'.[14] Crosland put his head above the parapet by taking up an invitation from *Tribune* – increasingly a mouthpiece for Bevan's views – to defend the Chancellor against accusations that he was betraying the socialist cause. In similar vein he wrote in the *New Statesman* that the defence programme had been accepted by the Cabinet in January and defended in public by Bevan as recently as February. More so than in later years, Crosland tried hard not to fan the flames of party enmity. Rather than a full-blown division between left and right, he argued, it was mainly a technical dispute between two views of future production prospects.[15] Bevan in turn used moderate language once out of office, and the 'Bevanites' remained for many months an indistinct grouping on the back-benches. But it was a turning point in Labour's history, marking the origins of a split that was to haunt the party for years to come.

Bevan's resignation confirmed Labour's loss of direction, and added to Crosland's sense of disappointment with parliamentary life. This was underlined in startling terms by his younger sister's new husband, the prominent historian A. J. P. Taylor. Crosland saw his sister Eve infrequently and did not attend her wedding, and he was not impressed when Taylor wrote to say that he had heard on good authority that Attlee spoke of Crosland as being a junior minister but for the fact that he was too often drunk in the Smoking Room.[16] Crosland believed that his heavy drinking, which had continued since his Oxford days, was none of his brother-in-law's business, but after a further trip to Strasbourg he received similar warnings from Taylor's friend, the Conservative Member Bob Boothby. During twenty-six years in the House, Boothby said, he had seen many brilliant and promising young men 'soak themselves out of public life', and he feared Crosland would become another. His behaviour at the Council of Europe had not gone unnoticed, especially when he arrived at an evening meeting with a hangover after staying in bed all day, and 'seemed rather proud of it'. Boothby added that he could not see the point of going to Strasbourg to sit at a bar, which could be done in this country, and he warned against 'chucking away a political career to which no limit can be set, as you are now doing'. He conceded it might not be his concern ('God forbid that I, of all people, should set up as a Censor of personal morals'), nor his duty to save the career of an opponent; but he wrote because of his regard for Crosland, his irritation at a waste of talent and his fear of 'you going the same way as too many others in the profession'.[17]

The advice was ignored, and when Attlee called a general election in October 1951 Crosland turned his attention to getting re-elected. The Prime Minister felt the government could not continue with a wafer-thin majority, and argued that to delay might produce diffi-culties of timing owing to a lengthy royal tour of Australia scheduled for the following spring. Several ministers wanted to struggle on, realising that Labour's prospects were not good. The campaign struggled to come to life; most of the arguments had been rehearsed in the election of the previous year. Crosland's address mirrored the party's national campaign in its defensive note. The Korean War, he said, had meant postponing hopes of social progress, but this was unavoidable; compared with the 'dishonest' pledges of the opposition, Labour still provided the best hope of combining 'rearmament with social justice and equality'.[18] The campaign in South Gloucestershire was lower key than in 1950 for another reason also: Crosland believed his majority was not under threat. He had diligently worked his way into the constituency, staying on his regular visits at the home of a local farmer and party activist, Jack Donaldson, whose family found him an entertaining but demanding guest, 'intolerable about such matters as meals and bathrooms'.[19] His confidence proved to be well-founded, for he held the seat with only a slightly reduced majority. But a small swing towards the Conservatives nationally was sufficient to allow Churchill to return to Downing Street with a seventeen-seat majority. Ironically, by piling up huge majorities in its industrial heartlands, Labour secured more votes – but fewer seats – than the Tories. Seasoned campaigners like Dalton were not downcast, believing the Conservatives would soon be in trouble. But Dalton's generation was destined never to return to office.

The start of Crosland's career in politics had not been an unqualified success but, with the patronage of Hugh Dalton, he was marked out as a future star. Dalton told Gaitskell in July 1951 that he was 'amazingly able . . . & is becoming as good a politician as he is an economist'. On sheer ability, knowledge and personality, Dalton believed, he was ideal material for a Treasury junior minister.[20] But others took a more cautious view. Earlier in the year when considering promotions Attlee said: 'Crosland. That's an able chap . . . But I think he'd better wait a bit.'[21] He was being asked to 'wait a bit' not simply because he had only been in the Commons for a year; Attlee also sensed that Crosland's brilliance was mixed with waywardness. The heavy drinking which some felt threatened his prospects reflected an inability to settle down to the routine of life at Westminster. John Freeman had this in mind when he said that Crosland might have been better returning to Oxford as a socialist don. This possibility was not seriously entertained once Crosland had secured a further term as an MP. Instead he was to turn in a more systematic way to writing, convinced that the task of opposition lay in mapping out the next stretch on the road to socialism. Over the next few years his view was that it was no longer sufficient for Labour to be 'the party in favour of what we did between 1945 and 1950'.[22]

6

The New Fabian, 1951–5

The opposition benches in the early 1950s were not the happiest of places for Tony Crosland. He did not endear himself to party colleagues by his attitude to parliamentary ritual. He was rarely seen in the House, dismayed by what he saw as the poor standard of debate and alienated by the internal in-fighting into which Labour lapsed from early 1952 onwards. Although identified as a strong 'Gaitskellite' in the left–right struggles that developed, he took little interest in the detail of disputes that focused mainly on foreign policy. His personal life was also complicated and unhappy, while boundary changes left him increasingly dissatisfied with his chosen constituency. On the other hand, Crosland's career did move forward in one crucial respect during the first half of the 1950s. He made a name for himself as a writer. Well before the end of the 1951 parliament, he had already become known for the force and clarity with which he addressed the problems and challenges facing post-war British society.

His reputation as an important socialist theoretician was based on two works, the first of which was published in 1952 as a contribution to the *New Fabian Essays*, edited by Richard Crossman. Crossman, emerging as a forceful advocate of Bevanism on the Labour backbenches, was like Crosland a fomer Oxford don. For some time the Fabian Society had been planning to produce an updated version of the original *Fabian Essays* written over sixty years earlier. Crosland had been involved since 1949, and was a regular contributor to a series of 'Problems Ahead' conferences organised in Oxford. In October 1950 he produced a draft of his final article, analysing what he called the 'nature of the Capitalist Crisis', and was congratulated by Dalton for managing to 'sweat out some Marxism which was still in your system'.[1] The final version of the *New Fabian Essays*, according to the editor, aimed 'to achieve a balance between theoretical analysis and practical application'. The task of restating the objectives of socialism and charting a way forward, Crossman said, was much harder than it had been for the original Fabians. The volume of information upon which arguments needed to be constructed was vastly greater and with Labour losing office while the book was being completed, the essays could not claim either 'finality or comprehensiveness'.[2] Although it contained contributions from figures such as Jenkins and Healey as well as Crosland, the book was not conceived as a Gaitskellite tract. It included essays by left-wingers such as Ian Mikardo and John Strachey, as well as Crossman. The project was far advanced before the Bevanite controversies erupted, though the unity it presupposed had largely disappeared by the time of publication in the summer of 1952.

Crosland's contribution, 'The Transition from Capitalism', contained the hallmarks of his later and best-known work, moving from a lucid analysis of what he saw as Britian's problems to an outline of proposed solutions. The early part of the essay, based upon carefully researched use of economic data, set out to show that British capitalism had produced a steadily rising national income since 1870. While still characterised by great social injustices, the system could not – as in classic Marxist theory – collapse of its own accord. In the last decade he believed a new type of post-capitalist society had been created under a host of influences, such as the expanded power of the state, the creation of welfare and employment opportunities unknown before the war, and greater variegation within the traditional class structure. There were, he acknowledged, difficulties in defining this new type of society. It was capitalist in that private ownership of industry still predominated, despite extensive nationalisation; but socialist in so far as minimum standards of welfare provision for all had come into being. This, then, was a pluralist society which, for want of a better term, Crosland called 'statism'.[3]

The latter part of the article moved to the present and the future. The success of Attlee's government in furthering working-class interests, notably through full employment and the NHS, raised the question of how far it was desirable to go beyond 'statism' to socialism. The answer to this, Crosland said, depended on how one defined socialism. His own preference was to reject the Marxist notion of socialism as the nationalisation of the means of production, distribution and exchange. Instead he endorsed the definition given in 1935 by G. D. H. Cole, the essence of which was that socialism was about equality, not simply equality of opportunity but 'equality of status in the widest sense – subjective as well as objective'. By this standard, Britain in the early 1950s had made strides forward in the recent past, but had not begun to approach the ideal of a 'classless or egalitarian society'. This was evident both from social data and from the 'deplorable' persistence of class antagonism, notably between workers and managers:

> The purpose of socialism is quite simply to eradicate this sense of class, and to create in its place a sense of common interest and equal status. This will require not only more measures on the economic plane, directed to the greater equalisation of living standards and opportunities, but also measures on the socio–psychological plane. It is here that the essential difference between statism and socialism lies, and it is in this direction that socialists must look for the main advance.[4]

Crosland followed with a brief sketch of policies for a future Labour government. There were, he felt, several areas of government activity which had rightly been emphasised in the aftermath of war, but which could in future be made a lower priority. These included the extension of free social services; more nationalisation of entire industries; the proliferation of economic controls; and further re-distribution of income by direct taxation. While more could be done gradually in all these areas, Crosland claimed that his version of socialism required new themes. Of these, the most important were: tackling the gross maldistribution of property, as opposed to income; reforming the educational system ('no other single factor is so influential in the propagation of class feeling'); and dealing with the deeply-ingrained psychology of poor industrial relations. Even a brief outline of future aims, he said, demonstrated how far there was to go to get beyond statism to a society free of class resentments. There were, moreover, formidable obstacles blocking the way. The pace of reform would be limited by the need to preserve social cohesion and by the appetite for change at a time of rising living standards. In the Britain of the 1950s, there was unlikely to be any revival of the angry dynamic of revolt against the miseries of pre-war capitalism that had manifested itself so clearly in 1945.[5]

Reaction to the *New Fabian Essays* was mixed, but Crosland's contribution was generally well received. From the political right, Robert Blake attacked the book's 'vindictive plea for equality', yet he conceded that Crosland had provided the most stimulating piece on home affairs. As so many socialists still used 'Marxist blinkers',

Crosland had performed a useful service in emphasising how wrong Marx had been in his predictions about the collapse of capitalism.[6] The *New Statesman* said the book would not much help the flagging cause of socialism, and American political scientists claimed that too much emphasis had been placed on economic aspects of equality. Where cultural issues had been highlighted – as by Crosland – they had not been assessed in any detail.[7] More encouraging was the reaction of several national newspapers. The *Manchester Guardian* described Crosland's essay as 'admirably lucid'; by contrast the chapter by Roy Jenkins on equality was criticised for not going 'deep enough'. Even *The Times*, which doubted if the volume would help Labour recover its sense of direction, ranked Crosland's essay alongside those of Crossman and Strachey as the most important in the book. Unlike the Bevanites, it noted, at least there was a recognition among the new Fabians that socialism needed updating to suit the circumstances of the 1950s.[8]

For Crosland this was the first occasion on which his writing received national, even international, recognition.[9] A year later he was able to attract similar coverage when he published the second item on which his early reputation was based, a full-length book entitled *Britain's Economic Problem*. In contrast to the broad scope of his Fabian essay, this was a closely argued 200-page account bringing to bear his economic expertise on Britain's balance-of-payments problem. Although published at a time when trade terms were improving, Crosland began from the assumption – borne out in subsequent years – that the question of long-term solvency had not been addressed. The first part of the book assessed recent events, weaving together a mass of statistical information on production, trade and the sterling area's dollar gap. In addition accounts were given of biennial crises that had occured since the war: the end of Lend-Lease in 1945, the convertibility crisis of 1947, the devaluation of 1949 and the gold drain of 1951. These crises were usually attributed to specific events; yet Crosland's case was that the long-term deterioration in the foreign exchange position had more deep-rooted causes, and would have taken place without war and rearmament. 'Unless this is widely understood, the nation will not apply itself to sufficiently radical remedies.'[10] The real difficulties as he understood them had come about because of gradual changes in world economic relationships. Most notable among these were a shortage of food and raw materials in relation to manufactured products; a shift in the character of demand for manufactured goods resulting from growing industrialisation; and increased global dependence upon North American goods at a time when the outside world became unable to balance its account with the United States.

What needed to be done? Crosland argued forcefully that orthodox solutions, such as short-term cuts in public expenditure or 'fiddling with the Bank Rate', were irrelevant. Rather than 'monetary juggling', the real requirements for solvency involved high investment and industrial modernisation. Hence he stressed the need for increased output in steel, coal and engineering – at levels not merely to cover worsening terms of trade, but also to allow a surplus for foreign investment. This in turn meant more effective planning. Here the tone became more partisan. The Tories, he claimed, were obsessed with monetary techniques and old-fashioned liberal slogans. Labour, he admitted, had been distracted by 'profoundly sterile quarrels' about the exact size of the arms programme. But there were signs that the party was recognising its dual role: to remain an agent of social reform whilst also putting before the country a bold long-term policy for economic regeneration. The latter required, among other things, changes to the machinery of planning, securing the right distribution of total investment between social and industrial expenditure, and ensuring the correct distribution of investment. If such changes were made, national wealth could expand rapidly. Without them, Britain would 'stumble along, a poor people, watching opportunity's bald cranium recede into the distance ahead'.[11]

The book was warmly received in many quarters. Hugh Dalton wrote in his diary that no other MP could have written such a good work on this subject, though its author had frequently lectured on it, 'both drunk and sober'.[12] Once again reviewers in the national press were impressed. Douglas Jay in the *Daily Herald* called it 'the best book since the war on the British struggle for solvency'.[13] Even more satisfying was the guarded praise from the financial press, not known for its sympathy with the Labour cause. The *Financial Times* noted how Crosland did not give 'two hoots' for the shibboleths of orthodox economists. The remedies he proposed, refreshingly, were mostly his own, though in the final chapter it felt he became too much the party man. The *Economist* too praised the willingness of the author to make bold suggestions irrespective of how far vested interests might be upset. The book at least served the purpose of demonstrating – what for some time had been in doubt – that economic realism might be reconciled with Labour politics.[14] The general tone of the reviews was summed up by *The Listener*, which praised it as lucidly written and readable: 'an excellent little book', which for students of economics was a useful antidote to remote theory and for the layman an intelligible guide 'through the forbidding complexities of balance-of-payments problems'.[15]

The early 1950s thus saw Crosland establish his credentials as an intellectual in politics. With a strong belief in the power of reason, his findings were grounded in thorough research and yet also stressed the need for remedial action. His emphasis on pragmatic Fabian-style reform, combined with the clarity of his style, ensured his easy transition from the academic world to journalism, writing for a wider audience at Westminster and beyond. This process was enhanced by his willingness to write for national newspapers as much as for Labour weeklies such as the *New Statesman*, the popularity of which was high among party activists in the early 1950s. By left-inclined papers such as the *News Chronicle* and *Reynolds News*, he was frequently called upon to provide accessible but informed commentary upon the Conservative government's economic policy. This gave him the chance to highlight what he saw as the failings of the Conservative Chancellor, R. A. Butler. Although post-war austerity was being left behind as world economic conditions improved, Crosland pointed to the likely effects of tax concessions which amounted to a 'major social change in the wrong direction', with increased inequality the outcome.[16] With some exaggeration – inevitable when trumpeting the success of a local MP – the *Bristol Evening Post* in May 1953 wrote that Crosland's book, together with his Fabian essay, placed him among 'the most considerable younger spokesmen of the Labour Party's so-called Right Wing which – as he implies – is now, in fact, the radical one'.[17]

In other ways too, Crosland gave the impression of being a rising star. He continued to enjoy the support of senior figures such as Dalton, who began to introduce him to others as a potential future Chancellor.[18] He also established close ties with Hugh Gaitskell, who was emerging as a credible candidate to succeed Attlee as party leader. In part the friendship developed through a similarity of outlook, as became clear when Gaitskell invited Crosland to become a member of the opposition finance team in the Commons. Long hours spent resisting the government finance bill in 1952 engendered a sense of camaraderie, which continued outside the House with the emergence of the 'Hampstead Set' – a group of mainly middle–class Oxbridge Labour MPs who met regularly at Gaitskell's house in north London. Although always a critical friend, Crosland developed an admiration for Gaitskell's political integrity and his capacity for private enjoyment. This admiration was reciprocated, and Crosland earned the patronage of one of the key players in the party leadership.

Roy Jenkins recalls that he personally found the early 1950s a time of isolation on the backbenches. Tribal divisions meant he barely spoke to Nye Bevan after 1951 and though building a reputation as an urbane and articulate Gaitskellite – publishing his book *Pursuit of Progress* in 1953 – he did not have the ear of any major figures. His friend Crosland was closer to Gaitskell; a recollection which hinted at jealousy about Crosland remaining the senior partner in their friendship, as he had been at Oxford. Dalton was friendly but only if it didn't involve making any choice 'between Crosland and me; when it did, I was nowhere with him'.[19]

More so than in later years, Crosland was also capable of delivering powerful speeches in the Commons. Once again he concentrated on the economy. During the debate on the 1955 budget, Crosland forcefully attacked the Tories for 'buying' extra votes at a high price for the reputation of the Chancellor and 'the financial security of the country'.[20] Sitting on the government benches, Edward Boyle observed that Crosland made consistently good budget speeches during the 1951–5 parliament. His 1955 effort he described as superb, one of the best sardonic debating speeches he ever heard in the House, Crosland alone on the Labour side going all out in attacking Butler for tightening monetary policy in February then reducing taxation in April.[21] Outside the House, Crosland was regarded as a fluent and witty speaker when he visited local Fabian societies and addressed undergraduates. In dealing with Bevanite interruptions at one university meeting, Hugh Dalton noted that he told his audience it was not so much a question of left versus right in Labour ranks as of optimists versus pessimists, an effective way of attacking the Bevanites for refusing to accept that society could be improved by anything other than old–style socialism.[22]

There was, however, another side to Crosland the emerging force in British politics. He may have been a capable parliamentary per-former, but he was a reluctant one. Once Labour had lost office in 1951, removing any prospect of imminent junior office, he became bored by the everyday routine of the House of Commons, and was a poor attender. His budget speeches were not accompanied by regular contributions throughout the year, and after his enthusiasm in opposing the finance bill in 1952 he took little part in any detailed committee work. As his friend, Hugh Gaitskell was concerned that Crosland's attitude did not endear him to less talented but more assiduous colleagues. And when Dick Crossman said he should not get so drunk when coming into the House, Crosland replied: 'How else is one to endure being here?'[23] Some of the reasons for this casual approach have been touched upon: he thought the standard of debate was low-level, and had made few new friends. He preferred to work in his flat fifteen minutes drive from the House, spending long hours drafting out in long-hand from the comfort of an armchair. As the parliament progressed, there was increasing frustration that Labour was failing to dent the government's popularity, and that concerted resistance in the Commons was not likely to enhance Labour's dwindling prospects of returning to power. This in turn was linked with a further cause of Crosland's disaffection: his dismay at finding that the Parliamentary Labour Party (PLP) seemed more concerned with rancorous internal arguments than with ousting Churchill.

Crosland may have gravitated towards the Gaitskellite wing of the party, but he remained an erstwhile admirer of Bevan and was far from happy about the division into tribal camps. His old Oxford tutor Robert Hall found him 'very blue' when it became clear that the row over defence looked certain to continue and broaden.[24] He resented being driven into a position which labelled him as 'right-wing'. Roy Jenkins told Crossman that the existence of the Bevanites and their popularity in the constituencies was a major factor in his and Crosland's loyalty to Gaitskell, to balance the union leaders who pushed him further to the right than was desirable.[25] Crosland had doubts about the orthodoxy of some of Gaitskell's economic thinking, and the strain of having to 'follow his leader' became clear early in 1955 when Gaitskell pressed for the withdrawal of the whip from Bevan for defying the party line. Together with Jenkins and Wyatt, Crosland wrote to Gaitskell claiming that the issue had been mishandled. They had supported him out of loyalty, but could be expected to do so only a limited number of times. This did not affect 'our feelings of both personal and political loyalty to you. We are pleased to be called "Gaitskellites"; we want you to be leader of the Party in the future and we shall do everything we can to see that you are.' The crux of the difference was that Gaitskell, unlike Attlee, seemed too willing to alienate many in the centre of the PLP whose support would be essential in any leadership bid.[26]

Two other factors threatened to undermine Crosland's likely rise to the highest ranks of Labour politics. Crosland's riotous personal life did not meet with approval in some quarters. In late 1951 his relationship with Hilary Sarson had temporarily ended, but mutual physical attraction brought the couple together again and they were married the following autumn. Hugh Dalton gave the marriage his blessing, agreeing that Crosland had been 'a playboy' long enough, but at the wedding lunch he proceeded to bellow in his loudest voice about other girls Tony had known. As the couple were leaving, with Hilary close to tears, he added for good measure: 'Well, I think we got them off to a thoroughly bad start.'[27] The 'bad start' continued with a disastrous honeymoon, and not long after moving into a flat in The Boltons, near South Kensington, cracks in the marriage began to appear. Feeling that at the age of thirty-four he had made a mistake tying himself to someone who did not share his intellectual or political interests, Crosland continued to see other women. After about a year Hilary moved out.

Although the divorce took several years, Crosland was free to resume the heavy drinking, smoking and womanising that had characterised his life in post-war Oxford. Woodrow Wyatt recalled that he could be seen with an ever-changing string of girlfriends, nearly always pretty, frequently fair-haired and blue-eyed. With his good looks and engaging smile, ready to amuse those in whom he was interested, Crosland had no shortage of admirers. 'He hardly ever loved the numerous girls he went to bed with,' Wyatt added. 'He did it to convince himself that he had triumphed over his homosexual side.'[28] Several of the girlfriends found their way back to The Boltons, where Crosland was free to arrange the limited amount of furniture that had not been taken by Hilary. Much of the floor-space was taken up by manuscripts spread around in neat piles. His most prized possessions were two armchairs, arranged either side of a gas fire, where Crosland would sit and write in longhand. The piles of paperwork would be carefully removed to the back of the flat whenever one of many parties was held. At other times Crosland would indulge his love of opera, which went back to a six-week period he spent in Rome during the war, or his growing fascination with jazz.

A later profile of Crosland noted that two sides of his personality

– his puritanism and his hedonism – seemed at war with each other in the 1950s.[29] Many colleagues in the Commons would not have known the writer who spent long hours working without a break. But they did notice the reckless *enfant terrible* drunk at the House, sometimes seen leaving with one of his conquests from his 'Duke's Daughters' period. Allied to his reputation as a dilettante was a truculence in conversation which some found off-putting. His teasing and sometimes cruel manner, especially with women, was much commented upon, as was his refusal to engage in small-talk, dismissing any conversation which held no interest for him. Even friends such as Roy Jenkins were reluctant to invite him into their homes. 'Famous for his flounces and his unconcealed disapproval of those he might be asked to meet', Jenkins wrote, 'he was too hazardous a guest for dinner parties.'[30] Whatever lay at the root of this behaviour, it did not seem to characterise someone with a single-minded determination to reach the top in politics. His semi-detached attitude towards Westminster was reflected in his decision to spend two months in the United States during the autumn of 1954. This allowed him to broaden his academic interests, taking in much new work being developed in sociology, but it meant missing almost a whole session of parliament.

A final factor which limited Crosland's potential as an aspiring politician was the threat that his constituency would, in the words of Hugh Dalton, be 'destroyed' by boundary changes. Crosland had encountered few difficulties in South Gloucestershire, visiting the constituency regularly, but he was alarmed when the Boundary Commission confirmed that some of his strongest areas of support were to be given to Bristol in return for unpromising countryside taken from neighbouring Stroud. At the beginning of 1955 his best guess was that redistribution would create a Tory majority of between 2,000 and 3,000, leaving him little time to decide whether to fight on or risk finding another seat where he would be unknown.

His decision was complicated by the intervention of Dalton, who made strenuous efforts to persuade the MP for a nearby constituency, Morgan Philips Price, to resign and take a peerage, so opening the way for Crosland to step in. Dalton's hopes were raised after getting Attlee – who again agreed that Crosland was 'a very promising young man' – to talk to Price and urge him to go.[31] By the time Price decided he would stand again, Churchill had resigned and the new Prime Minister, Anthony Eden, had called an early election.

Crosland was left high and dry. Dalton conceded that any 'last minute windfall' was unlikely, with other candidates ready to snap up favourable constituency prospects, but he felt that nothing more could have been done. He reflected that 'the cards have fallen . . . badly for you in this game', but had fallen well in 1950 and could do so again, so Crosland might yet win the battle against 'Giant Bad Luck. And politics, as you knew when you took it up, is often just a bloody switchback ride.'[32]

Dismissing the view of local activists that he might survive on the basis of a personal vote in South Gloucestershire, Crosland frantically looked elsewhere. Just six weeks before the election of May 1955, he was adopted as Labour candidate in Southampton Test, another Labour-held seat adversely affected by redistribution. Unusually, he was adopted in his absence, having gone to another selection conference the same day which made it impossible to get to Southampton in time. His first visit to the area was a week later in order to confirm his candidature.[33] In these circumstances, Crosland's campaign – like that of his party nationally – struggled to get off the ground. His election address admitted that the past four years had brought great prosperity, and tried to argue that the government had not made the most of its good fortune. As well as favouring the rich, the Tories were playing a 'trick' by going to the country so soon after raising the bank rate to its highest level for a quarter of a century.[34] But Labour appeals to the memory of 1945 did little to stir voters. It came as no surprise when the Conservatives became the first government for nearly a century to be returned to power with an increased majority. Press commentators had little difficulty in ascribing the result to a combination of Labour's internal feuding and the feeling of many working-class families that they were 'doing nicely, thank you'. In Southampton the Tory majority was some 4000 greater than it turned out to be in South Gloucestershire, and Crosland was left to reflect that he had made a bad mistake in not staying put.

Crosland's political future thus looked uncertain. He had made a breakthrough as a theoretician, though he was not yet in a position to shape official party policy. His reliance on support from senior colleagues had exacerbated his own inclination to be dismissive of the everyday grind of opposition politics. The patronage he enjoyed had not ensured his survival at a time of increasing Conservative popularity. Dalton's wife said that in the spring of 1955 her husband was like an elephant going through the jungle, making frantic telephone calls trying to find a suitable seat for his protégé, all to no effect. Dalton was no longer the force he once was, and it was during these years that Crosland came to rely more on Hugh Gaitskell. As an election drew closer, Dalton wrote in his diary that things had not gone well for Crosland of late, but at least he remained on good terms with Hugh, who 'is on the up grade. That will stand him well in the future.' He ascertained from Gaitskell that in the event of a Labour victory Tony might go to the Board of Trade, where his economic expertise could be utilised to the full.[35] But there was no Labour victory, and instead of enjoying the trappings of ministerial office Crosland found himself out of the House. His first attempt to build a career in politics had hit the buffers. Where was he to go from here?

7

The Future of Socialism, 1956

Tony Crosland's early years – his home background, his war experience, and the ease with which he mingled among the great and the good at Oxford and Westminster – all helped to make him ambitious and self-confident. These qualities helped him to recover quickly from the disappointment of losing his parliamentary seat in May 1955, as did the knowledge that he had another string to his bow: his writing. The journalist Henry Fairlie observed a couple of months later that he 'no doubt finds it easier to maintain his record of attending the House as little as possible now that he is not a member of it'.[1] Farlie added that Crosland was, however, making the best of his independence, writing a series of thoughtful newspaper articles, one of them predicting that Hugh Gaitskell would soon become leader of the Labour Party. This was borne out when Attlee retired late in 1955; Gaitskell easily defeated Nye Bevan and Herbert Morrison in the ensuing PLP ballot. Crosland also used the newspaper articles – which together with a small income from shares provided him with earnings after he ceased to be an MP – to trail the arguments he intended to deploy in a new book. In the aftermath of the 1955 defeat, he wrote, Labour was no closer than it was four years before to outlining 'any coherent view of what Socialism means in the present social context'.[2] This was the main purpose of the book he had been working on intermittently over several years. At the time of the 1951 election he told one reporter that it was his ambition to write a book on the future of British socialism, and defeat in 1955 allowed him to put the finishing touches to a manuscript that he sometimes worked on for twelve hours a day.[3]

The book was not conceived as a contribution to the power struggle in the party between Gaitskellites and Bevanites. Rather Crosland wanted to fulfil his ambition of emulating Bernstein by putting flesh on the bones of arguments outlined in his earlier writings. Most of the influences upon his writing had been at work over a period of many years. The small number of friends who read

56

the entire text in advance included those who had helped to shape his economic thinking in the late 1940s: Hugh Dalton, Robert Hall and the Oxford economist Ian Little. His views on libertarianism were also firmly established before the onset of Labour's factional warfare after 1951. What was being added to his thinking in the early 1950s was an interest in sociology, especially after his visit to the United States. Although critical of what he called the 'drivel' that was associated with this new academic discipline, Crosland was much influenced by the American writer Edward Shils and by Michael Young, head of the Labour Party's research department after the war and founder of the pioneering Institute of Community Studies in Bethnal Green. From these and other sociologists Crosland was confirmed in his view that he must be able to quantify the in-equalities of life; only when the data was thoroughly understood could practical, egalitarian remedies be proposed with conviction.[4] Some of his friends thought he went too far in his admiration for America, with its more open class structure and reformed brand of capitalism. Dalton complained that the manuscript contained too much transatlantic jargon, based on an excess of 'Teutonic-American – Sociological – Psycho – Pseudo – Analytico – Pathologico Reading'.[5]

The Future of Socialism was published by Jonathan Cape at the time of Labour's annual conference in October 1956, when the Suez crisis was coincidentally at its height.[6] The text ran to over 500 pages and was divided into five parts. The first went over much of the ground Crosland had covered in his article in *New Fabian Essays*, analysing changes in British society since the war and underlining his conviction that pre-war capitalism had been transformed beyond recognition. The second part looked at how socialism needed to be redefined in the light of such changes. It was here that Crosland distinguished between ends and means. Too often, he felt, particular groups – notably Marxists, but also others like the Fabians – had appropriated the term 'socialism' to describe the means by which they would bring about reform. But as such means had never commanded universal assent, it was best that any definition of socialism should stick to the ends in view – that is to basic aspirations and moral values. Using this yardstick, socialism for Crosland was primarily about welfare and equality. Why then was socialism as he defined it still relevant in 1950s Britain? His answer was threefold: because, despite improvements in living standards, social distress and physical squalor continued on a scale which restricted freedom of choice for many; because there persisted in Britain a greater degree of social antagonism and class resentment than in other industrialised nations; and because the distribution of rewards and privileges remained highly inequitable. The belief, he summed up, that further reform would 'appreciably increase personal freedom, social contentment, and justice, constitutes the ethical basis for being a socialist'.[7]

Part three consisted of one chapter only on the welfare objective of socialism, where Crosland stressed the need to continue improving a range of public services. More distinctive, occupying some one-third of the book, was the fourth section. This centred on the 'considerable social revolution' he hoped to see achieved through egalitarian reforms, for example to the education system and to the distribution of property. He was convinced that equality of opportunity was not sufficient and that, if access to grammar schools was widened, this would merely mean a change of personnel in a new meritocracy, not the alleviation of class inequalities. Hence the need was to democratise entry to private schools, abolish the eleven-plus and develop state comprehensive schools. But he was not in favour of 'complete equality of incomes, since extra responsibility and exceptional talent require and deserve a differential reward'. He personally did not wish to see 'the Queen riding a bicycle: nor the House of Lords instantly abolished, nor the manufacture of Rolls-Royce banned'. At which point to stop in the process of creating greater equality before reaching some 'drab extreme' he had no idea. Society would look quite different when the changes he proposed had been carried out. The whole argument would then need to be re-stated, and thought out afresh, 'by a younger generation than mine'.[8]

In part five Crosland turned to the economic implications of his argument for socialist policy in the years ahead, for example in relation to investment and planning. While urging the importance of securing growth for the realisation of socialist objectives, he spent little time on the balance-of-payments issue, having set out his views on this at length in *Britain's Economic Problem*. He underlined the extent to which his thinking on public ownership had shifted since the late 1940s. There was, he claimed, a continued need to nationalise certain industries, but old-style state monopolies were bad for liberty and 'wholly irrelevant to socialism as defined in this book'. They were not essential, in other words, to establishing social equality, increasing social welfare or eliminating class distinctions. Inequalities in the distribution of private wealth could be tackled in a pluralist society as well as in a wholly state-owned economy, with better results for social contentment. For him nationalisation was one of the means of achieving socialism, not an end in its own right. He looked forward to a society with 'diverse, diffused, pluralist and heterogeneous patterns of ownership'. Crosland also emphasised his view that questions of economic efficiency were of secondary importance. As Britain stood on 'the threshold of mass abundance', Labour might still require budgetary rather than monetary controls to maintain full employment and avoid inflation, but it was social reform that should be given top priority.[9]

As well as summarising his major recommendations, the conclusion to the book included some of its most striking passages. In a reflection of his thoughts at Oxford after the war, Crosland looked ahead to a time when economic and social change had gone so far that attention could turn elsewhere: to the spheres of 'personal freedom, happiness and cultural endeavour; the cultivation of leisure, beauty, grace, gaiety, excitement, and of all the proper pursuits, whether elevated, vulgar or eccentric, which contribute to the varied fabric of a full private and family life'. In essence he developed the libertarian case that was so much a part of his thinking since the war. Reform, he hoped, might come in two directions. First he wished to see cultural changes that would make Britain 'a more colourful and civilised country to live in', his preferences including 'more open-air cafés . . . later closing-hours for public houses, brighter and cleaner eating houses, more riverside cafés, [and] more pleasure-gardens on the Battersea model'. Secondly, in what amounted to an outline of the type of government legislation introduced a decade later, he called for the updating of restrictive laws on divorce, homosexuality, censorship, and rights for women. The socialist basis for such change, Crosland argued, could be found in the work of William Morris. Once more he had the Webbs in his sights, though in more temperate language than in the past: 'Total abstinence and a good filing-system are not now the right sign-posts to the socialist Utopia; or at least, if they are, some of us will fall by the wayside.'[10]

The book was not without its critics. Conservative-supporting newspapers attacked its 'tedious length', its 'specious jargon of sociology' and its 'preposterous and dangerous views'.[11] The most hostile reviews, however, came from the Labour left. In *Tribune*, Will

Camp wrote under the headline 'Socialism? How dare he use the word!' He attacked Crosland's work for its complacency about economic prospects, arguing that, with the Tories in trouble over the economy, a doubling of living standards over the next generation could not be taken for granted.[12] John Strachey called the book 'honest' and 'searching', but employed several criticisms. In addition to the charge of complacency – could Britain so easily become a kind of 'Swedish-American community?' – he spoke of Crosland's insularity, his assumption that 'the roaring tides of the world will never wash over our white cliffs'.[13] The main concern for Strachey – as he made clear in his own work *Contemporary Capitalism*, also published in 1956 – was Crosland's refusal to accept that the pattern of industrial ownership remained the key determinant of power within British society. In Strachey's eyes nationalisation continued to have a more central role – in terms of planning, the redistribution of wealth and the pursuit of full employment – than Crosland would allow. Public ownership, in short, remained more important than equality. 'As in Calvinism', said the journalist Alan Watkins of the Labour left's attitude to revisionism, 'good works were not enough – were irrelevant even – and justification came through faith.'[14]

But hostile voices were drowned out in a sea of approval. Reviewers vied with each other in their efforts to recall when such an important work of political economy had been written. For some it was the 'best book' since Labour lost office in 1951; for others it was 'the most considerable book' on socialism since the war; others again called it the key work on socialist theory since Evan Durbin's *The Politics of Democratic Socialism* in 1940.[15] What was most noticeable was the ability of the book to impress a wide swathe of opinion, well beyond the confines of the Gaitskellite right within the Labour Party. The *Financial Times* said Crosland had left his critics in the Labour Party flailing in his wake. For all its moderation and scholarly analysis, *The Future of Socialism* was far more radical than anything the Bevanites had produced, with their 'prescription of the mixture as before'. In *The Spectator*, Graham Hutton said that the author had showed what Labour might become if it stopped being 'priggish, envious, petty and class-conscious': it would benefit from Crosland's cultivated and 'wide-visioned' programme.[16] On BBC radio's European Service, William Pickles recognised the book instantly as a major contribution to socialist ideology; in his view it was 'the most important on its subject' since the German revisionist Bernstein was writing in the 1890s. It was the first thorough-going attempt since then in any language to re-examine the whole argument for socialism, prune away irrelevant parts and 're-state what is left in terms of modern facts and needs'.[17]

What was it that reviewers so admired? Many commented on the combination of virtues which Crosland's work contained: originality, breadth of vision, rigour, clarity and wit. As well as knowing economics, he was conversant with literature from several other academic disciplines such as political theory, sociology and industrial relations. He managed to write for a wide audience with style, and he combined an interest in social theory with a pragmatic concern for social change. Lord Pakenham, writing in the *Fabian Journal*, added to this list Crosland's ability to convey his message in a way that seemed removed from the partisan tone of most politicians:

> It says what many of us have been trying to say, but says it very much better. It provides an exhilarating economic exposition of a political doctrine. Above all, it reveals the rarest of qualities in a responsible politician writing about political things – a glorious, disinterested independence. There is never a moment in Mr Crosland's 500-odd pages when he appears to be considering either the news-value of his propositions or their effect on his own future usefulness; or when one can suggest a motive, apart from the free play of his reason, and occasionally his fancy, for his expression of view.[18]

This blend of qualities helps to explain why *The Future of Socialism* remained a highly acclaimed text for a generation to come. Twenty years on it was still being referred to as the 'main intellectual fount of modern British democratic socialism', and Edward Boyle was calling it 'the most impressive contribution by any politician to serious thinking on politics/economics/social science since the war'.[19] By the mid-1970s, however, against a darker backdrop of recurrent economic crises, some opinions were being revised and it was becoming more fashionable to point to shortcomings in Crosland's analysis. Many of the complaints made – that the book was largely indifferent to feminism and environmentalism, had no clear theory of the state or about the nature of political institutions – were anachronistic. As we have seen, Crosland's ideas were addressed to the circumstances of Britain in the 1950s, not the 1970s. In believing

Anthony Crosland

that the existing powers of the state – tested and vindicated in war – could be used to secure reform, Crosland was a child of his times; his starting point was widely accepted. With hindsight, it was easy to make the charge that he assumed too readily that continuous economic growth would provide the basis for uninterrupted progress towards greater equality. His work was flawed, it was said, because it underestimated the power of capital and had nothing to fall back upon if the neat edifice of redistribution and social justice began to crumble. But this argument was made by few at the time, and when a second edition of the book was published in 1964 Crosland was already admitting that he had over-estimated the ease with which high levels of growth could be secured.[20]

Bevanites were reluctant to re-open old wounds in 1957 at a time when the Conservative government was on the back foot; Bevan himself had made peace with Gaitskell in anticipation of Labour returning to power. As a result, the only really sustained attack on Crosland made in the months after publication came from the so-called New Left, which originated among those who abandoned communism after Russia's brutal suppression of the Hungarian uprising in 1956. Norman Birnbaum, editor of the *Universities and Left Review*, argued that *The Future of Socialism* marked a retreat from the duty of a socialist party to advocate fundamental change. Crosland was prepared for this type of onslaught. It was strange, he replied drily, to be accused of not wanting radical change when he was arguing for drastic reform in education, heavy taxation to finance social services, high levels of savings and investment, and measures opposing 'British philistinism and dreariness'.[21] The status which his book had acquired by the end of the 1950s was noted by the political scientist Bernard Crick in an article on socialist literature published in 1960. It was 'beyond dispute', Crick commented, that *The Future of Socialism* was the most comprehensive and important work of the decade. Its reputation had not been harmed, he added, by the 'almost diabolical status' the book had assumed in the mythology of the New Left, which made itself look ridiculous in challenging the statistical basis of Crosland's work. Just because there were still pensioners in poverty did not invalidate Crosland's analysis, which Crick concluded was more appropriate for the 1950s than the 'denunciation and sectarian polemic' of the New Left. Too many of this recent breed were 'dupes of the old Marxists. . . . It is, brothers, the revolution or nothing.'[22]

It was a remarkable personal success for a political writer under the age of forty, ensuring that Crosland would become the acknowledged high priest of 'revisionism'. This label was commonly used after the mid-1950s to define those who advocated not 'traditional' socialism but a mix of neo-Keynesian economics and progressive social reform. By the 1970s some revisionists refused to accept the particular emphasis Crosland put on promoting equality. But at the time, the reception given to *The Future of Socialism* could hardly have been warmer, for it provided exactly what the Labour centre-right had been looking for: an exciting synthesis of reformism and radicalism which went beyond Morrisonian 'consolidation', making socialism look relevant to the circumstances of the day and offering a balance between economic efficiency and social justice.

Gaitskell was immensely proud of his friend's book, which in the short-term gave theoretical underpinning to the type of policies the party leader sought to promote. In the years ahead it was to be an inspiration for a new generation of aspiring Labour politicians, including Roy Hattersley, David Owen, William Rodgers and Shirley Williams. Its success was magnified by the failure of the Labour left to provide anything comparable. In the words of John Campbell, *The Future of Socialism* was everything that *In Place of Fear* was not. Whereas Crosland's work became the 'Bible' for the moderate wing of the party, Bevan's political testament of 1952 failed to acquire a similar status among Labour fundamentalists.[23] Crosland even won grudging regard from Bevanites such as Dick Crossman, who conceded that his ideas were more radical than the promise to nationalise ICI: 'they are diabolically and cunningly left wing and Nye should have been clever enough to think them up'.[24] In many respects the book was a slow burner, its influence growing steadily over the course of the next decade. What it did not do, as we shall see in the next chapter, was to transform Crosland's career overnight.

8

Marking Time, 1957-9

The Future of Socialism was not a launch pad to instant political success. For a short while, Crosland could sit back and soak up the accolades. Hugh Dalton wrote in his diary that, with the book selling well and receiving generally positive reviews, Tony was 'very happy and cheerful . . . and is now pretty well off'.[1] His income was bolstered by royalties as sales from the book rose in subsequent years to over 20,000 copies, more than ten times the level of his later works. During the months after publication, however, Crosland's heightened sense of achievement receded. His next main contribution to political life, a report on the workings of the Co-operative movement, proved much less successful. And although he continued to have the ear of Hugh Gaitskell, he was aware that without a parliamentary base his direct influence in party matters was limited. Gaitskell did begin to steer policy in a more explicitly revisionist direction, but Crosland was not in a position to take much of the credit, and many around him still considered him to be – in the words of Dalton – a 'political problem-child'. Far from bringing Crosland immediate rewards, his elevated status as a theoretician left him uncertain as how best to channel his high ambitions; as in the late 1940s, he considered whether to abandon thoughts of a Westminster career altogether. This period of marking time was brought to an end only when fortune, which deserted him in 1955, came to his rescue at the 1959 general election.

Much of Crosland's time during 1957 was devoted to the Co-op. In 1955 the Co-operative Movement's annual congress had voted to set up an independent commission to find ways of revitalising methods of production and marketing. In the affluent society of the 1950s the Co-op found itself struggling to keep pace with the new world of large-scale retailing; its share of national retail trade had remained unchanged since before the war, while private companies were forging ahead. Gaitskell, as chairman of the commission, appointed Crosland as secretary to take charge of proceedings and to assume responsibility for the report. Crosland's research skills and thoroughness were much in evidence. He visited some twenty-five local co-operative societies in towns as distant as Cardiff, Glasgow, Harrogate and Bristol. When the task was completed, the commission paid tribute to the 'great energy, exceptional ability and complete intellectual integrity' of the Secretary. Among a mass of recommendations in his wide-ranging report, three priorities stood out: the need to revise management structures while retaining democratic control; the importance of slimming down the number of local societies to allow concentration on fewer and better quality products; and the suggestion of a retail development society to provide central direction and lead the drive towards an increased trade share.[2]

The *Economist*, in acknowledging Crosland's crucial role, called the report an 'impressive document', and praised the movement for its courage in publishing such a dispassionate appraisal of its operations.[3] Unfortunately for its author, several establishment newspapers could not resist the line that Co-ops were simply being urged to 'copy' private enterprise by adopting more efficient methods. This encouraged a backlash within the Co-operative movement. Those suspicious of any plan which would make the Co-op into a 'glorified quasi-capitalist concern' set their face against the comprehensive package on offer.[4] Exploiting the organisation's cumbersome structure, which allowed local societies to block early action, Crosland's opponents gradually stifled the momentum for reform. By the end of 1958 he could no longer contain his frustration. He publicly made clear that he regarded the decision of the central executive to set up further studies into key recommendations as amounting to 'a virtual rejection of the Commission's report'. Such delay, he added emphatically, would not stem the challenge from retail competition.[5] In this, his major contribution to public policy in the aftermath of *The Future of Socialism*, the outcome for Crosland was bitterly disappointing.

He was at least thankful that Gaitskell had given him a major task to undertake, and his association with the party leader ensured that he kept in touch with developments in Labour politics. Gaitskell had brought a new air of decisiveness to the leadership, exploiting the party's mood for unity by offering past antagonists such as Bevan and Harold Wilson important posts in the shadow cabinet. He also benefited from disaffection with the Conservative government; this survived Eden's departure in the wake of Suez and continued through 1957 as the new Prime Minister, Harold Macmillan, struggled to overcome unpopularity during a downturn in the economy. Crosland's link with the Labour high command was based in the first instance on personal friendship. Woodrow Wyatt recalled that while he, Roy Jenkins and Crosland were all on good terms with Gaitskell, there was no doubt who was the favourite. Like Dalton, Gaitskell enjoyed Crosland's outspoken teasing of his political seniors. 'There was', Wyatt added, 'a scintilla of platonic homosexuality in his affection for Tony, which Socrates would have understood. Hugh loved his mind but also his looks and the eternal undergraduate youthfulness of his raffish parties in The Boltons.'[6]

Crosland's influence was also based on shared outlook. He was pushing at an open door in urging Gaitskell to adopt revisionist policies. Although the party did not adopt wholesale recommendations made in *The Future of Socialism*, greater equality was a key concern in proposals which began to filter through in the findings of party committees from 1956 onwards. Crosland was also delighted when the annual conference in 1957 endorsed by a margin of almost four to one the influential document *Industry and Society*, which played down the adoption of further wholesale nationalisation. One of the authors of the document was Peter Shore, working at the time in the Labour Party's research department. He was surprised to find that some of his propositions were toned down after Gaitskell sent a copy to Crosland for revision, which he did by advocating the notion of the state gradually extending shareholding in major companies. The conclusions inserted by Crosland provided the party leader with, in Brian Brivati's words 'a politically effective fudge. If the Conservatives focused on Shore's part of the statement, then Gaitskell could stress that the only specific commitments on nationalisation were road haulage and steel; if the left attacked the lack of commitment to taking over the commanding heights, then the ambiguity of the idea of purchasing shares in companies that were failing the national interest could be played up.' It was a testimony to Gaitskell's high regard for Crosland, Shore recalled, that he should be allowed to intervene in this way when he was neither an MP nor a member of the party's National Executive Committee (NEC).[7]

This example of direct influence was, however, the exception rather than the rule. As an unofficial adviser, preoccupied with his work for the Co-op, Crosland had an impact on policy that was limited and episodic. His close ties with Gaitskell also proved to be double-edged. While Labour appeared on course for government, Crosland could take quiet satisfaction, and his behind-the-scenes role attracted little comment. But when things turned sour, and Labour's prospects of election victory receded, he became the subject of resentment and criticism. With 'Supermac' emerging as a formidable Tory leader on the back of an economic upturn in 1958, cracks began to reappear in the façade of Labour unity. Frustrated by this turn of events, the trade union group within the PLP in particular put much of the blame on the 'Hampstead set' – the Oxford-educated intellectuals who it was alleged decided policy over wine on Sunday evening visits to Gaitskell's home in Frognal Gardens. Many MPs, Crossman wrote in his diary, felt it was these advisers – including Roy Jenkins and Patrick Gordon Walker as well as Crosland – who urged Gaitskell to adopt a 'policy of saying nothing and playing safe', despite a recovery in Tory popularity.[8] Crosland found himself becoming a scapegoat. Instead of attacking the party leader, critics turned on his shadowy advisers, especially those like Crosland with no political base of his own from which to strike back against detractors. One of the most prominent of these detractors was the shadow Chancellor, Harold Wilson.

The mutual dislike between the Gaitskellites and Wilson – which was to play a key role in the later history of the Labour Party – had its roots in the factional struggle of the early 1950s. Bevan's stature and past record had earned him the wary respect even of his opponents. The same did not apply to Bevan's younger acolytes including Harold Wilson. In 1953 Wilson was in Paris on European business with several colleagues including Gaitskell, Jenkins and Crosland. Richard Crossman wrote in his diary that there was no danger of him, Wilson, being 'bought off by this gang' as he knew they 'hate him more than the rest of all us put together'.[9] What was such hatred based upon? Wilson's friends believed that the middle-class Gaitskellites were condescending about the shadow Chancellor's more humble background. They were certainly disparaging about his competence as an economist, despite the fact – as Wilson defensively pointed out – that he obtained the only starred double first in economics at Oxford between the wars. They were also scornful of the suburban domesticity of his lifestyle. One journalist who experienced Labour's in-fighting in the 1950s later wrote that the 'snobby Frognalites' affected to believe that Wilson had 'china ducks on his sitting room wall'.[10] As far as most Gaitskellites were concerned, Wilson's driving personal ambition was his cardinal sin; they believed that 'all his judgements are political' and that he had no overriding sense of purpose, as he showed by detaching himself from the Bevanites after 1955. In private, Crosland referred to him as 'dirty little Wilson'. Wilson in turn was among those who complained to friends that 'Our Leader' paid far too much attention to the likes of Crosland.[11]

The late 1950s may therefore have seen Crosland win admirers from afar as *The Future of Socialism* gained in reputation, but it was a different story in the closed world of Labour politics. Here his ties with Gaitskell increased the number who harboured resentments and jealousies, especially as Crosland refused to engage in 'squalid' efforts to please for its own sake.

His outspoken manner and unconventional behaviour were proving more testing than usual for his friends. Roy Jenkins recalled that in the years when Crosland lived alone after the break-up of his marriage he became remarkably inflexible about time, making social arrangements into major diplomatic negotiations. Another friend believed that his self-discipline while writing led him to measure time in very small blocks; when he said 'drop in at about ten to seven', he meant precisely that.[12] When he did consent to join a social gathering, Crosland was often an awkward guest. Woodrow Wyatt remembered one dinner party at which he suddenly announced to the assembled company, 'this is terribly boring'; he put his feet up on a sofa, where they remained for an hour as he pretended to sleep.[13] These same friends admit that at other times he could be immensely charming and amusing. Jenkins called him the 'most exciting friend' of his life, capable of suffusing a room with a great glow of warmth when in the right mood; and Wyatt recognised that his boorishness was often 'the pose of a pleasant man wanting to seem a tough Al Capone'.[14]

David Marquand, who later became an admirer, first came across him at an Oxford seminar in the mid-1950s: 'I took an instant dislike to him. . . . He seemed to typify what I most disliked about the Southern English mandarinate. He had a cut-glass accent. He was insufferably sure of himself. He was appallingly and gratuitously rude.'[15] In similar vein, A. H. Halsey, who in the 1960s became one of Crosland's education advisers, was put off Crosland at first acquaintance during his Co-op study, and described him with his exaggerated Oxford accent and flamboyant dress as 'a large, formidable, aggressive, outspoken man: always like the biggest and rudest boy in the playground'.[16] New relationships that Crosland formed at this time tended to be among those from outside the British political establishment. One such was with Susan Catling, the attractive American-born wife of Patrick Catling, a journalist working in London; both husband and wife became friends in 1957 when 'conviviality was active at 19 The Boltons, or in the Catling flat'.[17] Another acquaintance was the society hostess Ann Fleming, who frequently invited Crosland to parties at her Victoria Square home, teasing him into accepting by commending his 'provocative personality' and his 'unique and irresistible' manners. Gaitskell sometimes used Crosland's flat for his liasions with Ann, and she joked that when she went to bed with Gaitskell, she liked to imagine she was with the more debonair Crosland.[18]

Tony Benn, who had been a friend since his Oxford tutor helped him to secure the Labour candidacy for Bristol South East in 1950, speculated on Crosland's career after confirmation of Crosland's divorce came through in 1957. At a gathering, intended as 'some sort of celebration', Hugh Dalton and Roy Jenkins were the only two people Benn knew; the others were a 'sort of rootless crowd of nondescript men and rather sulky women' in their mid-twenties and thirties. At other times, Gaitskell was the only politician invited to parties at The Boltons, where other guests were economists, actresses or writers such as Kingsley Amis, who engaged in a violent argument with Patrick Catling over tenor saxophonists as jazz played in the background on the gramophone. Crosland, according to Benn, was a 'very unhappy person', still on the run from his strict upbringing and trying to catch up with his lost wartime youth, which at 'thirty-nine is rather silly'. Altogether Benn felt things did not augur well:

> He is unusually gifted as an economist and has a very clear mind with a very great faith in the power of reason. But the proof of his unhappiness is his curious death wish, which he showed when in the Commons, and which now takes the form of affecting to be bored with current politics. If he gets back into Parliament he will get high office. If he does not, then his life could be a very tragic one.[19]

Others who attended Crosland's parties paint a more upbeat picture, of a glamorous, almost bohemian world of lively jazz records, half-filled wine glasses and ashtrays spread around the flat.[20] But Benn's assessment did reflect Crosland's own self-disregard for his prospects. By 1958 he appeared to be increasingly detached from Labour politics. At one meeting of the Fabian Society executive committee, to which he had been elected in 1955, Crosland airily dismissed the argument that the Fabians were being eclipsed by the New Left, claiming that the political activities of the under thirty-five age group were of no great interest. 'All this was said in a most bored and offensive way', noted one observer, 'and was greeted with a titter of laughter.'[21] He gave the impression that he didn't much care what others thought of him, even if this meant that he was accused of lacking seriousness or conviction. For A. H. Halsey, his love of freedom was 'immoderate' and driven: 'Alcohol, cigars, women, even opera were avidly consumed. Life's candle was burned at both ends and in the middle'.[22] Part of the reason for this devil-may-care attitude was a genuine ambivalence over his future plans. He later admitted that after completing his work on the Co-op report, he did waver about whether to go back into politics. A return to academic life or a full-time writing career were attractive options: he had been out of the Commons for some time, and was not certain that he wanted to go back.[23]

Intensely annoyed by the emasculation of his Co-op report, Crosland was finally persuaded by Gaitskell that he could only build a long-term political career if he returned to the House at the next election. The party leader's determination on this score was evident in his brusque treatment of the Labour MP for Grimsby, Kenneth Younger, who was about to resign in order to become Director of the Royal Institute of International Affairs at Chatham House. At a meeting with Younger, Gaitskell immediately asked about the size of the Labour majority in Grimsby, and welcomed the news that it was above three thousand with the comment that the seat was 'a possibility for Tony Crosland'. Younger reported that the whole interview was over in about two minutes, with no pretence of regret about his own departure from the House or discussion of his own plans.[24] As in the case of South Gloucestershire in 1950, Crosland was the beneficiary of support at the top of the Labour hierarchy. In the selection conference that followed Younger's resignation, he won a clear majority over four other rivals, including another young hopeful, William Rodgers.

During August 1959, with an election likely in the autumn,

Crosland spent two weeks on a Grimsby trawler as it pitched on the North Sea. The whole experience, he recalled, reminded him of army days – the rugged physical life, the camaraderie and the good-natured arguments with the Tory-supporting skipper, each chalking rival slogans on the bridge blackboard while most of the crew remained indifferent to politics.[25] He did not have long to get to know his new constituency. The predominantly working-class citizens of Grimsby, as one profile writer observed, were 'fish-obsessed'. Though taking second place to Hull as a port, Grimsby was the home of some major concentrations of ships and capital, notably the Ross Group, which alone operated over forty trawlers. Working long days at sea, often in fog, gales or extreme cold, the local fisherman – rather like miners – had a low opinion of many who worked in less perilous trades. While locals might describe the Grimsby character as 'independent', outsiders were more inclined to call it 'bloody-minded'.[26]

In October 1959 Macmillan called the expected election, confident that 'never had it so good' prosperity would deliver another Conservative victory. Labour fought the election on what has been called a revisionist manifesto with a socialist peroration. Policy on public ownership was in line with the *Industry and Society* document of 1957, and pride of place went to social policies such as the end of selection in secondary schooling and increased spending on pensions.[27] Gaitskell fought a more vigorous campaign than Attlee had in 1955, but was always on the defensive after the Tories seized on his claim that improved social services would not require increased taxation. Grimsby was far from natural territory for an Oxford-trained intellectual, and Crosland may not have helped his own cause by introducing himself in his election leaflet as a 'writer and broadcaster'. His Tory opponent, Walter Pearson, was both a Grimsby man and a fish merchant. The difficulties of getting known in the town, combined with the general movement of opinion towards the Conservatives, meant that Kenneth Younger's comfortable majority was all but wiped out. After the drama of a recount, Crosland scraped home by just 101 votes, with the swing against Labour at some 4 per cent being well above the national average. Even so, in personal terms, the 'Giant Bad Luck' of 1955 had turned to Giant Good Luck in 1959. Crosland's ideas were gaining ground and he was on his way back to Westminster. Any personal satisfaction was tempered, however, by Labour's national defeat. As in the early

71

1950s, Crosland would have to develop his career from the opposition benches, and at a time when mutiny in the ranks was the order of the day.

9

'Mr Gaitskell's Ganymede', 1959-63

Crosland's conduct as an MP after 1959 was in sharp contrast to his behaviour in the Commons before 1955. He continued to dislike parliamentary routine and rationed the number of his speeches and appearances whenever possible. But there was less recklessness on public display, and his old Oxford tutor Robert Hall wrote that Crosland was 'trying for a new look'.[1] In part this was due to the narrowness of his victory in Grimsby, which compelled him to work hard as a constituency MP: he was conscious that another defeat like 1955 might put paid once and for all to his political ambitions. There was a further personal consideration in his more studied approach to life at Westminster. Gaitskell's high regard for Crosland had been much in evidence before the 1959 election. During the campaign Gaitskell instructed the party's publicity machine to build up the leading figures then ignore the 'second eleven' and go straight on to the younger generation, including Crosland, Jenkins and Healey.[2] Once back in the House, it was obvious that Crosland would figure as a potential minister in Gaitskell's plans, providing the party could broaden its appeal sufficiently to return to power. It was to this challenge that Crosland devoted most of his energy in the early 1960s. In the process he further enhanced his reputation as a writer, he displayed organisational qualities many never knew he possessed, and – despite jibes from opponents – retained his identity as a loyal but not slavish Gaitskellite. Crosland in his early forties looked set, it seemed, to realise his potential.

The third successive electoral defeat for Labour was a crushing blow. Unlike 1955, it was not possible to blame internal disunity, and some commentators concluded that the party looked obsolete in the face of rising living standards and the emergence of the so-called 'affluent worker'. Most of Labour's losses were concentrated in and around London and the West Midlands, areas that had prospered economically in the 1950s, whereas regions that experienced rising unemployment went against the national trend by recording a small swing against Macmillan, whose majority rose to an impressive 100 seats. Gaitskell pointed out that the party still commanded well over 40 per cent of all votes cast, but he could not prevent the outbreak of renewed in-fighting as the search for scapegoats began. Gaitskellites claimed that Labour suffered from its old-fashioned image as the party of nationalisation. The left, in turn, found it outrageous that those who dictated policy could claim that defeat made it necessary to move further to the right. Gaitskell himself stoked the embers of controversy by proposing in November 1959 that the party should amend Clause Four of its constitution – the aim, reprinted on membership cards, of securing the 'common ownership of the means of production, distribution and exchange'. Gaitskell tried to insist that his desire for an updated constitution would not rule out public ownership in future, but for many trade unionists and activists adherence to Clause Four was a basic article of faith. To attack such a vital symbol was like trying, in Harold Wilson's later words, to persuade fundamentalists to take Genesis out of the Bible.[3] During the period of blood-letting that ensued, Gaitskell's leadership came under direct challenge.

At the outset, Crosland was not much involved in the inquest into the 1959 defeat. The Hampstead Set met over the weekend following the election at Gaitskell's house, where discussions were conducted, as Roy Jenkins recalled, 'more casually than conspiratorially'. On the Saturday evening Crosland left early from a prearranged farewell dinner for Hugh Dalton to meet 'one of his actress friends', and the following day he was subdued like others and said 'practically nothing'.[4] When Gaitskell floated his idea of amending Clause Four, Crosland advised that it would be better to let sleeping dogs lie. Like other friends, he told the leader that it would 'start a battle in the Party that will cause far more trouble than the thing is worth'.[5] In spite of his private reservations, once Gaitskell went public with his plan Crosland came out as a strong loyalist and found himself under heavy criticism. After several months of heated exchanges – with Crosland helping to draft speeches arguing for a broadening of party aims – Gaitskell was forced to back down. As soon as a compromise form of words had been agreed, new battle lines were drawn up, with left-wing union leaders pressing for the adoption of a unilateralist defence policy. Crosland was again supportive in public, but the robustness of his private advice verged on the insubordinate. Defeat over Clause Four, he lamented, was being followed by an unplanned defensive action over the bomb. There were no positive reforms in sight, Gaitskell was more heavily criticised than at any time in his leadership and the morale of the right wing of the party was 'appallingly low'. If we cannot reverse the trend of the last seven months, he concluded, 'we shall certainly lose in 1964.'[6]

Gaitskell pointedly ruled out Crosland's suggestion of a supremo to provide him with better party intelligence, but he was happy to endorse a new grass-roots organisation, the Campaign For Democratic Socialism (CDS), which emerged as a bulwark against the unilateralist views of the left. Crosland played a critical role in the events that led to the formal launch of CDS in June 1960. His first contribution came as an 'ideological inspiration', helping to draft documents for the new group in conjunction with his old Oxford friend, Philip Williams. More surprisingly, he was also an organisational catalyst. He gave a clear lead at meetings held in his flat, insisting that those present work uninterrupted for several hours before anyone could have a drink. 'Look,' Crosland said, impressing young Gaitskellites such as Dick Taverne, 'forget about all this talk about intellectualism. We are apparatchiks.'[7] Other founders of the new movement such as William Rodgers were struck by a single-minded sense of purpose they had not detected before in Crosland, who clearly revelled in the challenge. One young enthusiast was told by Crosland that he 'had not felt so happy for years', finding great comfort in discovering so many others prepared to defend their views publicly.[8] In the autumn of 1960, some 20,000 copies were issued of a CDS manifesto which read almost like Crosland's personal credo. The aim, it stated, was to fight back against the 'disastrous' shift towards unilateralism in the party and to reassert a 'non-doctrinal, practical and humanitarian socialism – a creed of conscience and reform rather than of class hatred'.[9]

After his pivotal role in the early days of CDS, Crosland switched the main focus of his contribution to the Gaitskellite cause. Though he might playfully dismiss 'intellectualism', he produced a torrent of articles in newspapers and journals. More so than before 1959, his writing was dictated by Labour's in-fighting. In place of the broad brush arguments of *The Future of Socialism*, Crosland produced several populist pieces attacking what he called the 'conservative' orthodoxy of the Labour left. In the *News Chronicle* he was strident: 'Stop talking about mass unemployment – it's gone. Stop hankering after controls

– nobody wants them. Stop "knocking" today's prosperity – it's genuine'. He revealed that he preferred the name 'Social Democratic Party'; but, recognising that 'Labour' commanded the loyalty of millions of voters, he believed it was better to leave the name alone and concentrate instead on making the party's outlook and presentation relevant to 1960, not 1935. Without abandoning 'Socialist principles', Labour must seek to represent both the class-conscious Scottish miner and also the 'un class-conscious technician owning a car and living in a new Midlands housing estate'.[10] It was the forcefulness of his attacks on the 'increasingly irrelevant' left that made him the villain-in-chief among his detractors. 'Mr Gaitskell's Ganymede' was the phrase coined by the *New Statesman*: 'He is the cupbearer of the revisionist draught which has thrown Zeus and his court into a gloomy intoxication.'[11]

There was more substance to Crosland's work than populist polemic, however, and during 1960 he made two in-depth attempts to come to terms with the crisis facing the party. In March in 'The Future of the Left' he reflected on what he saw as the main causes of the 1959 defeat: the difficulty of dislodging a government which maintained both full employment and stable prices, and the extent to which Labour was suffering from its sectional, traditional class appeal. If, he said, detailed study of voting patterns confirmed that social trends were operating against Labour, the party had no choice but 'to adapt itself, without in any way surrendering basic principles, to the realities of social change, and to present itself to the electorate in a mid-20th century guise'. In any such process, it would be 'absurd' to claim that there was nothing left of socialism if nationalisation was demoted to a lower status. Differences, he said, would still be acute over issues such as the priority given to social welfare. For the moment it was not necessary to spell out detailed policies. The real need was to distinguish between the harmfulness of Tory un-regulated private interest and the fundamental character of Britain's affluent society. To dismiss the latter as 'evil' and 'rotten' was 'electorally imbecile' and arrogant on the part of those who enjoyed material benefits but wished to deny them to others. If Labour could adapt itself to new realities it would still find plenty of genuine battles to fight and 'might even get back into power, and have a chance to win them'.[12]

In May Crosland developed these themes in his second substantive contribution to the debate, a Fabian pamphlet entitled 'Can Labour

Win?' In this he noted that detailed studies of the election, for example the 'Nuffield' analysis carried out by David Butler, were confirming the importance of changes to the class system in determining voting patterns, as well as the crucial role played by party image. Unlike many colleagues, Crosland familiarised himself with the latest academic research, endorsing the view that while the Tories had lost many of the 'repulsive' aspects of their image over recent years Labour was too widely regarded as old-fashioned. He then went on to give some attention to areas of policy that might enhance Labour's prospects in the years to come, giving a high priority to creating genuine educational opportunity and suggesting radical reform in housing and urban planning. He reiterated that for some time to come the chief priority was not with detailed policy-making, which had been tried after 1955, but with rectifying Labour's 'one-class image'.[13] The pamphlet was sufficiently important to come to the attention of the Conservative Research Department, which described it as a 'first-rate bit of work'. Basking in the recent thumping victory, Tory strategists were confident that Crosland could not single-handedly refashion Labour's image. But it was conceded that his analysis was persuasive, notably his point that 'Conservative prosperity' – a trump card in 1959 – might become taken for granted by voters five years on, just as the achievement of full employment had lost its potency as a post-war election winner for Labour.[14]

Taken together, these two essays confirmed Crosland's reputation as the chief intellectual scourge of the Labour left. Many of his opponents were infuriated both by Crosland's message and by his languid style and air of certainty. Crossman, in restating the case for extending public ownership, attacked Crosland's 'mixture of Bohemian flippancy and economic punditry'. The two men had drifted apart since the days of working together on the *New Fabian Essays*. When a story appeared in the press referring to them as Labour's only great thinkers, Crosland – stung by continuing jibes about 'Bohemian flippancy' – made it clear that he regarded Crossman primarily as a 'vulgar journalist'.[15] For several months the Crosland–Crossman exchange reverberated. At one party meeting Crosland denounced left-wingers for hawking one of his articles around the Tea Room 'like a dirty postcard'. Michael Foot joined in the fray by arguing that the caution of the Gaitskellites was the prime cause of Labour's malaise. The party he said must reawaken a desire for radical change by unmasking the government's 'complacent optimism' and exposing the 'immoral assumptions' of a 'casino society'.[16] Spokesmen for the New Left were even more emphatic in denouncing what they called the 'Crosland revolution'. He and his supporters, it was claimed, had shown a gross failure of political imagination in failing to champion 'new horizons' among 'telly-glued, car-raving mindless consumers'.[17]

In October 1960 Crosland took stock of the debate. Some historians have claimed that the argument was rhetorical more than substantial; yet the vehemence of the exchanges pointed to fundamental differences of outlook and strategy. With the party conference looming, Crosland bemoaned that British Labour, unlike many of its continental counterparts, was in danger of drifting into 'fundamentalist irrelevance'. There were, he believed, three mistaken types of view which underpinned the left's resistance to change. One was an aversion to prosperity among many people who had never themselves experienced poverty: 'while a puritan government of one's own life is admirable, a Pharisaical attitude to the lives of others is revolting'. The second objection, which he also dismissed, was the idea that to change was to become immoral, power-centred and indistinguishable from the Tories. Finally, and most dangerous of all, was the view he attributed to Crossman that Labour need only wait, 'uncompromising and uncontaminated, for the inevitable capitalist crisis'. Many of the assumptions behind the case for greater public ownership, he claimed, were not proven, notably the belief that high Russian growth was due to the inherent superiority of the Soviet system. For Labour to withdraw to its winter quarters, he concluded, would be highly irresponsible and would condemn British people to another decade of Tory rule. An unreconstructed Labour Party, committed to 'all-out nationalisation and austerity', would find no way back to power and would not deserve to do so.[18]

By this time Crosland was preoccupied with the growing challenge to Gaitskell's leadership. Tempers frayed in the leader's circle as Gaitskell rejected Crosland's blunt advice to improve relations with senior colleagues, saying they could not be regarded as 'rational human beings'.[19] The reason for Gaitskell's tetchiness became obvious at the Scarborough conference in October 1960, when union block votes helped to ensure the passage of two unilateralist resolutions. Gaitskell famously pledged to 'fight and fight and fight again' to reverse the decision, but in the short-term he had to fight to secure his own position. Within weeks Harold Wilson challenged for the leadership, standing not on the basis of unilateralism but as a 'unity' candidate opposed to Gaitskell's 'confrontational' style. Crosland, aware that defeat for Gaitskell might ruin his own prospects as well as the party's, took a leading part in persuading any reluctant MPs to come into line. In order to push Wilson's vote as low as possible, he wrote to Gaitskell, 'we must resort to any degree of chicanery, lying, etc'.[20] In the event, Gaitskell – without too much recourse to 'chicanery' – secured a comfortable, two-to-one victory in the PLP ballot. For his part, Wilson had put down a useful marker for the future, but the contest left a nasty aftertaste. As Wilson's biographer Ben Pimlott notes, while the Gaitskellites 'never forgave him for his treachery, Wilson never forgot their hatred'.[21]

In retrospect, the leadership contest was the start of an impressive fightback by Gaitskell. During the following year he both restored his personal authority and put Labour in a position to benefit from a turn-around in electoral fortunes. The process was aided by the development of CDS, which actively promoted revisionist ideas among constituency activists and trade unionists. Crucially, some of the major unions decided in the interests of party unity to back Gaitskell in his effort to overturn the 1960 Scarborough decision on defence and return to a multilateral policy. This meant that Gaitskell could afford to ignore some of the advice given to him by Crosland, who urged him to isolate his irreconcilable opponents by expelling from the party '20 hard-boiled extreme Left, stretching from genuine fellow-travellers to Tribune extremists'. As in the past, Crosland's candid views were not always welcome to Gaitskell. Their main bone of contention was Crosland's belief that the party's middle-class elite was leading from too rigid a right-wing position, displaying 'no emotional desire to change any major aspect of the society in which we are living'. The dispute spilled over into the private life of the two men. Crosland expressed his fear that Gaitskell might be subtly seduced by the glamorous London world in which he now moved. In response to the jibe that he had experienced his own 'Duke's Daughters Period', Crosland said he was not Labour leader at the time.[22]

In spite of their differences, Crosland was delighted at the extent to which things started to go Gaitskell's way. Victory at the 1961 conference on defence helped to bolster a growing public perception that he was a strong leader, at the very time that Macmillan was flagging badly in the face of fresh economic difficulties. The party rallied behind a new statement of policy, *Signposts for the Sixties*, which Crosland told the PLP was the finest party document since the war, combining calls for both social egalitarianism and economic planning.[23] And Labour's revival at the ballot box – in by-elections and at local elections – was such that Gaitskell was being spoken of realistically as the next Prime Minister. Crosland could take satisfaction from his part in helping to ensure such a transformation. Writing to Gaitskell, he elaborated on his reasons for thinking that Labour's new policy agenda was encouraging. It struck exactly the right cautious note on nationalisation, he said, adopted issues that would appeal to a wide section of public opinion (some taken 'word for word from my revisionist article in the May *Encounter*!') and marked a welcome radicalism on the part of the leadership, so helping to win back valuable centre and centre-left support inside the party. All this also meant, Crosland added, that Labour's 'traditional Union-dominated proletarian class-image' would gradually be submerged by party identification with its 'fortunately bourgeois leader' and by the more classless appeal of a progressive agenda.[24]

It was not all mutual back-slapping between Crosland and Gaitskell. The two men were again at odds in late 1962 over the issue of Europe. Labour was under pressure to declare its attitude towards Macmillan's push for membership of the Common Market. The Gaitskellites, with varying degrees of enthusiasm, were advocates of closer European integration, and Crosland wrote to Gaitskell shortly before the party conference spelling out his view. The case for British entry, he believed, did not hinge on economic arguments: gain and losses would largely cancel each other out, though he hoped that the European psychology of rapid growth might rub off on Britain. The nub of his support was political: Britain needed to find a new role in the world and avoid the bitterness that could come from loss of empire and great power status. The idea of relying on the Atlantic alliance was a 'pipedream' and would lead to British isolation and decline.[25] Crosland's view – which was later to cause him great difficulty inside the party – was thus mildly though not fanatically pro-European. But as with Clause Four, Gaitskell refused to take his advice, and Crosland like others was surprised when at the conference Gaitskell made an impassioned speech against British entry. After rallying anti-Market forces, who tended to be on the Labour left, Gaitskell faced down bitterly disappointed CDS loyalists, telling them that Europe was a nuisance and should not deflect from the party's domestic agenda. Crosland certainly agreed that the Market was not an overriding priority, but this did not prevent the two men having some of their sharpest exchanges.[26]

Anguish over Europe was offset for Crosland by the success that accompanied the publication of his latest book. In November 1962 he brought together much of his thinking over the previous few years in *The Conservative Enemy: A Programme of Radical Reform for the 1960s*. As the title implied, this was a less wide-ranging study than *The Future of Socialism*. Rather, as he wrote in his preface, it was intended to supplement and update his earlier work by outlining 'a programme of radical, social-democratic reform for the middle 1960s'. This was done through a series of individual essays, about half of which had been published before, notably his well-known pieces on strategy such as 'Can Labour Win?' The principal 'enemy' before the nation, he asserted, was Macmillan's government, whose dismal record was such that Britain was gripped by a mood of national introspection. In this respect Crosland's work was in line with a growing body of 'state of the nation' literature, characterised by Penguin specials with titles such as *The Stagnant Society*; but with his usual candour Crosland pointed an accusing finger at his own party. He openly acknowledged what he had often told Gaitskell in private: the traditional Labour right had for too long lacked a genuinely radical appeal. Many elements on the mainstream and New Left, meanwhile, were 'conservative' in a more pernicious way, clinging to 'an out-dated semi-Marxist analysis of society'. Fortunately, he felt, there were signs of an emerging body of progressive, outward-looking opinion, which Labour needed to harness in order to lead the counter-attack against 'both conservatism and the Conservative Party'.[27]

On policy issues, the book was divided into two parts, the first dealing with familiar economic concerns such as the role of public ownership and wealth. He later called *The Conservative Enemy* 'much the angriest' of his works, and this was borne out by his chapter on 'Inequalities of Wealth', which began trenchantly: 'The contrast between the ample and often luxurious lives of the better-off classes, and the constricting circumstances of the 'submerged tenth' still

81

lacerated by poverty or filthy housing, is offensive to compassion and humanity, let alone to socialist principles.'

As ever, Crosland was keen to ground his analysis in verifiable data. In spite of post-war changes, he noted that less than 2 per cent of adults in Britain owned 50 per cent of total personal net capital, whereas 75 per cent of the adult population owned less than 9 per cent of wealth. His proposed remedies suggested that, were he ever to become Chancellor, he intended to emulate his early mentor Hugh Dalton by introducing radical tax reform. The existing tax system, he claimed, was 'scandously kind to property-owners', and could only be made more equitable by measures such as a comprehensive levy on capital gains and an annual tax on capital wealth. His proposals, he insisted – in contrast to many favoured by the left – were not designed as indiscriminate attacks on wealth. His aim was to create a more just and humane community by tackling the most hurtful contrasts in living standards and by removing 'the dead hand of inherited property. So far from penalising, they will positively foster individual initiative and enterprise.'[28]

The second section dealt with social and cultural issues such as urban planning and the role of the mass media. Whereas *The Future of Socialism* concentrated on state schooling, he turned his attention in this section to a problem that was to concern him as a minister – how an incoming Labour government should deal with private schools. Crosland's egalitarianism was nowhere more passionately expressed than in his attitude to the so-called 'public' schools. 'This privileged stratum of education', he argued, 'the exclusive preserve of the wealthier classes, socially and physically segregated from the state educational system, is the greatest single cause of stratification and class-consciousness in Britain.' Crosland echoed the view of social commentators such as Anthony Sampson, whose best-selling work *Anatomy of Britain* was also published in 1962. As Britain lagged behind its major industrial competitors, Crosland argued, public schools could no longer claim even to be providing efficient leadership for the country. The objectives of a Labour policy should be threefold: to assimilate the schools into the state sector, so that they played a full part in the national effort; to democratise entry procedures; and to limit the power of the rich to 'buy social privilege through buying a privileged education'. His main proposal for achieving these objectives was for schools to allocate a majority of places to non-fee-paying pupils from the state sector. This he felt should be secured by agreement if possible, since any imposed scheme was likely to cause a mass loss of teachers and so dissipate vital educational capital. While there might be difficulties in determining the scope and criteria for selecting free places, he was adamant that Labour 'must give a high priority to this reform'.[29]

Crosland's latest publication sold many fewer copies than *The Future of Socialism*, appearing in the bookshops too late to coincide with Labour's annual conference. *The Conservative Enemy* was clearly a less substantial book. It lacked the same freshness and originality of *The Future of Socialism*, and was open to the charge that it left large gaps in policy discussion, notably on trade union reform and foreign affairs. Yet ironically, the reception given to the new book was more consistently favourable. In part this was because Crosland's reputation was more firmly established than it had been in 1956. He was reviewed in every major national and regional newspaper, in weekly and monthly magazines and in numerous foreign journals. From overseas came some of the highest praise, with the *New York Review of Books* claiming his case was made with 'such precision, such fine discrimination and such literary grace – that it will be exceedingly hard to refute'. At home Crosland won plaudits from sympathetic newspapers and academic commentators, being hailed as 'a Socialist theorist and a political strategist in one' and as 'by far the most efficient socialist brain at work in Britain today', comparable in stature to Tawney and the Webbs.[30] Several reviewers commented on Crosland's appeal for 'floating voters' considering where to turn at the next election. One wrote that if Labour did return to power 'it will owe Mr Crosland an enormous debt of gratitude'.[31]

There was another key factor in explaining the response to Crosland's latest book. His critics from both right and left of the political spectrum, though far from silenced, were more muted than in the past. With Macmillan's government deeply unpopular, even the *Daily Telegraph* commented that Crosland's work – while throwing 'the odd flaming onion into the Tory lines' – was characterised by the virtues of being 'sensible, civilised, tolerant and generous'.[32] From the Labour left, there was little of the vitriolic language that greeted *The Future of Socialism*. In deference to the reputation Crosland had established, and seeking not to jeopardise prospects of election victory, his arch-antagonist Richard Crossman conceded that Crosland's 'furious moderation' had been successfully projected outwards to the public. And in *Tribune* Barbara Castle, while concluding that the verdict on the capitalist system was still 'guilty', acknowledged Crosland's great 'persuasiveness' and 'brilliance'.[33] Even the New Left found it difficult to maintain accusations that Crosland was an opportunist prepared to jettison principles for the sake of achieving power. There were complaints that his eleven-point programme for action set 'limited horizons' when two-thirds of the world's population lived on the verge of starvation.[34] But the haziness of New Left demands – with calls to bring 'the whole social product under social control' – served only to reinforce Crosland's conviction that his opponents had no comparable strategy for securing radical change.

At least one reviewer wrote that Crosland might soon have the chance to implement some of his ideas in government: 'The Treasury bench may well await him.'[35] Since 1959 the idea of becoming Chancellor one day had become fixed in Crosland's mind. In 1962 Gaitskell's wife Dora asked: 'Now that you have committed yourself to be a politician, Tony, what is your greatest ambition?' He replied: 'As every social objective I believe in depends on getting the economy right, I suppose one would like to be Chancellor of the Exchequer.'[36] With Jim Callaghan in position as shadow Chancellor, this ambition was likely to be a long-term aspiration. Yet there were those inside the party who believed that in a Gaitskell government, Crosland would find himself at the Treasury after a token period spent there by Callaghan. This view may also have reflected the thoughts of the leader himself. When Crosland was made Foreign Secretary years later, the economist Nicholas Davenport wrote to speculate about 'old Hugh's' thoughts on this promotion, considering that 'he wanted you at the Treasury'.[37] What was beyond doubt in late 1962 was the high esteem in which Gaitskell continued to hold Crosland, despite their differences over Europe. When he heard that his friend was being offered an Oxford fellowship to write a book about British government he was adamant: 'Good God. You can't have him. I need him.' The offer came to nothing at a time when Crosland's political ambitions were sharply focused: the least he could expect in the event of a Labour victory was a place in Gaitskell's first Cabinet.[38]

Gaitskell's first Cabinet was not to be. Only weeks after the publication of *The Conservative Enemy*, Hugh Gaitskskell died. Over the Christmas of 1962, Gaitskell had spent some time in hospital. The public were largely unaware of the seriousness of the rare disorder of the immune system with which he was attacked until news was announced of his death, aged 56, in January 1963. Crosland went on television to make an unscripted tribute. One might question, he said, whether he was a sufficiently radical leader. 'But', he went on, 'he was a leader. You had complete confidence in him. You trusted him. You knew absolutely where you were with him, and of how many politicians in Britain at the moment could you say the same?' The future Gaitskell had in mind for his closest ally had become academic. It was a huge blow to Crosland's personal life and political prospects

Looking ahead reluctantly, Crosland still had high hopes for the future. Since 1959 his reputation as an effective parliamentary speaker, as a hard-working constituency MP, and as one of the most prominent political writers of his generation, had developed significantly. One friend told him that at a lunch given by the editors of the *Universities and Left Review*, it was clear that the New Left considered 'Croslandism' as pubic enemy number one. This indicated, his friend added, that in 'the patois of the Left, you've arrived. Anyone who becomes an "ism" has achieved historical status indeed!'[39] Nor had he sacrificed his own identity. A newspaper profile of Crosland noted that his 'refreshing – almost reckless – honesty' saved him from being a slavish Gaitskellite; he was more the 'insubordinate subaltern'.[40]

Yet Gaitskell's death painfully exposed the weaknesses of Crosland's position. His tendency to rely upon the patronage of powerful figures, first Dalton and then Gaitskell, limited his development of a secure political base. He may have developed his reputation as a writer and impressed those who knew of his energetic commitment to CDS. But among colleagues within the parliamentary party, negative views continued to prevail. With the ear of the party leader, Crosland felt no need to ingratiate himself with fellow MPs in the Tea Room at Westminster, or at party gatherings, quite apart from his own temperamental antipathy to such use of his time. For some MPs he therefore retained a raffish, playboy image, the author of mostly highbrow works and someone remote from ordinary party members. Not surprisingly, there were those who resented Crosland's influence in high places without having to work his way through the ranks. Some thought he exploited his 'favoured son' relationship with 'Gaiters', as he called him, for example relying on Gaitskell's influence with the Speaker to catch Crosland's eye on budget day. Both men seemed unaware that this caused great resentment, especially as Crosland was known for his poor attendance at the House.[41] With Gaitskell's unexpected death, Crosland was not only mourning a dear friend. He also faced the prospect of being left politically high and dry, especially if the PLP should now choose a leader with no natural liking for the Gaitskellites.

10

Coming to terms with
Harold Wilson, 1963–4

Only days after Gaitskell's death a group of his followers met to
discuss what to do in the leadership contest that would follow. All
were agreed in their opposition to the favourite, Harold Wilson,
whom it was felt was a 'small man', lacking in purpose and vision.
But who should the Gaitskellites back? The obvious alternative was
George Brown, MP for Belper and the party's deputy leader since
1960. Brown was regarded as highly talented, ambitious and of
moderate views, but his working-class, trade union background
meant he had little natural affinity with many of the Oxford-
educated Gaitskellites, who also saw him as tactless and prone to
flying off the handle. One MP said of the choice between Wilson and
Brown: 'It's like a child being asked which step-mother he would
prefer.'[1] Several Gaitskellites welcomed the intervention of a third
candidate, the shadow Chancellor Jim Callaghan, even though the
splitting of the right-wing vote was certain to enhance Wilson's
chances of winning. It was a time of agonising for Crosland, faced
with unpalatable options. Unlike some others, he confronted the
issue head on, arranging a meeting with Brown to tell him that he
was likely to support Callaghan. His reasoning, he said, was that
Brown was too volatile, especially when under the influence of
heavy drinking. Gaitskell had grown accustomed to Crosland's blunt
reasoning. George Brown was not, and made his disappointment
clear in equally strong terms. He wrote to Crosland the following day
hoping he had not been too 'vehement' in his response and insisting
that he too cared passionately about the 'issues' involved in deciding
the leadership.[2]

Crosland realised that Callaghan was likely to be eliminated in the
first round of the ballot, but having committed himself he took an
active part in trying to win over support for his chosen candidate. His
fears were realised when early in February 1963 the result was
announced. Wilson's 115 votes put him well ahead of Brown on

87

eighty-eight and Callaghan on forty-one, underlining the point that a single candidate of the right might have been able to defeat Wilson, who garnered most of the left and centre-left vote. One of Brown's backers, Patrick Gordon Walker, wrote that the momentum was all with Wilson. The real problem was that George was 'too unpredictable', and as a result had not been able to convince several trade union MPs and those who supported Hugh on 'personal grounds'.[3] When the second ballot was held, Wilson defeated Brown by 144 votes to 103, with Callaghan's support dividing roughly two-to-one in favour of the winner. Crosland was left despondent, though for his favoured candidate it was not all doom and gloom. Rather like Wilson in his 1960 challenge to Gaitskell, Callaghan had secured enough votes to enhance his authority, and had put down his marker as a possible future leader. In the short-term, he had also done well enough to convince Wilson that he deserved a leading role in the new team, which was confirmed when he was asked to continue as shadow Chancellor. From this point onwards, Callaghan could look forward to being Chancellor in his own right; any talk about him keeping the seat warm for Crosland no longer had credibility.[4]

Crosland's dejection stemmed from his recognition that it was not simply the prospect of high office that had receded; it was the prospect of any office at all. Wilson was aware that he needed to work with the elected shadow Cabinet, only one of whom backed him in the leadership contest. In particular, he made a peace offering to the Gaitskellites by appointing Patrick Gordon Walker to the foreign affairs portfolio. But he had no intention of rewarding those such as Crosland who had been amongst his bitterest opponents. As and when vacancies for promotion came up, he began to promote friends from the left in order to redress the balance, with Dick Crossman, for example, coming in as spokesman for science. Crossman wrote in his diary that within weeks Wilson produced a 'psychological revolution in the Parliamentary Party and the Party in the country'. This he said was based on a more inclusive style than his predecessor, whose government would be 'a Gaitskell Government, hand-picked by him and woe betide anyone who did not toe the line'.[5] Crossman's gushing enthusiasm in comparing Wilson with Kennedy and the 'New Frontier' in the United States was also based upon a transformation in the leader's inner circle of advisers. The 'royal court', those who 'sprawled in armchairs, providing ideas, gossip and reassurance', now consisted of former Bevanites such as

Crossman, Thomas Balogh and Barbara Castle, while the Gaitskellites were firmly excluded.[6] Within a matter of weeks, Crosland had gone from the inner sanctum to outer darkness.

His dismay went deeper than the personal. He also feared that the painstaking work of the past few years in pushing revisionism within the party might be undone. With the loss of Gaitskell, the right within the PLP looked rudderless, whatever the composition of the shadow Cabinet. George Brown lived up to his reputation for un-predictability by disappearing for days after hearing news of his second-round defeat, and when he did re-appear he only reluctantly agreed to continue as deputy leader. Gordon Walker was not regarded as a strong enough personality to inspire followers, and Callaghan was seen as on the fringes of the Gaitskellite grouping. Wilson's style of leadership – maintaining the broad lines of agreed policy while keeping the left happy with traditional socialist language – further infuriated the right, for it struck them as lacking the clear direction that had always characterised Gaitskell, for better or worse. Hence when Philip Williams wrote to Crosland saying that if he stayed in politics – it would be understandable if he dropped out – he would have to accept the world as he found it, the reply was terse. Crosland was grateful for his friend's concern and advice, but he would not 'parley with Wilson'. He shared what Roy Jenkins called 'post-Gaitskellian indifference'. Jenkins said he could recall no contact of any sort with Wilson for several months after he became leader. Instead he found himself left to get on with writing a biography of Asquith and with his 'over-active social life'.[7]

Crosland too had an active social life to fall back upon, but before long he had to accept the logic of the advice from Philip Williams, who reminded him that he had frequently lectured the left on the need for realism. Wilson's popularity with the public as a down-to-earth moderniser helped to ensure that Labour's lead in the polls increased in the early months of 1963, when Macmillan suffered the further humiliation of France vetoing Britain's application for membership of the Common Market. In May, Tony Benn spent a couple of hours with Crosland and he noted in his diary the first signs of a painful process of coming to terms with Gaitskell's successor:

> I had a long talk to Tony about his attitude to Wilson, who he still thinks is a shit, but who he also thinks has done very well and would like to help in any way he could. I must try to pass this on to Harold since Tony

is too good to waste. But the simple fact is that with Hugh's death his old courtiers feel out in the cold – exactly as I felt with Hugh.[8]

For several months, there were few signs that Crosland would come in from the cold. In the meantime, he busied himself with a series of overseas conferences, speaking in Japan on the future of European socialism and in Turkey on common features of fast-growing economies. High levels of demand, high investment, a risk-taking entreprenuerial class, good education and central planning were all necessary, he argued, if Britain was to gain ground on its major competitors.[9]

By the autumn Crosland was more actively seeking ways of working with the new regime. The inducement to do so became stronger after Wilson's triumphant performance at the annual conference in Scarborough. His call for social reform twinned with the harnessing of the 'white heat of technology' heightened expectations that he would soon be Prime Minister. In the view of Crossman, it also provided an application of socialism to modern conditions which Gaitskell and Crosland had tried and 'completely failed to do'. Labour went away from the conference in high spirits and with a greater appearance of unity. Most of the Gaitskellites, recorded Crossman, accepted – albeit reluctantly – that Wilson was proving a great success, and many were anxious to improve their chances of serving in government.[10] Aware of the need to make his own way in the political jungle, Crosland stood for the first time in PLP elections to the shadow Cabinet. He was cautioned against this by his CDS ally Bill Rodgers, who told Roy Jenkins the day after Gaitskell's death: 'You are our leader now.'[11] This was a further reminder for Crosland of how far things had changed. Under Gaitskell he was secure in the knowledge of his 'favoured son' status; with Gaitskell gone he would henceforth have to compete with Jenkins for advancement. In the event he gained seventy two votes, eight more than Jenkins. Neither man won his way into the top twelve who made up the shadow cabinet, but they had signalled their desire to be considered for office. When Tony Benn suggested to the party leader that the shadow Cabinet was an old and unexciting bunch (with only Denis Healey under the age of fifty), Wilson said any ministerial team would be of his own choosing and would include some surprising names.[12]

If Crosland did figure in planning for government by the

beginning of 1964, a leading factor must have been the value of his economic expertise. One cloud on the horizon in Wilson's early months as leader was the tension between his two senior colleagues, Callaghan and Brown. The Treasury was concerned that a new ministry of production – charged with the task of producing a long-term plan to provide economic stability, and announced by Wilson at the Scarborough conference – would undercut its own authority. Both Callaghan and Brown, who was to head up the new department, sought allies where they could find them, including Crosland. The angry exchanges during the leadership contest were put to one side after Crosland defended Brown against 'malicious' left-wingers who criticised his handling of a TV interview responding to the death of President Kennedy in November 1963.[13] Callaghan, for his part, was grateful to Crosland for taking the initiative in arranging for distinguished Oxford economists to meet with him at Nuffield College regularly to discuss the likely economic problems facing an incoming Labour government. The general tone of the seminars was Keynesian, with much talk of the management of demand and economic planning, so providing Callaghan with useful intellectual preparation for office, if not a specific policy agenda.[14]

Crosland's relationship with Brown and Callaghan was in contrast to the coolness of his dealings with Wilson. Neither Brown nor Callaghan had been to university, but both had roots in the Labour movement of a type that Crosland first admired in Arthur Jenkins during the war. Partly because of their backgrounds, which meant they had no claim to academic pretensions, Crosland judged them less severely than he did Wilson.[15] With strong personalities of their own, neither man was intimidated by Crosland, whom Wilson at times found unnerving. In the case of Callaghan – who became Crosland's key political ally in the years after Gaitskell's death – it was a friendship that went back to the days of the Strasbourg visits overseen by Hugh Dalton. Callaghan's robust nature appreciated Crosland's 'reckless devil-may-care attitude, and his teasing manner which made me laugh a great deal. He was good company and although some were put off by his apparent lofty arrogance, his friends quickly saw that it was a camouflage behind which lay a deeply serious intellect.'[16] This long-standing friendship, con-solidated during the 1963 leadership contest, offered some possibility of Crosland going to the Treasury as a junior minister, if not as

Chancellor. George Brown had a similar regard, and later noted that in discussions about the establishment of his new department, Tony 'had come to be accepted as the probable Deputy Minister.'[17]

Crosland's chances of advancement thus looked better early in 1964 than they had a year earlier. There was still, however, the issue of his private life, with Wilson letting it be known that he preferred him to 'regularise' his domestic arrangements.[18] For some time Crosland had, in any case, been contemplating the question of marrying for a second time. In the early 1960s his relationship with Susan Catling developed after her husband Patrick left the family home at Hobury Street in Chelsea. There had been tensions in the marriage for several years, and about a year after his departure Patrick requested a divorce, saying that he had become involved with the singer Peggy Lee. Crosland was attracted by Susan's striking appearance – tall, blonde and with a strong personality. She also had journalistic and political interests, unlike Crosland's first wife, working as a profile writer for the *Sunday Express*. After hearing of Patrick's request for divorce, Crosland proposed, though Susan's first reaction was a mixture of pleasure and apprehension: 'he'd feel fenced in'. The issue was left unresolved, and when Susan's divorce came through, it was Crosland who 'grew uneasy'.

After hesitation on both sides arrangements were finally made, and the couple married at Chelsea Register Office in February 1964, with Dora Gaitskell and Ruth Dalton as witnesses. Susan Crosland recalled her anxieties:

> He moved body and other essentials into Hobury Street, retaining his own flat in The Boltons while I looked for a larger house. We'd assumed . . . that he would once in a way benefit from an 'adventure', without any disadvantage for anyone else. He was forty-five and hadn't tried to convince either of us that his promiscuity had altogether run its course.[19]

The existence of 'escape clauses' in their understanding was crucial, Susan added, as it meant that Crosland did not feel confined, as he had in his first marriage. Both parties were surprised when the 'escape hatch' of the The Boltons was not used. Crosland found that his flat no longer had the same appeal and by the end of the year the couple had moved into a £35,000 house in Lansdowne Road, a three-storey property on the western slope of Notting Hill which provided working space for Crosland and room for his wife and her two 'partly-grown children' from her first marriage, Sheila and Ellen-Craig.[20]

This second marriage proved to be a great success. Shirley Williams, who had known Crosland for several years, recalled that he had rarely before been able to call a woman his friend; most women were either attracted by his looks or recoiled at his rudeness.[21] Susan, she believed, saw his enormous charm but was also tolerant of some of his excessive behaviour. He expected his new wife to negotiate in advance the finer details of their social engagements. He grew increasingly reluctant to attend parties unless he knew who would be attending and might turn up in carpet slippers, which he considered more comfortable than shoes. In time Crosland came to prefer small gatherings at home, where guests could be carefully vetted. On these occasions wine would usually flow, though Crosland would affect to know nothing about it. One of his favourite quips was: 'Let's just have the carafe wine, and leave the vintages to Roy Jenkins.'[22] The transformation in the flamboyant figure of the 1950s was gradual but perceptible to some. According to the journalist Alan Watkins, Crosland became uxorious, unhappy when away from his wife for long on official business and sufficiently jealous to discourage her from continuing to work and from meeting with men friends. The greater stability in his private life was not apparent to all he came across in politics. When it was said that his second wife had 'mellowed Tony', someone asked: 'What can he have been like before he married Susan?'[23]

In the summer of 1964 politicians of all parties waited nervously for the general election. Macmillan's replacement as Prime Minister, Sir Alec Douglas-Home, was determined to make the parliament run its full course to the autumn. This, he hoped, would give him time to establish his own identity and take some of the shine off Wilson's popular image. Crosland's main concern was to work behind the scenes to influence Labour's economic strategy. He feared that the economic boom of 1964 – being stoked by the Conservatives in an effort to stave off electoral defeat – was certain to be followed by another sterling crisis and further restraint, continuing the cycle of 'stop-go' that had characterised the British economy since the war. If the ambitions of an incoming administration were not to be crippled, he believed it was essential that the pound be devalued immediately Labour came to power. His budget speech in 1963 had circled round this theme, and in alliance with other economists such as Nicky

Kaldor and Robert Neild, he urged the shadow Chancellor to act boldly. Callaghan, however, refused to be drawn. In public, Crosland was left to go as far as he could – without contravening party policy – in attacking Britain's poor balance-of-payments record, while also calling for more government planning. The planning theme was prominent in the abridged paperback version of *The Future of Socialism*, published in 1964, which admitted to undue optimism about growth in the first edition but which stuck to his main lines of analysis.[24] A completely new synthesis was premature, he felt, and was moreover difficult to contemplate while his first priority was to ensure re-election in Grimsby.

Crosland was well placed in his constituency when the election finally came in October 1964. Two years earlier the writer Richard West visited Grimsby and noted that a few people had said that any MP with a majority of only 101 votes would be keen to impress; but on the whole respect for Crosland appeared to be genuine and widespread. 'Even Grimsby Tories', said West, 'greeted his name with a mere grunt, meaning they could not think of anything rude to say of him – off-hand.'[25] At Westminster, Crosland devoted a far higher proportion of his parliamentary speeches to local matters than he had as MP for South Gloucestershire.[26] And his agent wrote in 1964 that the local party had no complaints about his attitude throughout the course of the parliament:

> Mr Crosland had been meticulous in making regular visits to the town, during which he made a point of seeing as many people as possible. He attended 'cottage meetings', canvassed during a council by-election and on other occasions, attended social functions and business meetings, and in general spared no effort in making sure that Grimsby knew who its MP was. Relations with the press were first-class, and much good publicity resulted. All this is not to say that he was content at that, for many people can know, and many can dislike, unless the work that an MP does in the House and with Government Departments, looking after the interests of Grimbarians both individually and collectively, is of the same quality. As to be expected, this criteria was more than adequately met.[27]

The agent also reported that Crosland was a 'really outstanding and hard-working candidate' in the final weeks of the campaign. Often in the company of Mrs Crosland, who added 'glamour' to the proceedings, he canvassed in every Grimsby ward personally and worked tirelessly as a link between all the wards on polling day. His election address was more sure-footed than in 1959, playing on the theme of 'time for a change' after thirteen years of 'tired and accident-prone' Tory rule and emphasising his commitment to the key Grimsby concerns of fishing and housing.[28] The electoral reward for all this activity came on 15 October. Nationally, Douglas-Home recovered some of the ground lost by the Conservatives earlier in the parliament. On an average swing of 3 per cent, Labour squeezed home with an overall majority of just four seats, gaining ground especially in Scotland and the north west. In Grimsby, the swing to Labour was not only above the national average; it was twice the level of that achieved in the east Midlands and the eastern counties region of England. Crosland's majority over his opponent Walter Pearson increased from 101 to 4,098, indicating an element of personal support which promised a more secure parliamentary base than he had known in the past. The dark days of early 1963 seemed a long way off amidst the wild cheering and celebrations in Grimsby on election night. As Harold Wilson went to Downing Street to become the first Labour Prime Minister since 1951, Crosland next had to endure – along with many other aspiring colleagues – an agonising wait. Would the telephone ring?

11

Into Government, 1964–5

Crosland returned to London on the day after the election to await his fate. The announcement of senior appointments brought few surprises. Callaghan would serve as Chancellor, Gordon Walker as Foreign Secretary and George Brown as head of the newly created Department of Economic Affairs (DEA). Crosland still entertained hopes that he might be appointed Callaghan's deputy at the Treasury; but he feared that his hostility to Wilson could see him excluded from the other appointments, and his nagging doubts increased as the hours went by without a call from the Prime Minister's office. At lunchtime on Saturday 17 October Roy Jenkins visited Hobury Street for a drink, and recalled in his memoirs that as they sat 'marooned in silence' he was relieved to discover that Crosland, like himself, had heard nothing.[1] The long wait finally ended for both men later that evening, not with a call from No. 10, but at a celebration party at George Brown's flat. Brown broke the news that Crosland was to be Minister of State at the DEA. Earlier in the day it had been decided that Robert Neild would become the Chancellor's economic adviser. One Treasury official believed this was an early indication of Wilson using divide and rule tactics. Crosland was a strong Callaghan supporter, and the Prime Minister did not wish to see the Chancellor build up a power base that might threaten his own authority. Brown was no doubt satisfied with the outcome, fearing that he would face a formidable team if Crosland were allied to Callaghan at the Treasury.[2]

The celebration of Labour's historic win at Brown's flat turned into a sour affair for Crosland. It was not that he was disappointed with the offer of his first junior ministerial post, the most that he could realistically expect. The Cabinet was inevitably dominated by centre-right figures such as Callaghan and Brown, whom Wilson tried to balance by bringing in allies on the left such as Crossman (Housing) and Barbara Castle (Overseas Development). There were places too for some of an older generation – for example Frank

Soskice, appointed Home Secretary – who had first served under Attlee. The average age of the Cabinet at fifty-seven was higher than that of the outgoing Tory government, and Crosland might have taken comfort from the fact that Denis Healey, who became Minister of Defence, was the only near-contemporary to be sitting round the top table. What Crosland was less pleased to discover on the Saturday night was that Roy Jenkins, whom he had grown accustomed to regard as his political junior, was being asked to run his own department, the Ministry of Aviation. Jenkins wrote in his memoirs of his delight at being told that he was not going to be 'a subordinate minister'. He added that he believed working for Brown was likely to be a recipe for 'emotional exhaustion'.[3] The competitive edge in Crosland's relationship with Jenkins, first evident after Gaitskell's death, sharpened with the knowledge that Wilson had given preference to the younger man. William Rodgers, appointed as a parliamentary secretary at the DEA, reported that his new ministerial colleague was 'furiously jealous' that Jenkins had got his own department.[4]

There was a second reason why any post-election euphoria was short-lived for Crosland. Unknown to the outside world, the previous night Harold Wilson – after only hours in Downing Street – had summoned Callaghan and Brown to a crisis meeting, and the three agreed after a brief discussion that there would be no devaluation of the pound. Whatever the economic case, the Prime Minister believed that on political grounds – with a slim majority and another election probable in the near future – Labour must at all costs avoid being labelled as the party of devaluation. Crosland went to George Brown's flat on the Saturday evening determined to urge the case for early devaluation, which he felt was both economically imperative and politically feasible, since it could be presented as an unavoidable consequence of Tory mismanagement. He arrived blissfully unaware that a decision had already been taken. A furious row developed, in the process of which Brown denounced Crosland as a 'traitor' for talking on the telephone to Callaghan about the day's events. Roy Jenkins recalled that he joined in on Crosland's side, though not as strongly as he might because he succumbed at the time to the 'infantile disease of departmentalism' and admitted he was thinking more about aircraft. For Crosland the exhilaration of the previous few days evaporated overnight. He was dismayed not only by the decision on devaluation but also by the injunction that the issue was settled and should not be raised again.[5]

The reality confronting the new administration was grim. In seeking to engineer a pre-election boom, the Conservatives had allowed imports to outstrip by far any rise in export trade, with the result that Wilson was greeted by officials at No. 10 with the news that Britain had a record balance-of-payments deficit. Economic policy under Wilson was to be constantly dogged by this legacy, necessitating a series of emergency measures throughout the parliament. In his first few days as a minister, Crosland took the unconventional step of writing to the Prime Minister outlining why he disagreed with the course being embarked upon. Within weeks, with sterling coming under pressure on the international exchanges – precipitating the first of several recurrent crises – the Chancellor appeared to be having second thoughts about devaluation, or 'The Unmentionable' as it became known; but George Brown remained firmly behind Wilson in refusing to reopen the question. It was Brown's department that had been given responsibility for finding alternative means of ensuring sustained growth. This aim was at the heart of the 'National Plan' announced by the DEA in 1965, produced only after overcoming great difficulties in the early months. On his arrival at the departmental buildings in Storey's Gate, Brown found himself with few officials and less furniture. His explosive outbursts made everyone so nervous that one civil servant failed to recognise a new arrival. 'Who are you?' demanded the official. 'My name's Crosland,' came the reply.[6]

Despite his reservations about the direction of economic policy, Crosland settled quickly into the routine of ministerial life. He was soon finding outlets for his expertise and experience. The Council of Europe, with members drawn from seventeen countries, threatened to denounce Labour for one of its first emergency measures, the introduction of a hefty import surcharge. The ministers of agriculture and trade, according to one of the Prime Minister's aides, 'received a mauling' when they tried to explain the position. But a skilful speech by Crosland in Geneva averted a humiliation; the new Minister of State rounded off a successful day by returning in time to persuade the House of Commons that British interests had been stoutly defended.[7] In a department with no established conventions, staffed by industrialists and academics as well as civil servants, Crosland flourished in the informal atmosphere, which Bill Rodgers described as a cross between Nuffield College and a Fabian Society seminar. Crucially, a strong mutual respect developed between Crosland and his boss. 'You knew where you were with Tony,' Brown later recalled. 'He was the one bloke who would fight me to my face – in the Department, in private.' Others might give in, then complain privately; Crosland would remain loyal if the arguments had been heard before any decision was taken.[8] In December 1964 Dick Crossman listed Crosland as one of only five ministers who was blossoming under the responsibility of office.[9]

Crosland's most valuable service, in the eyes of those who worked with him, was to establish the manner in which advice should be presented to the Secretary of State. In view of Brown's volatile temperament, this was essential in allowing reasoned discussion to take place on a range of issues, including devaluation, 'on which he [Crosland] refused to keep quiet'.[10] In mid-January 1965 Crosland sent Brown a typically forthright assessment of the economic prospects for the year ahead. There were, he said, only two 'mentionable' ways of tackling Britain's continuing balance-of-payments deficit. One was moderate deflation; the other was a combination of short-term expedients for two years until 'our long term DEA policies are really beginning to bite'. Forecasts for home demand were still tentative, he noted, but were currently set at over 3 per cent growth for 1965, which meant that no general measures of reflation were called for, in his view. Much though would hinge in the longer term on boosting exports. In the meantime, his advice was to keep up the momentum on prices and incomes policy, fight for two-tier interest rates to protect housing and 'push on with all our DEA prodding and planning and bullying'.[11] This paper proved, unexpectedly, to be Crosland's last serious contribution to the work of the department. Within days, he was leaving to take up a new post, one which carried with it a place at the Cabinet table.

The origin of this early reshuffle was the resignation of Patrick Gordon Walker. Despite being defeated at the election at Smethwick, Patrick Gordon Walker had been made Foreign Secretary in October 1964. A seat had to be found for Gordon Walker but, at the Leyton by-election in January 1965, he was again defeated in what was thought to be a Labour stronghold. He had no alternative but to resign. The Prime Minister decided to replace him at the Foreign Office with Michael Stewart, hitherto Secretary of State for Education. Wilson in his later history of the government wrote that he was sad to move Stewart, but felt Roy Jenkins should be offered education as he was the outstanding success among ministers outside

the Cabinet. When Jenkins turned down the post, Wilson recollected that the obvious alternative was Crosland, who combined
'economic brilliance' with a detailed interest in the subject.[12]
Crossman's diary noted that Wilson was prepared to adopt a pragmatic attitude towards talented Gaitskellite opponents of the past.
When his adviser George Wigg suggested Crosland over other
possible candidates, Wilson agreed he would be a positive addition to
the Cabinet.[13] At forty-six he thus became the youngest member at
Labour's top table, leapfrogging back over Roy Jenkins in the race
for advancement. Why then had Jenkins spurned the Cabinet post
only months after the October election victory?

According to his memoirs, Jenkins told the Prime Minister that he
was not greatly interested in education, and thought it would be a
disadvantage for it to be known that he had three children at fee-
paying schools. It occurred to him – an 'ignoble thought', he
conceded – that someone else would inevitably prosper by entering
the Cabinet ahead of him. Although Wilson said his rejection would
not prevent him being considered for other top jobs if suitable
opportunities arose, Jenkins also admitted to an 'inevitable stab of
jealousy' when he heard who was to take up the post. Crosland's
appointment meant, in effect, Jenkins surrendering his 'brief lead
over this great friend but formidable rival'.[14] What the Jenkins
account left out was the widespread assumption that Frank Soskice,
the incumbent at the Home Office, would not stay in office for long.
Nor did he mention how he sought to diminish Crosland's
appointment by making it clear to journalists that he had been given
first refusal. Woodrow Wyatt, a friend of both men, confirmed that
Jenkins was piqued that Crosland had entered the Cabinet before
him, just as Crosland had been disgruntled with the appointments of
the previous autumn.[15] The later parting of the ways between
Crosland and his oldest friend in politics originated in the early days
of the Wilson government when their rivalry took on a sharper edge,
with both looking to inherit the Gaitskellite mantle.

Crosland was reluctant to leave the DEA, where he felt his
economic training was at last being deployed. Brown was sorry to see
him go, and later wrote that one of the reasons for the subsequent
malaise of the department was that he had to take on too many tasks
after losing his first deputy, an 'exceptionally able administrator'.[16]
But Wilson's offer was too good to turn down. Here was an
opportunity for Crosland to direct high policy, and to do so in

an area that was central to his version of the socialist case for equality. One profile writer noted that it would be interesting to see how backbench colleagues and the educational world responded to the new minister. He had in the past attracted hostility as much as loyalty, notably because of his tendency to plain speaking – 'rather like the Regency peer who acquired a reputation for eccentricity by saying whatever he happened to be thinking at the moment'. What he had in his favour, as his writings demonstrated, was a clear idea of what he wanted to achieve. But if he was to become the most influential minister at the education department since Rab Butler he would have to overcome scepticism about his political – as opposed to his intellectual – toughness. Was he capable of dealing with the long administrative grind that would be necessary to secure change, and was he strong enough to reform the education service in the face of opposition?[17]

12

Secretary of State for
Education, 1965-7

The Department of Education and Science (DES) was located in Curzon Street, and was described by Crosland's PPS Christopher Price as a 'delightfully seedy building next to MI5 in what was then London's premier red light district'.[1] Crosland's early days at the department were spent getting accustomed to unfamiliar routines – such as the daily arrival of an offical car – and to establishing working relationships with new colleagues. All was not sweetness and light. Some civil servants were taken aback by the bluntness of Crosland's manner, and were soon made aware that he was obsessive about arriving at engagements on time; his car drivers suffered when traffic jams caused any delay. Officials also resented his willingness to use outside advisers – academics sympathetic to the Labour cause – who regularly visited his home, putting forward ideas that would then be tested back in the department. And he was intolerant of sloppy work. One civil servant who proffered 'completely incorrect advice' was given short shrift and was seriously ill after the humiliation became common knowledge in Whitehall.[2] But relationships steadily improved, and were given time to mature during Crosland's two and a half years at the DES; indeed he asked the Prime Minister if he could stay put after the election victory of March 1966 increased Labour's majority to ninety-seven. The chief official at the department, Sir Herbert Andrew, later spoke of his minister as 'eminently rational' and praised him for accepting that decisions could only be taken after consultation with the 'robber barons' of the educational world, such as the teachers' unions, local authorities and the university vice-chancellors.[3]

Crosland's junior ministerial colleagues were positive in their assessment. One of them, Denis Howell, recollected that Crosland quickly established command of the department. 'His style was quite delightful – relaxed, amused but always to the point.' What particularly impressed Howell and other juniors was that the boss was not constantly interfering in their own areas of responsibility. If they could persuade the minister of the merits of a case – which could be a daunting task – they were left free to develop policy along agreed lines. This, Howell believed, was the hallmark of a strong individual, who by the same token was sufficiently confident that he did not seek continual reassurance from colleagues. Aside from spending matters, Crosland brought few issues before the full Cabinet, preferring to get on with the task in hand. These qualities, allied with his passion for education, led Denis Howell to describe Crosland as a 'scintillating minister', the finest he worked with in the 1960s and 1970s.[4] What impressed civil servants and political colleagues alike was the minister's clarity and sense of purpose. In subsequent posts Crosland usually took time to settle in, and he believed it required at least six months to get a sound grasp of how a department worked. But at the DES he had already written extensively on the subject before he arrived, and felt confident of the issues requiring his early attention.[5] He soon made it clear to officials that top of his list was one aspect of education that had figured prominently in Labour's election manifesto – secondary school reorganisation.

The process of comprehensive reform was already under way when Crosland went to Curzon Street. For several years criticism had been growing of the 'eleven-plus' system which separated children into prestigious grammar schools and markedly inferior secondary moderns. Some local education authorities (LEAs) responded by ending selection and introducing comprehensives, but the process had not gone far. Only a tiny proportion of 6000 state secondary schools were as yet designated comprehensive, and in January 1965 – conscious of its small majority – the government went no further than stating that it would encourage local authorities to continue with reform. It also declared that the time was ripe for a fuller declaration of policy. Michael Stewart had begun drafting a circular before going to the Foreign Office, and Crosland's first major task was to finalise the details after consulting with various interest groups. Reg Prentice, one of the junior ministers at the department, wanted to 'require' local authorities to reorganise their secondary provision, but Crosland had argued as far back as *The Future of Socialism* that anything that smacked of immediate abolition of the grammar schools might discredit the whole process. Privately he told his wife he wanted to destroy 'every fucking grammar school in England' but Crosland was convinced that any new system would bed down more successfully if it could be achieved voluntarily. Hence when Circular 10/65 was issued in July 1965 its tone was firm but not harsh. The Secretary of State did not 'require', but instead 'requests local education authorities . . . to prepare and submit to him plans for reorganising secondary education in their areas on comprehensive lines'.[6]

The risk posed by Crosland's strategy was that it produced no immediate result. Local authorities were given a year to submit their plans, which meant that opponents of reform had time to mobilise. *The Times* spearheaded resistance, attacking Labour's commitment to the 'unrealizable ideal of equality' and highlighting examples of local opposition.[7] In an effort to maintain the initiative, Crosland made his first major pronouncement on comprehensive reform at the North of England education conference in January 1966. It was a vintage performance, starting with the assertion that every education system in history mirrored the society in which it was set. By this token Britain's post-1944 system had been 'educationally and socially unjust, inefficient, wasteful and divisive'. He reminded his audience of the mass of evidence which had built up against a process that branded 75 per cent of children as failures at eleven, and argued passionately for a system that would enhance social cohesion and give equal opportunities to all children:

> True equality of opportunity cannot be accomplished in one generation, or by education alone; it needs a wider social revolution. But as soon as we concede that measured intelligence is not a quantity fixed for life, and that it depends moreover partly on the child's environment, we must surely think it indefensible to segregate children into different schools at the age of 11. It is, of course, in the nature of things that as we grow to manhood we go different ways. Life itself is a selective process. But we must allow that process to work fairly; we must allow time for the beneficial influence of education to compensate for the deficiencies of upbringing and early circumstance.[8]

The Secretary of State also tried to remain on the offensive by issuing a fresh circular in March 1966, stating that he would not approve building projects incompatible with the government's stated objectives. Even so, the first six months of 1966 were a tense time at the department, especially as individual authorities began to submit plans which posed difficulties for Crosland. Liverpool and

Manchester were both Labour authorities who expected their proposals to be rubber-stamped by the minister, yet both were disappointed. Wilma Harte, the civil servant with responsibility for reorganising secondary schooling, noted that Crosland worked closely with his special advisory team of officials; without interfering unduly, he got to grips with the fine detail of controversial proposals. The result was that he had no hesitation in defending his decision to reject the Liverpool plan as unrealisitc. According to Wilma Harte, he demonstrated 'enormous courage' in saying no to a powerful Labour authority, and earned much credit in the educational world for sticking to the view that all schemes must be sound and defensible.[9] There was also the problem of what to do about authorities who rejected Circular 10/65 altogether, as Bournemouth did over the winter. The debate inside the department about whether to legislate against authorities who refused to submit comprehensive plans became so heated that at one point Crosland threw an ash tray at one of his ministerial juniors, though he did apologise subsequently.[10]

'Gosh! Here come those ghastly comprehensive rotters again!'

Garland, *Daily Telegraph*, 16 March 1966 (© Telegraph Group Limited, London 1966)

By the summer of 1966 the minister's voluntary approach began to pay dividends. By the time the deadline for submitting plans arrived, the majority of LEAs had complied with Circular 10/65; those who refused to produce schemes or who presented plans retaining eleven-plus selection numbered less than twenty. Commentators were agreed that this was a 'points win' for Crosland: he had established momentum without major opposition, even if the whole project would take many years and massive rebuilding to complete. In spite of a strong swing to the Conservatives in local elections during the spring of 1967, the *Times Educational Supplement* concluded that by the time Crosland left the department, 'a great shove towards comprehensive schools has been given'.[11] Wilma Harte had no doubt that this owed much to the qualities of the minister. He was fortunate in that hardline opponents were not taken seriously among educationists. West Riding could have caused trouble, but 'Bournemouth was a joke'. Crosland had nevertheless cleared some tricky fences: he had created an appearance of change, and he had won the argument by making comprehensives appear the norm; it was now selection that was regarded as difficult to justify. 'The great push had taken place,' concluded Wilma Harte. 'By the time he left the important work had been done.'[12]

Crosland was less successful in dealing with the independent sector, about which he felt equally passionate. *The Conservative Enemy* had contained a strong attack on independent schools and Crosland spent much time on his arrival at Curzon Street making the case for reform of the public schools. Labour's aims, he noted, were to destroy or weaken a system that enabled the upper-middle class to purchase educational and social superiority, and to ensure that the private sector fitted with the new national system of comprehensives. The party hoped to create 'socially and intellectually mixed semi-independent semi-state boarding schools'. But how was he to achieve such an outcome? The outright abolition of private schools he regarded as a non-starter. It was, he said, 'hard to justify on libertarian grounds'; and it was illogical to close some 400 schools when an additional two million children were expected in the school population over the next decade. Nor was it sufficient, he believed, simply to 'squeeze' the schools by closing tax loopholes. The only viable way forward, he argued, was to take up Labour's manifesto pledge to set up an independent schools commission. This had twin advantages: it enabled the possibility of a voluntary settlement, so preventing any mass exodus of teaching staff; and it gave time to firm up the details of a workable scheme, which Labour lacked when coming to office.[13]

In July 1965 the Cabinet gave approval for the decision to appoint a Commission 'to advise on the best way of integrating the public schools with the State system'. By the end of the year Sir John Newsom had been appointed chairman, and the commission had been charged with the task of securing reform consistent with the government's objective of maximising private schools' contribution to national needs and creating a socially mixed entry.[14] Thereafter Crosland could only watch from the sidelines, though he tackled head on accusations that he was a 'class traitor' for turning on the school system of which he was a product. In public debate he resisted those who claimed that educational inequality was inevitable, saying that this was an 'anti-democratic conception'. In private he also had clear views of what he hoped the Commission would come up with, telling one journalist that he looked for some three-quarters of public school places to be distributed free of charge in accordance with clearly-defined procedures. For Crosland the problem had particular personal relevance, because at the time of his second marriage his wife's children were being educated privately. He was increasingly intolerant of colleagues who advocated comprehensives while sending their own offspring elsewhere, and it was agreed that Susan Crosland's youngest daughter would go to a local comprehensive when she reached eleven.[15] But his desire for substantial reform was ultimately to be thwarted. The Commission reported after he left the DES, and its proposals for limited assimilation were considered too costly to act upon at a time when pressure was intensifying for expenditure cutbacks.

How far could Crosland be held responsible for this disappointing outcome? He was later asked why, if he so deplored the class nature of British society, he had not abolished public schools when he had the chance. Yet abolition had not seriously been on the agenda. It was not official party policy, and it posed immense practical difficulties. Crosland said that finding places for the 6 per cent of children who were educated independently would be a strange order of priorities when many children still worked in Victorian school buildings.[16] This underlined the reason why he was unable to succeed in his more limited objective of integration. Herbert Andrew, Permanent Secretary at the DES, later wrote that the issue of comprehensive schooling inevitably demanded great attention and the lion's share of resources; in a world of competing priorities, it was not possible to reform all aspects of secondary education at the same time.[17] Aside from deteriorating economic conditions by the time the Commission reported, Crosland believed that the Cabinet had been lukewarm in support. He teased colleagues by calling himself 'the only radical in the Government', and Wilma Harte later reflected that the government as a whole gave the appearance of being unable to decide 'whether these schools were so bloody they ought to be abolished or so marvellous they ought to be made available to everyone'.[18] In 1970 Crosland concluded, more in hope than anticipation, that 'the problem is still there and we shall eventually have to come back to it'.[19]

When it came to a third area of policy preoccupying the minister at the DES – higher education – the story was one of mixed fortunes. The Robbins Report of 1963 had called for the creation of a large, undifferentiated system of higher education to accommodate the burgeoning demand for degree-level work. There was much sympathy for this in Labour ranks, but under the influence of official advice Crosland announced at Woolwich Polytechnic in a provocative speech in April 1965 that the government favoured not a single but a 'dual system', based on the 'twin traditions' of autonomous universities on the one hand and the public sector, as represented by leading technical colleges, colleges of education and polytechnics, on the other.

As ever, he presented a closely argued case: there was, he said, a growing need for vocational and industrially based courses at a high level which universities alone could not meet; no other major power downgraded technical colleges in the way that Britain did; and it was desirable that part of the higher education sector should be responsive to social needs and under some form of government control. The Woolwich speech drew flak from two quarters. For some in his own party it left him open to the charge that he was hardening in higher education the type of divisions he was keen to eliminate at secondary level. And for many vice-chancellors, Crosland's language raised fears about their future, especially his claim that Britain needed to get away from its 'snobbish caste-ridden hierarchical obsession with University status'.[20]

After he left office Crosland admitted that he made an 'appalling blunder' at Woolwich, creating bad feeling which he had to work hard to rectify. He thereafter found negotiating with the vice-chancellors difficult. His PPS recalled that he would put on a 'supercilious drawl' when he felt that university heads were trying to patronise him, and gave the impression that he regarded all universities as being 'as effete and remote as Oxford and Trinity'.[21] On one occasion he complained to his wife about the vice-chancellors going 'on and on and on' as if their institutions were not already privileged and successful: 'I can understand about micro-economics. I can understand about sex. What I *cannot* understand is the desire of human beings to hear their own voices. Also, if one is to be truthful, I'm not frightfully interested in the universities.'[22] In public the minister deliberately used more temperate language, though he remained convinced that the general thrust of policy remained 'utterly right'. In 1966 he announced the creation of thirty polytechnics as part of the new 'binary system' of higher education. The polytechnics would be different from, not inferior to, the universities, especially in responding to the needs of technology and industry. Allied to this was the work done in creating the Open University (OU), the brain-child of Crosland's sociology mentor Michael Young. This was primarily the responsibility of Minister for the Arts, Jennie Lee, whose relations with the Education Secretary were distant. He would complain in private about that 'bloody woman', but he left her free to develop the OU concept well aware of her popularity within the wider Labour movement as Bevan's widow.[23]

Higher education was thus an area of extensive but controversial reform. Many were dissatisfied with the outcome. Traditionalists in the universities who believed their institutions should have a monopoly of degree-level work voiced disapproval, and polytechnic leaders were soon complaining that they were being treated as the poor relations of the system. Crosland had sympathy for the latter view, reflecting on his policy after he left office that left-wing critics failed to see that a unitary system would not produce instant parity because universities were so far ahead in terms of resources and buildings. In a situation where the proportion of working-class students in higher education had hardly risen since the 1920s, he insisted upon his 'profound belief that Polytechnics could greatly contribute to *equality* in education'. He recognised that there were growing pressures for polytechnics to imitate universities rather than to become regional centres with an emphasis on vocational courses.[24] But as one educationist noted in 1971, this had more to do with a drift in policy after Crosland left the department. Crosland deserved credit for at least moving beyond the old conception that universities alone were synonymous with higher education. Indeed his championing of greater access for working-class students, notably for part-timers and women, was arguably 'the most radical, most specifically socialist policy the Labour government had in education'.[25]

During the summer of 1967 the chance to switch jobs came, and Crosland hesitated before leaving a department in which he felt policies were going well. Comprehensive reform looked irreversible, the polytechnics were being established, and the independent schools commission was due to report within a year. He was also proud of his success in other areas of policy: for example in securing approval for a large-scale building programme in educational priority areas; in tackling the problem of teacher supply; and in establishing the Social Science Research Council.[26] Not all of those who worked with him were impressed by what was left behind. One of his advisers, A. H. Halsey, said that his background ensured he had no understanding of further education and that he had been insufficiently tough in dealing with the public schools; his main redeeming feature was that his successors were worse.[27]

After Labour lost office in 1970, education also came to be regarded by left-wing critics as one of many areas where high expectations had been dashed. Brian Jackson, writing in the *New Statesman*, described Crosland as a 'gifted, serious man struggling through the treacle of the Wilson government, lifting hopes with many small, brave gestures, but achieving so very little, despite himself'. Seven out of ten children still had no access to a comprehensive school, the consequence Jackson said of Crosland's misguided decision to 'request' not 'require' local authority action. As for the public schools, the minister had wasted £75,000 on a commission which shunted the question into the sidelines. Crosland, he concluded, had not emulated Rab Butler, who had triumphed despite similarly lukewarm support from the prime minister of the day.[28]

These harsh verdicts were not generally held either within the educational world or among those with whom Crosland worked. One of his officials, who served thirty-five ministers at the department over the years, later wrote that Crosland stood out for 'a rare combination of qualities: brains, courage, perspective and compassion'.[29] Cabinet colleagues admired his persistence in securing a rising share of funds in the face of stiff competition from other departments. By mid-1967 education was claiming a similar proportion of spending as defence; and even when cutbacks were being demanded, colleagues noted Crosland's success in challenging Treasury figures. Barbara Castle, by no means a strong admirer, wrote in her diary that Crosland had made a 'magnificent' case: 'it is pretty clear to me that he will get off very lightly. I ought to do a bit more of that kind of thing myself!'[30] Ministerial and party colleagues were agreed that much had been achieved in a small space of time, particularly in helping to promote equal opportunity through comprehensive education. Crosland's success was also evident in consistently high opinion poll ratings for Labour's education policy.[31] There was, in other words, a consensus that Crosland had confounded those who felt he did not have the temperament to make a successful administrator. Indeed one of the Prime Minister's aides said that for a while as the reform programme forged ahead, he was 'probably our most popular minister'.[32] But beyond the purely departmental concerns, Crosland's wider reputation as a politician – in Cabinet, the parliamentary party and the country – developed erratically in the mid-1960s. In order to understand why, it is necessary to appreciate the broader difficulties of the government, in particular the economic problems that were beginning to erode confidence in Harold Wilson and his administration.

13

Plots and Crises, 1965-7

Tony Crosland's life was busy and fulfilled as Education Secretary. At last he was at the heart of the decision-making process, and he revelled in a hectic daily schedule of work at Curzon Street, attendance in Cabinet and at the House of Commons, evening meetings with various educational groups and full constituency engagements. His enjoyment of running his own department was commented upon by profile writers, who spoke of him as 'informal, glamorous, intellectual'; a new-style socialist who reflected the popular mood of the 1960s – half-Americanised, personally liberated, undogmatic.[1]

This was also a period when his domestic life became more settled. In some of the most intimate passages of her biography, Susan Crosland paints a vivid picture of life at Lansdowne Road, where the Secretary of State was to be found in his old pullover and slippers, whisky and cigar in hand. He would often arrive back late at night from the Commons to mull over events of the day before returning to his ministerial boxes and his avid reading of the political weeklies until the early hours.

Susan Crosland charts the development of her husband's relationship with Sheila and Ellen-Craig: spending time with them watching *Gideon's Way* on a newly rented television set and taking responsibility for breaking the news of the death of their grandfather, Susan's father, in America. On Sunday afternoons the adults insisted on a siesta, and the girls had to reduce the noise level from the gramophone. On one occasion Tony Benn turned up for a chat with Crosland, with bicycle clips still attached to his trouser legs. Crosland agreed to spend half-an-hour with Benn. 'If you'd walked in five minutes later, Susan and I would have been in bed,' he declared. Susan Crosland provides a particularly candid account of some of the furnishings at Lansdowne Road:

> The study had the atmosphere of his sitting room at The Boltons – the same Victorian chandelier, the same floor-length gold-velvet curtains.

. . . Most horizontal surfaces were covered with methodically-organised papers, files, books. Books lined two walls, a drinks tray on one shelf. On the remaining wall hung two large austere black and white portraits by Auerbach either side of a nearly lifesize drawing that Tony had commissioned – me, standing, wearing high-heeled sandals only.[2]

There were still reminders of Crosland's earlier behaviour and he occasionally spoke to his wife with the impression that he was addressing a public meeting. 'No one wants second helpings, Susan', he would boom out at dinner parties, wanting to get on with conversation. But friends observed that the happiness of his marriage helped to make him a more rounded personality, with a moderation alien to the bachelor of the 1950s. He told one colleague he needed eight hours sleep every night to work effectively, and after an attack of what he called 'mild sub-jaundice' during the 1966 election campaign he made efforts to change his drinking and smoking habits. While he had no intention of giving up such 'civilized + pleasure-giving pursuits', he sought at least to moderate his consumption. Smoking, he noted, was 'certain to give chronic bronchitis' unless he could cut down to two to five cigars per day.[3] Instead of socialising, Crosland was more likely to be indulging what his wife called his 'passionate . . . affair' with *Match of the Day*. He went to great lengths on Saturdays not to be told the result of games prior to screening, and sometimes enlisted his stepdaughters' help to say that the Prime Minister was on the telephone if he wanted to slip away from guests to watch a match. His passion was such that he complained to the Director-General of the BBC about the 'dreadful Kenneth Wolstenholme', though he admitted his was probably a minority view of the commentator who famously covered England's 1966 World Cup victory over Germany.[4]

In many respects the mid-1960s were good times for Crosland, with ministerial success allied to personal contentment. For the Labour government, however, events began to go badly awry after the 1966 election, and this was one of the factors which limited Crosland's progress in the broader political arena beyond his department. It was not for some months after he became Education Secretary that he began to make an impression in Cabinet. This was a direct result of his conviction that it was best to keep silent unless he had a well-informed point of view. Crossman noted in his diary that about half the Cabinet could be described as 'tiddlers', rarely contributing to general discussion. Callaghan, however, told Crosland he was being too modest: his 'knowing nothing' left him better equipped than many others, and Callaghan was pleased to see his friend did begin to join in and become an 'opinion-former'. By April 1965 Crossman noted that Crosland was more confident than seemed likely a few weeks earlier, 'and is emerging in Cabinet as a man with something important to contribute on the economic side'.[5] Unfortunately when he did begin to speak up it was with a message that neither Prime Minister nor Chancellor were keen to hear. Although the Cabinet was not allowed to discuss 'The Unmentionable', Crosland did little to endear himself to Wilson by implicitly returning to the issue of devaluation in several of his Cabinet interventions.

He was also outspoken in criticising the package of moderately deflationary measures adopted by the government in the summer of 1965. In an effort to improve Britain's financial stability, the Chancellor presented ministers with a programme that cut local government spending and called for a standstill on the expansion of public building programmes. Barbara Castle noted in her diary that, with one eye on the need to prepare the ground for a general election, there was little choice but to accept. But to 'her delight', it was Crosland who jumped in to put the case for higher public expenditure as the *raison d'être* of a Labour government. The cuts package might be inevitable, he said, but colleagues should recognise that it could lead into stagnation and Tory policies. Castle passed him a note asking if he still favoured early devaluation, to which he whispered in reply that he did, but that he had promised Callaghan he would not press this.[6] Crosland's robust style was also praised by Crossman, who sympathised with the view that deflation would undermine the potential of the government's much-trumpeted National Plan. Crosland, he noted, was the only minister who 'comes right out with these honest-to-God economic judgements'. This bluntness did not win favour with the Prime Minister, who was determined to defend the existing parity of sterling at all costs. Some in the Cabinet were of the opinion that Crosland had isolated himself by 'banging on about The Unmentionable'.[7]

After Labour was re-elected in March 1966 Wilson's wary, suspicious view of his young colleague was brought into sharper focus. Before the election, the Prime Minister's personal popularity remained high, and he went to the polls arguing that the economy was being put back on to an even keel. But in spite of his considerably increased majority, Wilson was soon under pressure. A seamen's strike undermined the prospects of a successful incomes policy; sterling fell to its lowest level for twenty months; and the publication of figures for gold losses turned nervousness into panic on the foreign exchanges. In the 'July crisis' of 1966, the Cabinet split between those who backed Treasury plans for a more drastic deflationary package and those who believed devaluation was unavoidable. On 12 July the Chancellor announced his intention to reduce public spending by half a billion pounds – not an enormous sum in relation to total expenditure, but sufficient if carried through to damage the government's reputation, especially coming so soon after the election. Ministerial divisions, according to Crossman, crystallised after Crosland said that it was imperative to avoid a repeat of the previous summer, with inflation tackled by cutting spending.[8] The pro–devaluation case appeared to be gaining ground. Crosland was joined by an articulate group of ministers, including George Brown, Crossman and Castle; the last two were important, in Crosland's view, because they could not be tarred with the Gaitskellite brush. As the Prime Minister left the country for a pre-arranged trip to Moscow, the Westminster air was thick with rumour. At one point it was thought that Callaghan and senior Treasury officials were on the point of switching camps.[9]

When Wilson returned to the country on 19 July he immediately chaired a marathon four-and-a-half hour session of the Cabinet. Unable to keep devaluation off the agenda, he was determined to flush out his opponents and ensure Cabinet approval for his preferred option of economy cuts. Barbara Castle wrote in her diary that Crosland had the best of the argument and looked like winning it, but 'one after another the "do nothing" brigade mowed us down'.[10] Much was made of the claim that if Labour was dubbed the 'party of devaluation' the government would be in danger of disintegrating. Crosland realised that the argument could not be won if Wilson and Callaghan stuck to their guns. The Chancellor wobbled for no more than a day, and when the votes were counted around the Cabinet table only six of over twenty hands went up in favour of devaluation – Crosland, Jenkins, Brown, Crossman, Castle and Benn. George Brown heightened the drama by threatening to resign and marching out, but he returned the following day. Crosland's desire for a radical shift in economic policy had again been frustrated. Amidst stunned silence on the Labour backbenches, Wilson announced the new package of cutbacks. Labour had abandoned the National Plan in favour of financial orthodoxy. George Brown, who soon after left the discredited DEA to become Foreign Secretary, reflected that it was 'undoubtedly the turning point' in the life of the government.[11]

It was certainly a turning point for Wilson. From this moment on, distrust seemed to spread, in the words of one MP, 'like some mysterious viral infection from the Prime Minister to his colleagues', slowly undermining the Cabinet's sense of unity and purpose.[12] Wilson told Callaghan that he believed a conspiracy to unseat him had been organised during his absence in Moscow. This he said had been led by the 'European devaluers' Crosland and Jenkins, who had taken in some of the 'naive left'. Crosland and Jenkins had been heavily engaged in trying to persuade others of their case that devaluation could only be effective if linked to a fresh application to join the Common Market. Barbara Castle in particular supported this line of argument: after hearing that Callaghan wanted to leave the Treasury – worn down by the crisis – she proposed Crosland as his successor, much to Wilson's annoyance.[13] But if there was inevitably fevered discussion, there was no evidence of a direct conspiracy to oust the Prime Minister. One of those who may have been implicated as a pro-devaluer, Tony Benn, claimed this was paranoia on the part of No. 10. Over lunch some time later Crosland denied entirely any knowledge of a conspiracy, which was not his way of doing things. He told Benn he had never been an admirer of Wilson, and that over the past few months 'we appear to have been entirely without a strategy and I think he's been very bad'. On the other hand it was difficult to quarrel with his electoral record, and on balance he might be the best type of Premier one could hope for in peacetime. On the leadership issue, Crosland added, he thought Callaghan had ambitions and Jenkins also, but 'none of these things was in sight over the next five years'.[14]

Where did this leave Crosland's standing inside the Cabinet? The Prime Minister respected his expertise, but counted him among those who needed to be carefully watched. When Wilson set up a special Cabinet committee to co-ordinate economic strategy – one of the demands of the devaluation rebels – Crosland was pointedly excluded. In Wilson's eyes, matters were made worse by Crosland's forthright manner, notably when he blurted out that No. 10 was mainly responsible for the press leaks of which the Prime Minister complained. Dick Crossman recorded:

There was an awkward silence and I think this has cost Tony dear in his relations with Harold. Still, he had the courage to say it. This is the fourth Cabinet running in which he has played an active part, talking not just as a departmental Minister but as somebody who understands economics and rates himself equal with the PM, George Brown and James Callaghan, somebody who has forced his way into their stratosphere.[15]

Crossman's admiration was shared by other colleagues around the Cabinet table, although there was also another rising star. George Brown told Cecil King of the *Daily Mirror* that after the July crisis Wilson was no longer regarded as infallible. The succession was being discussed, and while Brown acknowledged that he was not in the running (and made no mention of his arch-rival Callaghan), two candidates being talked about were 'Jenkins and Crosland, in that order'.[16]

Why was Roy Jenkins, Home Secretary since late 1965, forging ahead of his older friend as the front-runner among potential future leaders? Both were regarded as successful departmental ministers – with Jenkins encouraging the type of libertarian reforms outlined by Crosland in *The Future of Socialism* – and both could hold their own in Cabinet. But elsewhere on the political stage, it was Jenkins who shone brighter, becoming one of Labour's most effective debaters in the House of Commons. His meticulous preparation contrasted with Crosland's more cavalier attitude, especially if he regarded a debate as 'frivolous'. In July 1965 he was humiliated after winding up for the government in a debate used by the opposition to attack Labour's record since coming to power. Crosland spent less than half an hour preparing, resenting any time given to what he saw as mere ritual, and he made the elementary mistake of finishing before the allotted time. This allowed Conservatives to jump in and maul his speech, leaving Labour backbenchers silent and downcast. The following day he had to face newspaper accusations that he was an 'elegant lightweight', badly outclassed by heavier hitters.[17]

Jenkins also spent more time cultivating media contacts. Crosland had no 'spin doctors', whereas Jenkins employed John Harris as a special adviser at the Home Office with particular responsibility for relations with the press. This meant Crosland had a low profile among party activists and the public, which was reinforced by his reluctance to appear on television. Disliking the sound of what he called his own 'lah-de-dah' voice, he resented the notion of developing a public persona for the screen. When accused of looking aloof and bored when tackled by TV presenters, he said it was no wonder. 'They don't do enough homework and then ask these footling questions.'[18]

Equally important was the willingness of Jenkins to spend time building up a coterie of supporters inside the parliamentary party. Crosland did meet occasionally with a small group of MPs new to the House, including David Owen and David Marquand. But as Education Secretary he spent more time with outside advisers, and those who worked with him confirmed that he was reluctant to spend time in the Tea Room or bars at Westminster rallying the troops.[19] If he was at the House during the evenings, he mostly worked in the room allocated to him as a minister. All this proved disappointing to new MPs such as CDS stalwarts Bill Rodgers and Dick Taverne, who found Jenkins approachable but Crosland more likely to 'blow hot and cold'.[20] By temperament, some claim, Crosland did not have the right 'fingertips' for politics, failing to see that supporters hoped for their own advancement. Roy Hattersley, later one of Crosland's closest allies, recalled that he first became a friend in the mid-1960s. In spite of the warmth of his relationship with Crosland, Hattersley regarded his real patron to be Roy Jenkins, who made efforts to persuade Wilson that he was worthy of promotion. It was this type of encouragement which helped to make Jenkins a growing focus of loyalty for many on the Labour right.[21]

Neither man could yet be regarded as a serious threat to the Prime Minister. One of the reasons for Crosland's refusal to 'gather troops' was his belief that any change in leadership was a remote possibility. He believed the question would not arise until well into the next parliament, and that Callaghan's seniority and high profile made him the clear favourite to succeed. In spite of his troubles as Chancellor, Callaghan also retained a command of the party in the Commons that put him well out in front, Crosland told Cecil King, and he and Jenkins would have to wait.[22] Colleagues confirm that in private Crosland was fatalistic. In weekly gossip sessions with junior ministers he might be scathing about Wilson and the 'kitchen cabinet', but he recognised that the Prime Minister remained a formidable force: 'a bastard, but he's a genius'. At the same time, he would have harsh things to say about those who voted for Wilson in 1963 but were now complaining.[23] If Crosland saw no point in pressing any leadership claim, what he did resent was others seeking to exploit Wilson's declining popularity by jostling for position. He told Tony Benn he was 'sick' of ministers using aides to leak to the press what jobs they would like, notably Roy and Jim, whose ambitions for the Foreign Office were 'so well known as to be almost boring'.[24] At one point, August 'silly season' speculation prompted several stories about Callaghan, Jenkins and even Crossman as leadership contenders. Crosland turned on his PPS: 'Why the fuck don't I ever read about Crosland for PM; what the hell are you doing about it?'[25]

Implicit in all these developments was a gradual but perceptible cooling of relations between Crosland and Roy Jenkins. Wilson's security as leader had hitherto been enhanced by the knowledge that his two most senior colleagues, Callaghan and Brown, were never likely to combine against him. As events went sour in 1966, he became concerned that a threat might emerge in time from the two younger Gaitskellite pretenders. As we have seen, during the July crisis of 1966 Wilson was anxious about the close co-operation of the 'European devaluers'. Fortunately for the Prime Minister, such examples of harmony between Crosland and Jenkins were becoming the exception not the rule. David Owen, new to the House in 1966, was invited to join the 1963 Club, an informal grouping which met to maintain Gaitskell's legacy. At the club's regular dinners he rapidly made two discoveries. One was that hostility to Wilson was deep-seated and went back a long way, to the 1950s; the other was that there was strong personal rivalry between the two 'great men' of the Club – 'delphicly conducted but nevertheless ever-present within a friendly gathering'.[26] Both Jenkins and Crosland, Owen noted, were highly ambitious and the jealousy was mutual. Crosland became increasingly irritated with the club being used as a forum for promoting the leadership ambitions of his great rival.[27]

Although the two old friends could still be seen playing tennis together in Labroke Square, careful observers noted that the tension between them was in danger of breaking into the open. In July 1967 Crosland gave a widely reported speech at Norwich reaffirming his belief that socialism required high and growing levels of public expenditure. Since 1964 he had given few indications in public that he was in any way at odds with the direction of government policy. Reporters inevitably asked questions about his motives. Was this a bid to secure a greater share of resources for his department in unresolved Cabinet battles? Was it a plea for Labour to mend its deflationary ways and look to economic expansion? Or was it some sort of effort by Crosland to heighten his personal profile? Dick Crossman noted that the first of these was unlikely, for Crosland had already settled the education budget with Callaghan before making the speech.[28] Alan Watkins, the journalist who was closest to Crosland, frequently meeting him over drinks, wrote that the speech had much to do with his relationship with Jenkins, which became cooler if not antagonistic the more Jenkins was touted as a future Prime Minister. It was an open secret, Watkins said, that Crosland disliked the government's deflationary strategy. But his willingness to stay silent in public was tested beyond endurance by a speech by Jenkins a few weeks earlier trumpeting growth. This was 'almost more than flesh and blood could stand', and it prompted Crosland to remind listeners that he had stronger credentials in arguing that Labour's case had to be based on more than successive years of spending cuts.[29]

Crosland's speech reverberated across the party. It was welcomed by some on the left as being consistent with everything he had said in the past, whereas disillusionment with Wilson was based on his apparent abandonment of his pre-1964 radicalism. The irony was much commented upon: in the past it was Crosland who was attacked for allegedly jettisoning socialist principles; now he was being lauded for attempting to restore idealism and a sense of direction. Some commentators were perplexed. If Crosland was looking to extend his political base by building bridges across the party, it was noted, he had a strange way of going about it. He was notorious for having no time for summer evenings spent drinking beer on the Commons terrace; worse still, he was 'occasionally observed drinking wine'. As it was once said of Lord Chandos, Crosland was 'a man who has long since given up any vestige of a desire to please'.[30] Crosland was unlikely, in practice, to have spent much time calculating the reaction of the left. His speech was rather an outpouring of long-held views, its timing prompted by pique that so much attention was being given to the leadership claims of others. Wilson, he believed, was unlikely to be toppled and colleagues might be better employed getting on with their jobs. In the summer of 1967 Crosland told Dick Crossman that he had ceased to know Jenkins intimately and that he was 'behaving in a very funny and remote and ambitious way'. Crossman was greatly surprised to find that 'Roy is running his drive for power completely on his own'.[31] By the end of the year, the rift between Crosland and Jenkins was set to widen dramatically.

14

Missing the Chancellorship, 1967

One habit from his bachelor days which Crosland maintained after marriage was holidaying on his own. On his first summer break with his second wife and stepchildren, it was agreed that Susan would take her children to visit relatives in the United States, which she continued to do every year, and this left her husband free to resume his practice of spending time alone, reading, walking and soaking up the sunshine somewhere in Europe. 'Extreme conjugal intimacy, in our view', wrote Susan Crosland, 'was assisted by periodic recharging of the batteries.' Most of Crosland's holidays in the decade after he married Susan were spent in Italy, France or Spain but in August 1967 he was in Cyprus when his sightseeing was unexpectedly interrupted. The Prime Minister telephoned him from his own holiday retreat on the Scilly Islands and asked him to become President of the Board of Trade.

Wilson quickly outlined his reasoning. He said he wanted to bring Crosland into the team of economic ministers to help deal with the balance–of–payments; and that with the DEA in decline it was essential for the Board of Trade as the remaining economic department to be invigorated by someone of energy and expertise. Crosland was reluctant to give an immediate answer and asked for time to weigh up the options. On the one hand, he was reluctant to leave the DES, where reform was proceeding and morale was good; nor did he have a high regard for the Board of Trade. On the other hand, here was an opportunity to have influence in the formulation of economic policy, and the Trade portfolio was traditionally regarded as a stepping stone to the Chancellorship. Before coming home he sent a telegram to his wife: 'mixed feelings but on balance must be right'.[1] Within days newspaper profiles were appearing of the forty-nine-year-old minister about to move in Wilson's latest reshuffle. He was described as a 'tall pale man with a smart voice and hair combed thickly back like a speedway rider's'. Crosland, it was said, appeared to be making a sideways move, but there was no doubt it might help him in his ambition one day to become Chancellor.[2]

The future of the Chancellorship was not only in Crosland's mind at the time of the reshuffle. Wilson told the disgruntled outgoing President of the Board, Douglas Jay, that he was being asked to resign because of his age. But underlying Jay's removal was the continuing press build up, especially in the *Daily Mirror*, of Roy Jenkins as the likely next Chancellor and possible Prime Minister. A few days after the reshuffle Wilson told Crossman he was highly satisfied with the outcome: 'I've got seven potential Chancellors, and I've knocked out the situation where Jenkins was the only alternative to Callaghan.'[3] Back from his curtailed holiday, Crosland began to have second thoughts about the wisdom of accepting his new post. He, too, confided in Crossman, telling him it had always been 'his nightmare that he might be pushed into this ghastly Ministry which was nobody's business', and where any restructuring to make it more effective would be an 'appallingly dreary' task. But, he said, he had no real choice; he felt he had been got at while on holiday and had to come into line. Crossman tried to cheer him up by repeating what the Prime Minister said about seven potential chancellors, adding that at least it put him on a level with Roy in his chances of going to the Treasury.[4] Callaghan himself made the same point in writing to congratulate Crosland on his 'step nearer the centre'. You will still, Callaghan wrote, 'have to put up with me – but you would prefer that than having to put up with Roy – and as you have been told you are not prejudiced – on the contrary I would say.'[5]

The move to the Board of Trade therefore put Crosland in the running for the Chancellorship in a way that did not apply while he remained at Education. What no one guessed in August was the speed with which the question of who might succeed Callaghan would come to the top of the political agenda. During the autumn, pressure on sterling once more intensified. Crosland again pressed the case for devaluation, this time on the Cabinet's Steering Committee for Economic Policy, which he joined as Trade minister. Wilson, in a gesture that was unthinkable in the early days of the government, invited Crosland to lunch in his flat above No. 10, and told his guest he had 'an open mind' on whether devaluation was now appropriate. 'One hasn't the faintest idea', Crosland told his wife, 'whether the bastard means what he says even at the moment he speaks it.'[6] He found his first meeting at the Economic Policy Committe 'rambling + diffuse + hopeless', but it was in this forum that events came to a head in November. Crossman noted that it was Crosland who made much of the running on devaluation, finally helping the Chancellor to persuade Wilson that it was better to jump rather than be pushed.[7] The President of the Board of Trade was among a small group of ministers charged with maintaining secrecy before the official announcement came: sterling was to be devalued by 14.3 per cent in relation to the dollar. His initial response was one of relief and anti-climax; the battle for devaluation had been won, though for him it came three years too late.

The greatest humiliation in the days that followed was reserved for the Prime Minister. His television statement – especially his bizarre claim that the 'pound in your pocket' remained unaffected – was savaged by the press and opposition alike. But devaluation also raised the question of the Chancellor's position. On the evening of the broadcast on 20 November Crosland was at No. 11, and reported back to his wife that Callaghan was inclined to resign within the next week. He added that 'Jim talked in front of the others about my being Chancellor in a week or so. He says that he and Harold have agreed that the odds on this are 95:5.' Susan Crosland was taken aback to find that her husband's long-time ambition might soon be realised; with two daughters in the 'throes of adolescence', she had hoped such a move would come later rather than sooner. As Callaghan waited for devaluation to be completed before resigning, there were indications that Crosland had emerged as front-runner in the race for the succession, ahead of rivals such as Jenkins, Healey and Shore. He opened for the government in a hastily arranged debate about economic policy in the Commons on Tuesday 21 November, and told his wife afterwards that Callaghan was dropping hints about his candidature to officials at the Treasury. The Chancellor had also emphasised to Wilson that Crosland was his preferred successor, both because of his record on devaluation and because – unlike some colleagues – he understood that it was not a soft option.[8]

Even so, the matter was not yet cut and dried. On the evening of Thursday 23 November, Callaghan told Roy Jenkins it was unlikely he would get the post, as seemed probable earlier in the year. He said that Crosland was favourite, and Healey was considered an outsider, and implied that this reflected Wilson's thinking. It was bad fortune, Callaghan commiserated, that this should happen at a time when Jenkins was not on good terms with the Prime Minister.[9] That same evening Crosland urged Callaghan to sleep on things over the weekend before making any final decisions. 'If I find next week that I've talked myself out of the job,' he said to his wife, 'it will feel very odd.' When he returned from his Sussex farm, Callaghan told Wilson he had reconsidered: he did not wish to go to the backbenches as hitherto intended. In staying on within the government, his preference was for the DES, but the Prime Minister felt this would be interpreted as demotion and as a snub. He was anxious to avoid a major reshuffle, and if he promoted Crosland from Trade, 'this would create a chain reaction'.[10] In these altered circumstances, it was agreed that the best course was for Callaghan to move to the Home Office in a straight swop with Roy Jenkins. On the evening of Tuesday 28 November Jenkins was called to Downing Street and immediately accepted the offer of the Treasury. The Prime Minister told him he was the first choice for the post, though – Jenkins recalled – he 'did not say *when* I had become his first choice (my guess is that it was only the day before)'.[11]

The news came as a devastating blow to Crosland. Salt was rubbed into the wound when it was announced, only two hours after, that Crosland as President of the Board of Trade was to attend a meeting in Paris to deputise for Callaghan, who had just relinquished his responsibilities at the Treasury. Roy Jenkins wrote in his memoirs that this must have been 'one of the most thankless missions ever undertaken by a member of the Cabinet'. Calling briefly at Lansdowne Road to collect an overnight bag Crosland bleakly told his wife: 'It's the greatest fall I've ever had in my life.'[12] Others attending the meeting in Paris were in no doubt about the 'emotional strain' he was experiencing over the whole episode.[13] His dismay was based not only on his conviction that his credentials for the job were superior to those of his younger friend; it was also that his hopes had been raised by the whispers of the previous few weeks. When the two men met for the first time after the announcement in December, Crosland made no attempt to conceal his distress. He told Jenkins he would never have gone to the Board of Trade if he had known of this outcome, and that his one wish now was to move to a non-economic department. Any credit in the economic sphere for the remainder of the parliament, he said, would inevitably go to the new Chancellor or the Prime Minister. In view of all that happened, Jenkins recollected, Crosland behaved 'remarkably well'.[14]

Why was Roy Jenkins favoured and Crosland denied the prize when it seemed within his grasp? One view is that the outcome was never really in doubt. Jenkins was simply the 'best man', superior in Cabinet and the House and competent in economic affairs. 'Nobody except Crosland himself', claims John Campbell, 'thought that Wilson had made anything but the obvious choice.'[15] Jenkins as a reforming Home Secretary had clearly become the darling of many on the right of the PLP. Yet he readily conceded that Crosland was better qualified as an economist, and more than once expressed anxiety that he was not part of the ministerial group which made the final decision on devaluation. Crosland's involvement in these discussions had raised his profile and his prospects. In early November Crossman recorded that the Prime Minister's regard for Crosland had risen, adding that 'Tony looks to me like the man booked for the Treasury'.[16] Crosland's candidature, in other words, was serious, and his position as front-runner appeared to be confirmed in the week after devaluation was announced, especially as he made a reasonable job of defending the government in the House.

We should not attach too much credence to the idea that Wilson preferred Jenkins on personal grounds. Ben Pimlott claims that Wilson had more liking for the biographical and historical interests of Jenkins than he did for Crosland's more theoretical concerns, and that Wilson and Crosland found it difficult to get on: 'Crosland had the kind of charm that bewitches a certain kind of man or woman, and makes another, chemically different, kind feel insignificant. Wilson was disconcerted, rather than charmed by Crosland's self-assurance; and irritated by the arrogance with which he seemed to take his own future progress in politics for granted.'[17] Jenkins wrote in his memoirs that, while he had fierce arguments with Wilson at times, they could at least converse socially 'about minutiae which Crosland regarded as puerile: railway timetables or Wisden-like political records'.[18] But a case could equally be made for saying it was Crosland who had more in common with Wilson: his identification with his working-class constituents, and his disdain for the type of social life with which Jenkins was associated. In reality, Wilson had never felt comfortable with either of his Gaitskellite colleagues, though journalists recall that he said harsher things about Jenkins than he did about Crosland.[19]

To understand why Crosland was pipped at the post, attention needs to be focused on the weekend of 25-26 November, when two key developments took place. First, Callaghan wobbled on the issue of returning to the backbenches. Once he had determined to stay on in government, Crosland's prospects were considerably diminished. A straight swop with Jenkins at the Home Office, as far as Wilson was concerned, solved two immediate problems: it preserved Callaghan's dignity by giving him another high office of state, and it minimised government changes. The Prime Minister's determination to limit the extent of the reshuffle was also influenced by the storm of criticism in the newspaper press about his leadership and the ability of the government to survive the humiliation of devaluation. Under fierce attack, Wilson needed to act decisively but without appearing to panic. Another reshuffle could be interpreted as desperation, and it was in these circumstances that the case for Jenkins suddenly became overwhelming. Wilson needed to bolster his administration by turning to the one figure whose public popularity remained high. The need, in short, was for a 'political' Chancellor more than an 'economic' one, even if this meant building up further the image of Jenkins as a possible alternative leader. The Prime Minister's closest advisers were equally swayed by the needs of the moment. Some months later Dick Crossman told Crosland that as Leader of the House he had pressed for Jenkins, saying that Roy was a more formidable enemy and so it was right to 'buy him in'.[20]

The Chancellorship was thus a hard political calculation. Crosland had reason to feel that he had been let down by Callaghan, whose desire to repay his friend for support in the 1963 leadership contest was not sufficient to tip the balance in Crosland's favour. His reluctance to contemplate going to the Board of Trade undermined the chances of securing the outcome he initially hoped to engineer.[21] The Prime Minister was no doubt relieved that Callaghan would not be returning to the backbenches, where he might become a focus for discontented MPs. In any calculations about preserving his leadership, Wilson may have felt that there was no ideal solution. Hitherto he had been proud of his ability to balance potential rivals and to multiply their numbers, as he had done by giving Crosland the Board of Trade. But in promoting Jenkins he was setting him up as the single crown prince, at least until such time as Callaghan's reputation might recover. Yet this, he may have reasoned, was the price that had to be paid. It met the desperate need of the moment for the government to have an appearance of a fresh start, and it was better than finding that in any future crisis Crosland as Chancellor was making common cause with Callaghan on the backbenches. This may have been a clinching factor for the Prime Minister.

A Crosland–Callaghan alliance was one to fear, whereas it was almost inconceivable that Jenkins would combine with Callaghan; the latter were often barely on 'spitting terms'. Political rivalry combined with mutual personal dislike. Callaghan felt Jenkins was an elitist snob, while Jenkins was to say of Callaghan that he could think of no one who combined 'such a powerful political personality with so little intelligence'.[22]

The final weeks of 1967 were a defining moment in the history of Wilson's administration and in Tony Crosland's career. As the government's popularity plummeted, question marks hung over Labour's ability to win any forthcoming election. It was bad enough for Crosland that he had to watch the government being pilloried, knowing that he had argued for devaluation three years earlier. To compound the misery, he knew that the chance of reaching the one senior office he most sought had gone, possibly for ever, along with the chance to forge policy in the crucial remaining period of that parliament. The bitterness he felt about having his dream shattered was to linger for a long time to come, and was to have important consequences for the party as a whole. As Roy Jenkins concluded:

> . . . it would be idle to pretend that these events of November 1967 did not leave a scar on Crosland which had the effect of crucially damaging the cohesion of the Labour right over the next eight or nine years. Had he and I been able to work together as smoothly as did Gaitskell and Jay or Gaitskell and Gordon Walker a decade before it might have made a decisive difference to the balance of power within the Labour Party and hence to the politics of the early 1980s.[23]

In the short-term, Crosland had no choice but to try to come to terms with what had happened. As the second most important economic minister in the Cabinet, he had the task of working closely with the new Chancellor in the aftermath of devaluation. As Callaghan had warned in the summer, he would now have to 'put up with Roy'.

15

Anchored at the
Board of Trade, 1967–9

The months after devaluation witnessed a shift in the balance of forces inside Wilson's Cabinet. Callaghan was temporarily eclipsed, and the Prime Minister's other great rival of earlier years, George Brown, was removed from the running early in 1968 after finally acting upon one of his resignation threats. Wilson tried to balance the promotion of Roy Jenkins to the Treasury by pushing on allies such as Barbara Castle, who became Employment Secretary. But there was no doubt that the new Chancellor was in a strong position. In the aftermath of devaluation he was free to determine the direction of economic policy for the remainder of the parliament. He chose to follow an orthodox Treasury line: if Britain could eliminate its balance-of-payments deficit, he believed, this would show that devaluation had worked in restoring industrial competitiveness. In order to reach the promised land, Jenkins pledged himself to 'two years hard slog', beginning with fresh expenditure cuts and the most deflationary peacetime budget since the war, increasing taxation by nearly a billion pounds. The aim was to endure all the pain rapidly in order to leave time for economic and political recovery before the next election. For Tony Crosland, licking his wounds after failing to become Chancellor, it was to be his most frustrating period since becoming a minister.

In January 1968 Jenkins presented the Cabinet with details of cuts which the Treasury insisted were necessary to accompany devaluation. Crosland was in no mood to co-operate. He questioned the basis of Treasury calculations, and objected to a series of separate decisions being requested without an assessment of the across-the-board impact on economic policy. He followed this up by calling for a detailed look at how resources were divided between civil and military expenditure and between taxes and public expenditure. The new Chancellor was forced to go away and come back with figures which rebutted Crosland's claim that only about half the proposed cuts were necessary.[1] Instead of falling into line, suitably chastened, Crosland actively opposed one of the most controversial of the proposed cutbacks: the postponement of a manifesto commitment to raise the school-leaving age to sixteen. Along with another former Education Secretary, Michael Stewart, Crosland led the resistance. He conceded that postponment would affect no more than 400,000 children. 'But they're not our children. It's always other people's children. None of us in this room would dream of letting our children leave school at fifteen.'[2] His relations with the Chancellor were hardly improved when he threatened what he called 'blackmail', saying he would switch his vote on another close issue unless there was a rethink. Jenkins agreed this was the hardest of the proposals to endorse, but believed if any one of them was altered the whole exercise 'would be dead'.[3]

When the Cabinet met to vote, the balance of forces was tipped by Crosland's successor at the DES, Patrick Gordon Walker, who claimed it was his duty to support the Chancellor. One of the defeated minority, Lord Longford, Labour leader in the House of Lords, resigned in protest, and Crosland went back to Lansdowne Road much disheartened. Gordon Walker, he said, had 'lost his nerve', while many of the so-called 'left' such as Crossman and Castle had been strangely silent. Throughout the whole exercise, Crosland's behaviour had been what Tony Benn described as 'niggling'.[4] Some colleagues were critical of his stance, arguing that he knew better than most that devaluation was no soft option and yet chose to question the Chancellor's judgement at a time when the government needed to close ranks.[5] For backbench supporters of Jenkins, Crosland was simply 'messing about' and being 'too clever by half'. Other observers claim it was hardly to be expected that he would come into line so soon after the enormous blow he had suffered.[6] The failure to become Chancellor had left him dejected and on the sidelines. As rumours of plots against Wilson multiplied, with talk of turmoil in the City and the need for a national government, Crosland remained detached. He told Tony Benn there was nothing much to worry about and that some of the wild rumours were simply the 'City being silly'.[7]

Crosland's sullen attitude to Cabinet business persisted for some time. His standing with the Prime Minister, which had improved in his early months at the Board of Trade, deteriorated again in 1968, especially after the resignation of George Brown as Foreign

Secretary. On the night of 14 March, amidst grave concern about the need for further devaluation, American financiers urgently requested the closure of the London stock exchange the following morning. The Prime Minister hastily arranged a midnight meeting between the Privy Council and the Queen, a necessary prelude to announcing a public holiday on 15 March, so ensuring the closure of the stock market. The Foreign Secretary was not present at the midnight meeting, and flew into a rage upon hearing the news, gathering together a small group of ministers in the early hours. Crosland was among them, and shared Brown's indignation that they had not been consulted when they were only a few minutes away attending an all-night sitting of the House. After a shouting match with Wilson on the telephone, Brown led a mini-delegation to Downing Street, where the air was thick with accusations and recriminations. Wilson accused Brown of calling an irregular meeting of ministers, a 'cabal', and implied that the Foreign Secretary could not be contacted because he was drunk. Brown in turn accused the Prime Minister of lying in saying that 'efforts had been made' to invite him to the midnight meeting.

Tony Benn was present at No. 10 and wrote in his diary that as the argument dragged on the sense of a power struggle taking place became more noticeable. Crosland and Michael Stewart made it clear they were unhappy about the lack of consultation, while the Chancellor remained detached; Benn thought this was because he had his 'eye on the main chance and thinks Harold will destroy himself'. Eventually the Foreign Secretary stormed off, leaving his post and the Cabinet for good. Benn recorded:

> At 6am I came home. I gave Tony Crosland a lift and he hotly denied there was any alliance to replace Harold. He and Roy were at daggers drawn and there were great disagreements. But I'm sure Tony, in his heart, thinks Harold will go. Tony took an optimistic view of our economic situation and didn't take too grim a view even of the gold panic. But with the Bank Holiday, the Cabinet split, gold suspended, and the pound in the front line to the dollar, I should have thought the possibility of the Cecil King-type crisis which we predicted a month ago is very real.[8]

In the event, a further financial crisis was avoided, though the episode led to fresh suspicion of Crosland by the Prime Minister.

Within a month he was excluded from Wilson's 'inner Cabinet', a shifting group of up to ten senior ministers who met informally in order to take a broad view of government policy and to suggest new initiatives.

The Prime Minister told Dick Crossman that Crosland was being punished for intriguing with Brown at the Foreign Office, alleging that what he had done was 'very wrong' and that there was a tape of what had been said. Crossman confessed to being bewildered by this, though the issue surfaced again two days later in conversation with Roy Jenkins, who repeated the story but without shedding any further light on Crosland's so-called 'crimes'. Crossman ascertained from this discussion with Jenkins that 'Tony isn't as close to Roy now as some people believe', and he came away with the impression 'that Crosland and Healey are right out on a limb as the men whom Harold sees as the chief conspirators against him'.[9] As in the July crisis of 1966, Crosland's style was not one of seeking to mobilise forces behind the scenes. A few weeks later he told Crossman that any allegations against him were 'complete and absolute invention', and that he didn't know how such nonsense could spread. Wilson, he added, was an 'ass' to exclude him from the inner Cabinet, though he was not too disappointed as there did not seem to be any improved co-ordination of government strategy. Nor were Crosland and Healey the only individuals under a cloud. As Tony Benn noted, Wilson's defensiveness was such that he routinely suspected colleagues of plotting. Harold, he said, was 'very paranoid' and lived in constant fear of the day when four senior ministers would come and say that they refused to serve under him.[10]

Wilson's fears were driven by the knowledge that dissatisfaction with his leadership was mounting on the Labour backbenches. After disastrous local elections in the spring of 1968, a small group of right-wing MPs – including the likes of Hattersley, Taverne and Marquand – began to take soundings. They gathered the names of over one hundred MPs who wished to see a change of leadership, and in June Patrick Gordon Walker, who had recently resigned from the Cabinet, recorded that a 'conspiracy' was gathering pace. Roy Jenkins was kept apprised of these moves from the start, and it was also agreed 'to tell Callaghan and Crosland of the number of backbenchers with whom we were in touch'. But the President of the Board of Trade was only loosely involved in these developments. Any discussion about who should be the preferred successor revolved around the names of Jenkins and Callaghan, and it was the Chancellor who continued to be the one consulted about when and how to strike. By the end of the parliamentary session Wilson was seeming more secure and it was agreed that the conspirators had 'missed the bus' for the time being.[11] Crosland's attitude continued to be fatalistic: the party was stuck with a leader who – as he wrote in some private jottings on a new book about the Prime Minister – had no real interest in socialist or political theory, no governing set of principles, and no serious concern for equality.[12]

In the meantime, Crosland was left with little option but to immerse himself in the job he had held since the previous autumn. One of the reasons he had been reluctant to go to the Board of Trade was that it was a department with such wide-ranging interests. These included external trade; responsibility for individual sectors of the British economy such as shipping, civil aviation, tourism and the film industry; and the co-ordination of areas such as regional policy and the distribution of investment grants. Crosland did not get off to the best of starts. The range of responsibilities at the Board was daunting for any newcomer, and the minister's desire to inform himself fully before acting gave some colleagues the impression of indecision. And when he did act decisively, announcing that he would reopen consideration of Stansted as the 'third London' airport, it was to the consternation of civil servants. Some of his officials never forgave Crosland for what they considered to be a 'mad' move, re-igniting a controversy they hoped had been settled.[13] Nor did he have much good news to announce during his early months in the post. Trade figures remained poor and he had to admit in December 1967 that, while his department was inundated with inquiries from exporting firms, some sectors of industry were reacting slowly to the opportunites opened up by devaluation.[14]

Gwyneth Dunwoody, a junior minister at the department, recalled that while Crosland was not initially pleased to be there, he warmed to the task when he recognised that it did present an intellectual challenge. There were several areas of the Board's work, she noted, that he found appealing and to which he devoted himself, for example the securing of bilateral trade deals, the development of monopolies and merger policy and negotiations with overseas bodies such as EFTA, the European Free Trade Association which Britain helped to establish in the 1950s as a counterweight to the EEC.[15] Crosland's overriding concern was to ensure that devaluation produced an improvement in the balance-of-payments position. To this end, during 1968 most attention was given to external trade, including contingency plans for policies that might be adopted to strengthen the trade balance in the event of a fresh downturn.[16] By the late summer the signals from industry were becoming more positive. The *Director* magazine said that if the Board of Trade was on the way to recovering from the loss of status it suffered in the early days of the DEA, this was thanks in no small part to the 'drive of the long-distance runner who is now in charge'. Companies again looked to the Board for its informative bulletins on economic prospects and as a vital sponsoring department, and there was a new-found optimism that devalution would prove successful on the export side, even if this was not yet reflected in official figures.[17]

In time, Crosland established successful working relationships with most of his colleagues at the Board. Officials came to appreciate the care he took in reaching decisions, and one noted that many a dull meeting was enlivened by trying to work out what the minister's raising of an expressive left or right eyebrow signified.[18] Junior ministers approved of Crosland as they had at the DES. Crosland proved adept at delegating tasks and allowing others to get on with them while he took a broad overview. Bill Rodgers, by 1968 firmly in the Jenkins camp, agreed that Crosland was an excellent head of department, fair to juniors such as himself and generous in allowing others to receive praise for their own endeavours. Gwyneth Dunwoody, who became fond of her boss, recalls that life was never dull: provided one stood up to Crosland and was not put off by his formidable intelligence – or his sometimes 'docker-like' vocabulary – he was an immensely stimulating minister.[19] An even warmer tribute was paid by Professor Wilfred Beckerman, an Oxford Fellow recruited as the President's special economic adviser. Beckerman found Crosland to be a man of 'charm, warmth, humour, vitality, breadth of vision, enjoyment of life and generosity of spirit'. What marked him out from other politicians, he felt, was a lack of vanity: a willingness to give credit where it was due and to listen to views he considered important with 'not the slightest interest in people's status'.[20]

Crosland may have impressed those he worked with at the Board of Trade, but he remained out of favour with colleagues in Cabinet. The Prime Minister told Crossman in September 1968 that he regarded Crosland as a disappointment, often contributing an idea in

Cabinet but not a policy or a decision. There were also periodic spats with the Chancellor. According to Roy Jenkins, Crosland prevaricated over the proposed tightening of hire-purchase controls. In a special committee dealing with the issue, Crosland was 'half in favour, half against, but always opposed to an immediate decision on any particular course. His view (very typically) was that we ought to do something different from the proposition currently under discussion, maybe more drastic, maybe less, but certainly much later'. As a consequence, Jenkins added, action was delayed longer than it should have been, and it was Crosland who ultimately suffered in the Commons as he was the minister who had to announce the change on hire purchase restrictions.[21] Others in the Cabinet were similarly critical. Barbara Castle, who saw Crosland as a dynamic minister while at the DES, now called him a 'curious bird', someone who said a lot of the right things but who never 'really fights'.[22] She also noted his habit of waggling his foot violently throughout Cabinet meetings – an apt indication of his mood. A year on from the devaluation episode, with the government limping along and the economy in the doldrums, it was apparent that Crosland was still smarting from the failure to become Chancellor.

At Labour's annual conference in the autumn of 1968 he addressed a fringe meeting in terms which showed he had lost none of his capacity for plain speaking. He bluntly asked what had gone wrong for the government: why had the triumph of March 1966 turned into deep unpopularity by 1968? The obvious diagnosis, he asserted, was the correct one. Inheriting a sluggish economy, the government had decided not to alter the exchange rate. Decoded, this amounted to saying, for the first time in public, that he had been right about devaluation all along. Instead, the belated measures chosen had, he claimed, in terms which would not endear him to Wilson or Jenkins, resulted in the longest period of slow growth since war, averaging only 1-1.2 per cent per year. Although standards of living had been cushioned by overseas borrowing, the sense of 'crisis and failure' persisted. In looking to what should be done, Crosland argued that economic recovery alone was not sufficient. It was also necessary to reaffirm the party's 'social-democratic ideals' and apply them to existing social problems, for example by getting rid of slum primary schools. The tendency to believe change was too difficult, unpopular or costly needed to be resisted. Labour should not always defer to public opinion, as it had recently over independent schools; it should

135

seek to change attitudes.[23] This was the authentic voice of the radical iconoclast, the manifesto of a would-be alternative Chancellor. Yet the conference speech went largely unreported; journalists were not listening as they had been at the time of the Norwich speech the previous year. In 1968 Crosland had become a marginal figure; indeed during the year to come there was a danger that he would be pushed out of the Cabinet altogether.

16

Strife, 1969-70

In January 1969 Crosland spent a week in Italy with his wife, recuperating after breaking his elbow in a fall on some slippery leaves. He returned to find the government embroiled in a major controversy over trade union reform. Following an upsurge of unofficial strike activity, the Employment Secretary Barbara Castle secured Wilson's backing to publish a White Paper as a precursor to legislation. *In Place of Strife* proposed that the government should be given powers to compel employers to negotiate with trade unions; failure to do so could result in arbitration and legally binding awards. In return, unions would be asked to accept penal clauses such as strike ballots before official stoppages. Union leaders angrily denounced such proposals, the first of their kind since the war, and the Labour left eagerly took up their cause. In the words of one left-wing MP, Ian Mikardo, the White Paper was 'completely out of balance', requiring sacrifices from those on the shop-floor but calling for no restrictions on highly paid professionals or on unearned income. 'The document which Barbara had called *In Place of Strife* was instead a provocation to Strife.'[1] There was no shortage of strife inside the party in the first six months of 1969. In the face of growing opposition, Wilson had to look for a way out, proposing a watered-down version of the White Paper. Rumours of plots to oust the Prime Minister circulated again, and the press made much of divisions inside the Cabinet. Senior figures including Crosland, it was alleged, were stirring up trouble among disgruntled ex-ministers on the backbenches such as Douglas Houghton, who had been sacked as Minister without Portfolio and was a long-time ally of Callaghan.

Crosland's attitude to the White Paper was based on pragmatism. In the face of rising industrial unrest, he was one of those in Cabinet who urged the need to modernise the trade union movement, but he believed it would be madness to undertake such contentious reform so late in the parliament. He was also concerned that the proposals as drafted would not work, and might result in a situation where the intended penal clauses would be ineffective and unofficial strikes continue to grow.[2] He joined with five other members in Cabinet to sound the alarm bell: the proposals, it was said, had been slapped on the table with the intention of being pushed through as quickly as possible; they would cause conflict with the unions in a vital pre-election year; they were, in short, 'crazy and doomed to defeat'.[3] Castle believed that with the backing of the Prime Minister and the Chancellor she would be able to forge ahead. What she had not calculated on was the resolute opposition in particular of Jim Callaghan, who was soon in almost open rebellion, holding his own meetings with trade union leaders. Wilson was so incensed he removed the Home Secretary from a new and smaller inner Cabinet formed in the spring. This snub nearly prompted Callaghan's resignation and Westminster was awash with rumours that he was about to mount a direct challenge for the leadership.

By June 1969 opposition inside the Labour movement forced Barbara Castle to retreat. The White Paper was dropped, and instead a face-saving formula was announced under which a 'solemn and binding' commitment was given that member unions would observe the guidelines on unofficial stoppages issued by the TUC. The outcome was another humiliation for the Prime Minister, especially as the TUC's lack of compulsory powers meant that its undertaking, 'though no doubt solemn, could hardly be described as binding'.[4] Wilson's fury at the result stemmed in part from his belief that Callaghan had not only been looking to topple him but had promised Crosland the job of Chancellor in a new government. 'There was', he told Barbara Castle, 'a secret pact between them based on their joint disloyalty'.[5] Dick Crossman told Castle to abandon her talk of threatening to resign alongside the Prime Minister; if it became known that another leader might be invited to form a government, then Callaghan and Crosland would have their chance. Crossman continued in his diary that:

> Tony has never forgiven Harold for making Roy Chancellor and has never lost hope that if Roy goes he will be Chancellor in his place. His best chance would be the breaking up of this Government and Callaghan's taking over. Though this sounds a terribly remote possibility I can't help thinking that it has been at the back of Tony's mind during the course of the last six months, when he has switched from demanding stronger anti-trade union measures to being 100 per cent pro-Callaghan.

Harold is right, Tony and Jim do see a lot of each other and I know it because my room in the House is on the same landing as theirs. They are in cahoots with Douglas Houghton, the Chairman of the Party, and it has been their triangle which has really endangered Harold in this crisis.[6]

As in previous moments of crisis, however, fears among Wilson's entourage were largely without foundation. Callaghan was asked if he was prepared to stand against the Prime Minister, but said he thought there was insufficient support inside the PLP for an immediate change. He was also wary of enhancing the chances of Jenkins, for he was aware that agitation on the backbenches was most widespread again among confirmed Jenkinsites.[7] Crosland still maintained his links with disaffected MPs, and indeed opened discussion at a 1963 Club dinner in May 1969 'with a very frank statement to the effect that at the proper time Harold must be got rid of'. What, he asked, was the point of just meeting and moaning? 'All you do is fucking talk', he blurted out at one stage.[8] He was not, however, suggesting immediate action, and his comments about a lack of planning confirmed for his listeners that their efforts to maintain secrecy had been successful. Crosland, in other words, was no more directly involved in a conspiracy than he had been before. In the event, less than fifty of 138 MPs canvassed by conspirators such as Gordon Walker said they would definitely come out against Wilson. The Chancellor, again better informed about all this than Crosland, once more cautioned against triggering a leadership battle, fearful that it would be Callaghan who benefited.[9] Neither of the Prime Minister's two main rivals were prepared to make the first move.

Over the summer there was much talk about Wilson exacting revenge. The names of Callaghan, Crosland and another opponent of *In Place of Strife*, Richard Marsh, the Minister of Power, were all mentioned as possibilities for demotion from the Cabinet. In July Tony Benn recorded a conversation in which the Prime Minister lashed out at Crosland and Marsh among others for leaking to journalists. 'He said', Benn continued, 'that he was going to do major restructuring and heads would have to roll. He asked if I would keep an eye out for plots and said that Ministers were meeting in secret and the Campaign for Democratic Socialism was still active'. Benn concluded that Wilson had 'gone mad' and 'is finished'.[10] But the Prime Minister did have some sympathy for his views from Dick

Crossman, to whom he also complained. Crossman got the clear impression that Wilson was 'infuriated', and agreed that Crosland was being more than usually irritating in Cabinet. He seemed to be 'thoroughly browned off, sick at not being Chancellor, sickened by the Chancellor's policy', and was being inefficient as well as nonchalant, 'just not seeming to mind' and in a peevish mood that led him to leak. Crossman admitted that he too tended to leak when feeling frustrated and on the fringe of things; this was all rather different, he felt, from the case of Marsh, who had simply been 'promoted far beyond his merits'.[11]

An indication of Crosland's frame of mind came in September 1969 when he engaged in his coolest exchanges yet with Jenkins. The Chancellor sparked the row by attacking Crosland for announcing trade figures in the House without proper consultation with the Treasury. Jenkins wrote that this behaviour was 'almost unbelievable', and he curtly added that with such actions 'you can hardly expect good relations between the Board of Trade and other Departments'.[12] Crosland replied that he was first astonished then saddened to receive 'so hectoring and pompous a communication from an old friend and Cabinet colleague'. He had been tempted to reply in kind, but felt this would only make matters worse:

> There will always be some tension between the Treasury and the Board of Trade, the Chancellor and the President, and no doubt us two personally. But as virtually everyone in the Treasury knows perfectly well, you are very lucky to have had me at the Board of Trade in the last two years; and the degree of constructive tension between our two departments is just about right.

Crosland added that he would continue the Board tradition of commenting on trade figures, and noted that his statement had been warmly praised by the Prime Minister and by economic commentators. He proposed to forget this 'rather undignified correspondence' and hoped relations would improve in future. Jenkins, for his part, feared that if Crosland was sacked he would be blamed for the outcome, though his line with Wilson on this was that it would be a foolish step.[13]

By the end of the month Crosland had left the Board of Trade, though not the Cabinet. Fearful that demotion would damage his department, he set out for the Prime Minister the case for extending the Board's powers as a counter-weight to the Treasury.[14] Wilson summoned him to Downing Street and told him confidentially that he had been working since July with officials to restructure several departments. The DEA was to be wound up and the Board of Trade would be diminished, but parts of both would go to a new ministry embracing housing, transport, local government and regional planning. Crosland was not wildly enthusiastic: 'Harold always makes things sound better than they turn out to be.'[15] When the changes were announced early in October, newspapers hailed the creation of two 'super-ministries', with Crosland as regional overlord and Tony Benn as industrial overlord at an expanded Ministry of Technology. Dick Crossman noted that the reshuffle was a far cry from the fevered talk of the summer. Marsh had gone, but Callaghan stayed where he was with his reputation much restored by his 'victory' over union reform and his handling of events in Northern Ireland, and Crosland appeared to have been promoted.[16] Crosland himself was not so sure. He told Tony Benn he was disappointed to see the Board of Trade 'cut up' and suspected it was another publicity stunt. Benn described him as 'obviously very sick about it because he doesn't think there is anything in the job'.[17] This view was echoed by Barbara Castle, who was delighted that Crosland would no longer interfere with her concerns at Employment. Wilson said to her with relish, 'It will stop him meddling so much in economics.'[18]

What then was the legacy of two years at the Board of Trade? If many colleagues had found him 'niggling' in Cabinet, Crosland could claim to have done reasonably well for his department. With the economy at last showing signs of improvement, he was satisfied that the Board had played its part in helping to boost export growth. His own reflections on what he had achieved emphasised a strengthening of the Board's prestige and morale, which were low when he took over. Although the task had been made easier by the demotion of the DEA, a department does react – he added immodestly – to having an 'able, vigorous & ambitious Minister'.[19] This was not his assessment alone. One of his junior ministers, the industrialist Wilfred Brown, complained in no uncertain terms to the incoming President of the Board, Roy Mason, about his habit of taking credit for things long in the pipeline. You were lucky, he told Mason, to come to the Board 'when so much fruit was about to fall off the tree. Your lack of generosity to Tony Crosland really infuriated me.' Unlike in the days of Douglas Jay, the Board had become a dynamic department giving a real lead to British industry. Crosland had encouraged a host of beneficial changes, Brown insisted, such as the extension of budget credit, reform in the regions, and liberalisation of trade in Eastern Europe. It was under Crosland, in other words, that the attitude of industry to the Board had 'swung from criticism to high praise'.[20]

Soon after taking over the newly created Department of Local Government and Regional Planning, Crosland received a note from the Prime Minister asking him to join his reshaped inner Cabinet. 'Funny man, Harold,' Tony said.[21] This did not mean he was particularly back in favour or rising any higher in the Cabinet hierarchy. He remained in the middle ranks, anchored beneath the likes of Jenkins, Callaghan and Healey in any ministerial pecking order. He was reconciled to this remaining the case until the end of the parliament, and elaborated in conversation with Crossman on his fears about the new department. The details, he revealed, had been decided in his absence on a trip to Tokyo. He came back to find that it had been publicly announced that the full integration of the department – amalgamating responsibilities from other ministries – would not be a high priority. Permanent secretaries were being transferred from their old posts, leaving 'Tony with apparently no one at all'; and he was being told to concentrate on local government reform and pollution. No wonder, Crossman noted, he was fed up: 'he knows absolutely nothing about local government and has no interest in the job. . . . He is a macro-economist, interested in the budget, a natural Chancellor, in fact a disappointed Chancellor, and I think he will remain a disappointed Chancellor all his life, unless of course Roy becomes Prime Minister.'[22]

After three months in the post, interested observers were still wondering why the Prime Minister had decided on such a vast new department. According to William Plowden, writing in New Society, some said it was to neuter the increasingly embarrassing DEA, some to punish Crosland by giving him an impossible task, and some that with a huge new government building becoming available in Horseferry Road, it was necessary to find 'a huge new tenant to fill it'. Whether by accident or design, Plowden believed, it had potential to be the best solution to the vexed problems of planning and development. There were sound administrative reasons, he noted, for bringing together responsibilities for regional policy and local government, and for including transport, as this acknowledged the relationship between land–use and movement; the location of motorways for example was vital to regional questions. Whether improvements in decision-making would result depended, among other things, on how well Crosland co-operated with colleagues such as Anthony Greenwood, who for the time being retained the statutory powers he previously exercised over Housing. There was of course good reason to co-operate, since all concerned would not wish to share the fate of the DEA, but thus far it was clear that Crosland's 'empire' lacked the neat hierarchical arrangements that characterised the Ministry of Technology. In effect, Plowden concluded, the final shape of the Department was far from settled, and would not be so until Crosland had tackled the one issue that was taking up most of his time – local government reform.[23]

In early February 1970 Crosland published a White Paper on local government reform which accepted the broad outlines of the 1969 Redcliffe–Maud Report. This committed the government to major changes such as the amalgamation of town and country districts under all-purpose unitary authorities, with the establishment of metropolitan authorities for large conurbations. Crossman noted that, despite being new to the job, Crosland had lost none of his talent for mastering his brief: it took him only an hour to gain acceptance for the Maud recommendations from a Cabinet committee.[24] Crosland later wrote that his main achievement at the Department of Local Government and Regional Planning was to steer the plan smoothly through the party, helped he felt by his stylistic improvements to early drafts of the White Paper.[25] He was not, however, rewarded with much credit for his efforts. Morale among Labour local authorities was low and resistant to change. More important, any legislation was certain to be complex and would not take effect for some time. Crossman noted in his diary that the White Paper launch itself was a 'flop', written off by most newspapers as unimportant as it referred to events which would take place in 1971-2 at the earliest, 'when' – he said gloomily – 'we shan't be in power'.[26] As the months went by, Crosland found himself becoming more absorbed in aspects of his latest job, especially work on the environment. But it was not his finest hour as a minister. Richard Marsh, bitter at his sacking from the Cabinet, told Cecil King that Crosland 'sits with a secretary, a telephone, four volumes of the Maud Report and nothing to do'.[27]

During the spring of 1970 Labour ministers were increasingly preoccupied about the timing of a general election. At long last the Chancellor had something to show for his policy of 'hard slog'. Interest rates were being reduced and the balance-of-payments position had been transformed, showing a large annual surplus. Jenkins was also credited with a politically astute spring budget. 'Roy, don't be a Stafford Cripps,' said one colleague, but the Chancellor insisted on only modest tax reductions in order to minimise risks with the recovery now under way. The opinion polls, which had showed Tory leader Edward Heath almost twenty per cent ahead at times, suddenly narrowed. After modest Labour successes in the local elections, Crosland was in a minority arguing for delaying an election until the autumn, claiming that by then voters would have experieced a more sustained rise in living standards.[28] The Prime Minister opted instead for June, believing that to delay would miss his best opportunity to secure a third successive victory. As in the previous two campaigns, Wilson set the tone for Labour, this time presenting himself as the 'safety first' candidate, urging voters not to allow recovery to be jeopardised by the untried and 'extreme' nostrums of the opposition. Every effort was made to exploit Heath's stiff television manner: 'He had not sung a duet with Ena Sharples at the *Sun* television awards dinner. He had not been on *Sportsnight with Coleman*.'[29]

In Grimsby, Crosland echoed the cautious tone of Labour's national campaign. After claiming successes locally, notably in implementing while at the Board of Trade the recommendations of a committee on trawler safety, he attacked the strident, 'almost hysterical', language used by the Tories. By contrast, Labour offered 'responsible Government', promising to combine economic recovery with continued social reform.[30] This helped to maintain Crosland's healthy majority in his constituency, but it did not cut much ice elsewhere in the country. Four days before polling, the government announced trade figures which, after nine months of surplus, showed a deficit for May. Heath's charge that there was no sound basis to Labour's so-called economic recovery suddenly struck a chord. Jenkins recalled his feeling that 'this one might be slipping away from us', but like most ministers he was stunned to find that the result produced 'defeat out of the jaws of victory'.[31] On the largest uniform swing at any post-war election, the Conservatives were returned to power with a majority of thirty over all other parties. Labour lost seventy seats, and its share of the total vote fell back to

1959 levels. The 'family doctor', Harold Wilson, 'for all his reassuring skills, had not quite succeeded in healing the scar tissue over the wounds of 1966 to 1969'.[32]

For Crosland election defeat sealed more than two years of frustration stretching back to his failure to become Chancellor late in 1967. Before then he had made a great impression both as a departmental minister and inside the Cabinet. Since the trauma of seeing the one job he really wanted going to a younger rival, he had continued to be a competent administrator, but around the Cabinet table his reputation had waned. Some regarded him as indecisive; others believed he had taken over George Brown's mantle, that of the talented yet unpredictable force never quite living up to his potential. Dick Crossman summed up the view of colleagues when he described him as 'a man with no future outside politics who yet makes himself awkward in politics'.[33] Crosland's disenchantment in the late 1960s amounted to more than a feeling that his personal talents were not being put to best use. He shared the view put by the journalist John Cole that Labour's election campaign was a disappointment in its Baldwinesque appeal to 'safety first'. Wilson and Jenkins, Cole said, had abandoned any attempt to persuade voters that Labour remained committed to greater equality of the type that Crosland and Gaitskell had tried to make the party's 'guiding beacon. Now no beacon was visible at all.' It was in order to restore a sense of direction that John Cole prepared an editorial for the *Guardian* in June 1970 which urged the Prime Minister to make Tony Crosland Chancellor: 'The article was not required, and his opportunity never came.'[34]

17

'A Full–Time Politician', 1970–71

When Labour lost power in 1951 under Clement Attlee, the party looked back with pride at the government's achievement. It was a different story in 1970. Disillusionment with the record of Wilson's government was widespread, and the leadership had to find ways of restoring the battered morale of party workers, as well as reaching out to disaffected voters. These tasks looked to be beyond Harold Wilson. After winning two out of three elections, Wilson remained secure as leader, at least in the short-term, but he was unable to provide anything like the unity and enthusiasm of the early 1960s. He spent his first six months out of office writing up his 'personal record' of the Labour government. Crosland later read it with 'horrified fascination: he's learned nothing and forgotten nothing'.[1] This hiatus encouraged senior party figures to set out their stalls for the future. Wilson might not be under immediate threat, but another election defeat was certain to end his leadership. Crosland noted that Tony Benn did not seem too downcast; he welcomed the opportunity to begin appealing to left-wing sentiment away from Westminster. Benn himself, attending a meeting of the fomer inner Cabinet only a week after the election, said 'one could already sense the edging of candidates for position, particularly Jim and Roy'.[2] Crosland told Jenkins he would have to consider carefully whom to vote for if both stood for the deputy leadership of the party, made vacant after George Brown's loss of his parliamentary seat. In the event Callaghan decided not to stand and Jenkins easily defeated the candidate of the left, Michael Foot. By choosing to build up his power base on the NEC, the importance of which was enhanced in opposition, Callaghan continued to lurk 'like a big pike in the shadows'.[3]

Like other Labour ministers, Tony Crosland had not steeled himself for a decisive defeat, and his wife confirms that he was 'stricken for a couple of months'. During this time he considered looking for jobs in industry or the academic world to compensate for the sudden two-thirds cut in his salary, but no suitable offers materialised.[4] He also reflected on his future during his summer holiday, though he did not impress one fellow tourist who wrote to ask if it was fitting for an ex-minister 'to wander around Amalfi in old khaki 8th Army shorts', with tummy protruding and maroon trunks showing down one leg.[5] By the time he returned from Italy, Crosland had taken stock and settled on a new course, one that he was to pursue for the rest of his life. He would do more than just remain in politics; he would try to leave behind the difficulties of the previous two years by raising his personal profile and furthering the causes he espoused. He would become what he called 'a full-time politician'; he would take the task of opposition seriously and devote himself to politics with a single-mindedness that had not applied when he last experienced Labour losing office back in 1951.[6]

Personal calculation and doctrinal conviction pointed him in the same direction. Though he might conceal his ambitions behind a flippant façade, Crosland had always wanted to influence the party at the highest level. Hitherto he had set his sights on the Chancellor-ship, and with Jenkins no longer at the Treasury – though he remained shadow Chancellor – this ambition could be rekindled. And if, as seemed the case in late 1970, Wilson was not the force he once was, there might be other prizes to consider. In looking ahead, he realised that Callaghan or Jenkins remained the most likely successor whenever Wilson gave up the leadership. Beyond that there might be all to play for. If he wished to become a serious contender for the leadership in the longer-term, it was essential to broaden his appeal within the party, and in particular to try to step out of the shadow of Roy Jenkins. Clearly his past did not permit him to make the type of appeal to left-wing activists that Benn was launching; nor did he wish to do so, but on ideological grounds he had little sympathy with the Wilson–Jenkins economic orthodoxy of the late 1960s. In his eyes, there was no inconsistency in restating his ideas with a view to attracting support in the centre of the party. If in the process he could win over some of the Labour right – those outside the ranks of dedicated Jenkinsites – then so much the better.

There were several indications of Crosland's new strategy. One was his decision to stand for the first time in elections to the constituency section of the NEC. He narrowly failed to be elected during the autumn of 1970, coming runner-up in eighth place. In spite of numerous speeches to local Labour parties, he slipped to ninth in 1971 and was never able to secure a seat. A second illustration of his desire to establish a clearer political identity came in his exploitation of 'Grimsby man'. Many grew weary of Crosland's increasing tendency to dismiss arguments with which he disagreed on the grounds that they struck no chord with 'my constituents in Grimsby'.[7] Much was made of Crosland as the friend of the fisherman, the football-lover who did his best not to miss home matches in the town. This type of populism was derided by some as inverted snobbery, the over-zealous idealisation of working-class life by someone whose background was altogether more privileged. Others, though, were convinced that Crosland's feelings for Grimsby were genuine, and that those who patronised local voters or party workers would quickly be regarded as phoney. Marcia Williams recalls that one working-class MP for a mining constituency told her that he and others felt entirely at ease with Crosland, something that could not be said of 'many of his friends on the Right'.[8]

Herein lay a key feature of the Grimsby connection. Crosland believed that the Jenkinsites were losing touch with the concerns of working-class voters, and that this had much to do with Labour's malaise. It was essential in electoral terms to highlight the concerns of fishermen in Grimsby; it might also serve to broaden his appeal in the party. Rather than plucking a populist approach out of thin air, he therefore gave greater emphasis to views that had been held for many years. In early 1970, with Labour still in office, *Guardian* journalist Peter Jenkins had accompanied Crosland on a visit to Grimsby to investigate his 'implausible claim to be a first-class constituency MP, man of the people and all that'. Jenkins was taken aback by what he experienced. Crosland, he noted, was up 'disgustingly early', was irked by the lack of fresh fish for breakfast, and launched into a succession of meetings with constituents and local notables; he coped easily with an icy and rough ferry crossing (unlike his companion) and appeared to be well known on the streets. 'I questioned tactfulness', the journalist added, 'of greeting mature constituent with words "Glad to see you're getting through the winter."' Peter Jenkins acknowledged that only the most pressing government business prevented Crosland from meeting his obligations in the constituency. He could not challenge the minister's claim that he was 'devoted' to Grimsby: it might not be the most beautiful town in Britain, Crosland once said, but it was a place of 'enormously strong personality'.[9]

148

A further indication of Crosland's intention to widen his appeal came in his speeches and writing after the 1970 defeat. Wilson received short shrift when he requested that former ministers should stick by the record of the 1964 government. Tony Benn with a new boldness said that 'when the boat is sunk you can't exactly rock it', and Crosland was among those who claimed that the freedom to 'think aloud' was justified if done in a constructive spirit.[10] To the public this gave the impression of a largely unchanged front-bench team squabbling over the causes of defeat and the remedies required. As far as Crosland was concerned, it provided a welcome return to former habits. Freed from office, he was able to spend more time working at home, thinking through his ideas in the light of recent experience. By the end of September 1970 he was giving his first considered outline of Labour's future objectives. These he summarised as the traditional social welfare goal of tackling poverty; a more equal distribution of wealth; a broader concept of social equality; and strict control over the environment to tackle pollution. In a sideswipe at the strategy pursued particularly after 1966, Crosland insisted Labour should face head on, not bow to, public concern about high welfare spending, pointing out that the share of public expenditure on social services was lower in Britain than in most European nations.[11]

At a press conference called to launch a Fabian Society pamphlet early in 1971, Crosland made a pitch for greater backing in the centre of the party. In his efforts to outline Labour's way ahead he was trying to steer a course between two extremes: those 'obsessed by popular short-term attitudes, tending towards cynicism and a loss of radical will power' and the 'sentimental bourgeois section, trying to lead the party into all sorts of new and wrong directions'.[12] His pamphlet, *A Social Democratic Britain*, began with a veiled attack on the orthodoxy of Labour's economic policy. He also admitted to 'personal error'. He admitted that he had been too complacent in *The Future of Socialism* about growth – which he continued to believe was essential to securing social advance – failing to foresee that successive governments would use deflation ('deliberate *reductions* in growth') as their primary means of regulating the economy. This was as true of Wilson's administration as of its predecessors: the annual growth rate over the previous five years had been lower than in the 1950s, a 'wretched showing, for which all of us who were in Government must share responsibility'. If Labour was to do better next time, then

149

it would not do to give priority to the balance of payments over the search for ways of ensuring higher economic growth.[13]

Some of this candid assessment of his own government's performance had been hinted at in speeches before 1970. Similarly, it was not unusual for Crosland to reserve some harsh words for the Labour left, especially those whose response to defeat was to encourage an agenda that included participatory democracy. These ideas he believed distracted from the quest to secure economic growth; most people, he reiterated, were less interested in politics than in leading a 'full family life . . . And a good thing too'. What was novel in Crosland's argument was the virulence of his attack on environmental pressure groups who claimed that growth was the root cause of escalating pollution. He agreed that attention must be paid to concerns such as cleaner rivers and safer pesticides; and also that tight planning was essential to ensure that both industry and the consumer met the costs of the pollution they created. This was not, however, an argument for being hostile to growth, without which none of Labour's social objectives would be realisable. Many environmentalists, he wrote, were from affluent backgrounds and were indifferent to the needs of the majority, as evidenced by the view that international travel could be greatly curtailed:

> Yes, indeed. The rich would proceed in leisurely fashion across Europe to the Mediterranean beauty spots where they would park their Rolls Royce and take to a boat or horse-drawn vehicle. As for my constituents, who have only a fortnight's holiday, let them eat cake and go back to Blackpool.[14]

If the pamphlet was designed to raise Crosland's profile by deliberate provocation, it succeeded. Environmentalists reacted furiously. Crosland saw environmentalism as securing equal access to good homes, parks and the countryside, and he was scornful of middle–class activists who would turn up at protests in their Jaguars.[15] He responded to J. K. Galbraith's comment that he was being silly by saying: 'I have thought closely about this while in my bath, but do not really see what, at my age, I can do to cure this distressing disability.'[16] Nor was Crosland upset to find that some on the left acknowledged his attempt to distance himself from the Jenkinsites. Richard Clements in *Tribune* attacked his 'snide' attacks on the Labour left, but added that unlike many of his old Gaitskellite pals, Crosland was no deflationist. In particular, Clements noted, Crosland's insistence that any future Labour government should not sacrifice growth to the balance of payments was likely to bring him into conflict with some of those who were formerly his 'closest allies'.[17] The Fabian pamphlet thus had some success in giving Crosland a more distinctive voice. One backbench colleague called him 'the voice of sanity in Labour ranks' and newspapers such as the *Observer* praised his contribution to the debate not only about Labour's future but also about the relationship between growth and the environment.[18]

Even so, any attempt to carve out a separate niche within Labour's senior hierarchy was certain to take time, and was not made easier when it was discovered in 1971 that Crosland was suffering from high blood-pressure. A specialist told him that this was not unusual considering the stresses he experienced as a minister. 'Nothing to do with the nation's affairs,' he replied. 'If anything is responsible for altering my blood-pressure, it's my wife's children and their friends, most of whom . . . are deranged or delinquent – often both.'[19] For a few colleagues this marked a stage when Crosland lost some of his 'vivacity'. The 'daring imaginative intellectual saboteur' of the 1950s, it was claimed by Jenkinsites, would have set about a more thorough-going rethink of all his ideas.[20] No similar expectations were made of Roy Jenkins, who in the aftermath of defeat contented himself with the claim that Labour had been a 'reasonably successful government in very difficult circumstances'.[21] Crosland did at least set out why his objectives remained unchanged from the days when he was writing *The Future of Socialism*. In the mid-1950s, he noted, fresh thinking was essential after Labour suffered successive heavy defeats, and affluence represented a sharp break from 1940s austerity. In the 1960s there had been no such dramatic shift: Labour had made steady progress, but glaring social inequalities remained, and it was upon these that attention should be focused.[22] Allied to this was the theme implicit in his Fabian pamphlet. His strategy remained valid because he was not persuaded it had been tried: the disappointments of the last Labour government could be avoided next time round if priorities were changed. If his views on policy prevailed, in other words, the mistakes made since 1964 could be rectified.

Some critics believed Crosland had not said enough about *how* a higher level of growth was to be achieved. If he stood accused of failing to provide a comprehensive agenda for change in the 1970s as he had fifteen years earlier, then a further part of the explanation lay in his responsibilities as a shadow minister. He believed that the four separate government posts he held in five and half years after 1964 were 'far too many', not allowing him to carry through meaningful change in any one department except Education.[23] In a further indication of his determination to be a 'full-time politician', he resolved to take seriously his role shadowing Environment, aiming to build up the basis for a programme that might be enacted when Labour returned to power. Before 1964 he had no comparable commitments to those he assumed for the enormous environment brief, especially in relation to housing. He began by proclaiming: 'know nothing about housing'. He then proceeded to immerse himself in the subject, telling Harold Wilson that he would spend much of his 'personal' as well as his parliamentary time on housing.[24] In place of education specialists, Lansdowne Road became the venue for frequent meetings with experts in the housing field, and before long he was producing discussion papers setting out the principles that should guide Labour's future housing policy.[25]

A year after the initial shock of losing power Crosland could claim that he had adjusted well to the demands of opposition. He was beginning to stake out new political territory, reaching out to the centre of the party without alienating the right, and he was working on a departmental brief that would prepare him for a return to power. He was not persuaded, however, that the party as a whole was in good shape. Labour continued to languish in the polls against a backdrop of Edward Heath's tough new trade union laws which helped to provoke an atmosphere of industrial militancy unknown since before the war. In September 1971 Crosland went on record as admitting that the party was not yet in sight of formulating 'a better set of policies than those which we had in June 1970'. It was time, he urged, to wake up to the seriousness of the situation and to give more attention to the 'solid work of preparing for the next Labour Government'. His explanation for what had happened was two-fold. In the first place, the party's policy-making machinery was cumbersome and slowed down the development of fresh initiatives. The second stumbling block was more intractable, and it was the cause of great personal difficulty for Crosland, damaging beyond repair his relations with many former allies and associates on the Jenkinsite right. For several months, Crosland lamented, the vital task of formulating a new Labour programme had been overshadowed by the attention given throughout the party to a single issue – that of the Common Market.[26]

18

The Common Market Debate, 1971

In the second half of 1971 Crosland's attempt to broaden his political base suffered a major setback. His strategy came unstuck when confronted with an issue on which it was impossible to remain on good terms with *both* the centre and the right of the party. In what his wife called 'his most unhappy period in politics', Crosland found himself estranged from many of his longest-standing friends and allies. There was great irony in Europe being the catalyst for a damaging split. Crosland had long been an advocate of British membership of the Common Market, which Edward Heath as Prime Minister pressed for tenaciously after 1970. He had differed with Gaitskell on this, and during the mid-1960s he and Roy Jenkins were together feared by Wilson as the 'European devaluers'. His case throughout was based not on any likely economic benefits but on the political need for Britain to readjust to the loss of Empire. 'Churchillian pipe dream[s]', he wrote, were the cause of disasters such as Suez, and the effect of saying no would be that Britain would be left as an isolated and declining power.[1] However, whereas in 1962 Crosland could remain friends with Gaitskell despite Europe, in 1971 he was unable to sustain his friendship with Jenkins. The Common Market debate brought to the fore all the tensions and jealousies that had bubbled beneath the surface since Jenkins leapfrogged Crosland to become Chancellor in 1967. While that key moment was controlled by others – Callaghan in resigning and Wilson in choosing a successor – Europe marked a parting of the ways that Crosland and Jenkins chose, and which was to leave each of them wounded.

During the summer of 1971 the issue grew in importance as it became clear that Heath was determined to press ahead with British entry, in spite of divisions within both main parties. On the Labour side, the enthusiasm of the Jenkinsite right for joining the Market was in stark contrast to the hostility of many on the centre-left. Wilson bided his time, but sensed a threat to his authority when Callaghan

Anthony Crosland

came out against entry, echoing Gaitskell's 1962 speech by talking of the dangers posed to the 'heritage of Chaucer'. An alliance between Callaghan and the anti-European left, Wilson believed, could pose a serious challenge to his leadership. In May Crosland told Roy Jenkins that he was in favour of entry but not at the cost of diverting attention from domestic political concerns.[2] At this stage he looked at the problem in relation to how it would affect the party as a whole. He wrote a private note outlining the dilemma. He wanted the Tories to secure British entry but feared that Labour's pro-Europeans would be greatly damaged if they were seen to be defying mainstream party opinion, and especially if they were accused of sustaining in power a reactionary Conservative government responsible for rising unemployment.[3] Before long, he would have to make a hard choice. Should he line up behind Jenkins, who regarded British entry as a matter of high principle, or should he back the majority who believed the defeat of Heath's government was the priority?

Pressure mounted in the run-up to a special party conference held at Central Hall in London during July. As Labour began to line up into pro- and anti-factions, Crosland disappointed friends on the right by taking a cautious line. It would be foolish, he insisted in private conversations, to allow Europe to endanger party unity. Labour's first duty was to defeat the government, which looked incapable of getting all its supporters into the division lobby to back British entry. Membership of the Market, he maintained – with what Jenkins called a 'peculiar sense of proportion' – was less important than economic and social reform at home. 'I do not support things with enthusiasm if I do not feel enthusiastic. You may like this or not. That's the way I am.'[4] In this frame of mind, he drafted a speech setting out his views and justifying his 'sense of proportion':

> . . . if I list all the things that I have fought and written and argued for over more than 20 years – greater equality, the relief of poverty, more public spending, educational reform, housing policy, the improvement of the environment – I do not find that any of these will be decisively affected one way or another by the Common Market.[5]

Urged by pro-Marketeers not to make a speech that would damage their cause, Crosland confined himself to addressing a private meeting of his local party in Grimsby.

News of his thinking leaked out, however, and Crosland suddenly faced the charge that he was deserting the European cause. On 11 July James Margach of the *Sunday Times* splashed a story with the headline 'Crosland, Healey No to Market'. Denis Healey had announced that he was reversing his earlier attitude by saying he would vote with the anti-Marketeers when the crucial division came in the Commons during the autumn. Margach correctly reported much of Crosland's view, including his assertion that if it came to keeping Heath in power by voting for membership he would not do so. The article was doubly damaging. In the first place it contained the assertion that Crosland would vote with the anti-Marketeers, which he had not determined to do; second, it made reference to Crosland's concern that an 'elitist' faction of right-wing intellectuals was in danger of becoming separated from the main body of the Labour movement.[6] The 'elitist' jibe was greatly resented by Jenkinsites, and within days colleagues were writing to express their concern at what appeared to be a volte-face. One fellow MP warned that he was causing 'irreparable damage' to the high regard in which he had previously been held inside and outside parliament.[7] Much to his dismay, Crosland found that press reaction was to contrast the 'conviction' of Jenkins with the 'ratting' of Crosland and Healey. It was easy to pillory those for whom entry to the Market was apparently fine under Labour but unacceptable under the Tories.[8]

By the time of Labour's special conference on 17 July party divisions were openly on display. Wilson sought to ward off any threat from Callaghan by declaring himself against entry on Heath's terms, even though this meant bringing himself into conflict with his deputy leader. 'Poor Harold', someone was overheard saying in the Tea Room. 'If he drinks, the water is poisoned; if he doesn't, he will die of thirst.'[9] While the Jenkinsites could rely on warm praise from sections of the press, indications that they would defy majority opinion infuriated many in the party. Tony Benn said Jenkins would never be forgiven by the left if he split the movement, and Wilson in a moment of anger said: 'I'll smash CDS before I go.'[10] The pro-Marketeers in turn, feeling beleaguered, vented much of their anger on Crosland. While the behaviour of Wilson and Healey was only to be expected, Crosland's apparent abandonment of his past Euro-enthusiasm amounted to a 'betrayal' by the high-priest of revisionism. He stood accused of being 'indecisive', a 'turncoat' and an 'opportunist'. At a stormy meeting of the 1963 Club, Crosland was given a rough ride and his motives were questioned. It was alleged that he was driven by jealousy of Jenkins and that he had become simply a careerist, devoted to personal advancement. Crosland lost his temper, saying he could go round the table and apply equally malicious interpretations to the motives of others; 'no doubt we all have moral frailties.'[11]

" .. AND HE MARCHED THEM DOWN AGAIN .... "

Garland, *Daily Telegraph*, 29 July 1971 (© Telegraph Group Limited, London 1971)

It was a painful parting of company between Crosland and some of his oldest allies. As a busy minister in the 1960s, Crosland had found little time to scribble down more than a few private jottings; in opposition he increasingly set out his thoughts in hand–written notes. In September 1971 he wrote a detailed account reflecting on why the European issue had proved so difficult. He admitted that over the winter of 1970–71 he had been hoping that negotiations for British entry might fail, as he suspected Europe would come to dominate all else. On the record, to journalists and in the House, his position was that he 'mildly want[ed] to join', but that the Market was not his top priority. In early 1971 he was becoming less persuaded of the merits of membership, and had tried to say this –

'though badly' – at the meeting of the shadow Cabinet and NEC in May. In June some of his friends were urging upon him the importance of dissociating himself from the 'Right Europeans', and the whips' office made it clear that he couldn't vote with the pro-Marketeers and somehow back the party. This left him contemplating the possibility of a speech to clarify his views. There was, he conceded, an element of political calculation in this: how would his attitude bear upon his chances of getting elected on to the NEC? On the other hand, other politicians routinely made the same type of calculations. It was no secret that 'Roy's boys' – a well-organised clique led by Rodgers, Marquand and others – were devoted to making Jenkins leader of the party.[12] So why had it turned sour for him?

The answer to this, Crosland felt, lay partly in events beyond his control. In particular the leaking of his draft speech generated feelings of betrayal, for he had yielded to requests from colleagues that he would not go public. He could see why former friends were so angered. They thought he intended all along to deliver a speech, they were bitter about his attack on an 'elite' (comments made casually, he noted, over a drink with Margach), and they believed he was defecting at a critical moment in order to win favour with constituency activists ahead of NEC elections. The lesson of all this, Crosland believed, was that he should either have kept as silent as possible, or at least not wavered in public about his intentions. While accepting he had played his hand badly, he had no regrets on the substance of the case or his motivation. 'Both over Europe and more generally', he wrote, 'my major political need is to establish positions independently of 1963 Club, Roy etc: can't continue as No. 2 to Roy'. He reassured himself that charges of behaving 'immorally' were unfounded. He agreed this would have been true if he had acted entirely against his convictions, but this was not the case. The real core of the trouble, he concluded, was that because 'Europeans didn't know my views, thought I was going against personal convictions; so did everyone else'.[13]

The debate continued until in late October the Commons carried a pro-Market resolution by 356 votes to 244. Sixty-nine Labour MPs voted with Edward Heath, so ensuring victory, while a further nineteen abstained. Crosland was one of the latter, which left him open to the additional charge of cowardice. Far from keeping a low profile during the debate, Crosland sat on the opposition front bench, making it plain that his was a calculated abstention. He told his wife that the only cowardly aspect of his behaviour was not saying publicly that he felt the case for joining the Market was weaker than ever on the most recent figures. But stung by these latest attacks on his integrity, he issued a crisp press statement:

> My position is simple. I have long been on balance in favour of entry though I think that going in will make far less difference than either the extreme pros or extreme antis imagine. I could not suddenly stand on my head and vote against what I had felt for many years past, even though I felt it more moderately than some of my European colleagues. On the other hand I could under no circumstances desert my Party and vote with the Tory government which is pursuing such disastrous domestic policies. So the only logical course – and the only course sanctioned in the situation by Labour Party Standing Orders – was to abstain.[14]

Some Jenkinsites were never to forgive this action. What substance was there to the various charges they made against Crosland? David Owen, at the time a supporter of Jenkins, later agreed it was highly ironic that Crosland should be accused of not wanting 'to put his head over the parapet'; his war record made this particularly inappropriate.[15] Crosland can also be defended against the accusation that he was cynically abandoning deeply held views. However poorly he handled events, friends such as Philip Williams confirm that he had been more lukewarm about Europe than Jenkins for many years past. Just as the pro-Marketeers were sincere in believing that Europe was of such importance that it transcended party barriers, Crosland believed with equal passion that it was not. Harold Lever, Paymaster General when Labour lost office in 1970 and a more detached Euro-enthusiast, contradicted two supporters of Jenkins who were assailing Crosland and threatening revenge:

> In your heart of hearts you must know that Tony's character has not suddenly changed in some abominable way. I don't agree with his stance on Europe, but that's nothing to do with integrity. It has to do with standards developed outside politics which he brought into politics with him. He is under the control of his own principles, a dangerous thing in a leader, I accept. The meaner, more squalid elements of politics he despises. I must tell you that I despise them too.[16]

This is not to deny that Crosland was influenced by jealousy. Ever since the traumatic events of November 1967 he had struggled to accept that Jenkins was the crown prince of the Labour right, and his irritation was increased by fresh comparisons in the press between the 'principle' of Euro-enthusiasm and the 'expediency' of Euro-doubters. For some, however, the jealousy was understandable. David Owen later recalled that Crosland had spent a long time tolerating the 'monumental insensitivity' of some of the Jenkinsites, who paraded Roy's leadership claims in front of Tony and made no effort to get the two to work together.[17] By the same token, Crosland admitted the element of political calculation. Even so, accusations of 'careerism' he found difficult to accept from those who were dedicated to the leadership ambitions of Jenkins. If Crosland had been concerned with nothing more than boosting his chances of getting on to the NEC, his best course of action would probably have been to vote with the anti-European majority in Labour ranks. Indeed, he was told by Callaghan that abstention was a mistake, as he was missing the chance to establish himself thereafter as a 'Party man, forever distinct from the Jenkinsite Right'.[18] One of the reasons why Crosland suffered from the Europe episode, it became apparent during the months that followed, was that in personal terms he had not been calculating enough.

In the short-term, his reputation within the party was damaged. He had alienated old friends on the right, and by abstaining he had not gone far enough to win any compensating credit on the centre-left. As the PLP prepared to vote in the annual shadow Cabinet elections, there were rumours that the Jenkinsites would attempt to use their fifty-plus votes to remove Crosland and replace him with someone more 'loyal'. In the event he remained on their slate of candidates, but fell from third to eighth place, losing twenty-nine votes from the previous year. He was in no doubt that Europe was the cause: the *Sunday Times* story, he reflected, had been highly damaging, giving an impression of 'calculating backsliding'.[19] His support also fell in elections to the NEC, and he again failed to win a place. Crosland was not alone in suffering over Europe. Most press coverage in the aftermath of the Europe debate centred on the anger of mainstream party opinion with the pro-Marketeers, which Wilson harnessed by threatening expulsion if the 'rebels' persisted in helping Heath with the detailed legislation required to take Britain into Europe. One incensed MP said that at least Ramsay MacDonald had the decency to leave in the 1930s: 'this shower has deliberately wrecked the party [and] saved a Tory Government under pressure'.[20]

Faced with such hostility, Jenkins needed friends where he could find them. He sensed that his leadership ambitions might be permanently blighted if he could not rebuild bridges with old friends such as Crosland. As the dust settled on the Europe vote, the two men dined alone and Crosland came away with the impression that he was being courted. If Tony would join his group, Jenkins said, it would be possible to attract wider support and so build a majority within the party, one capable of defeating the main alternative contender Callaghan and the emerging standard-bearer of the left, Michael Foot. Crosland in his private notes on the dinner felt he was being offered the unofficial deputy leadership of the right. 'I'm much better at tactics, you're much better at policy,' Jenkins said in his efforts to persuade. When it became clear that Crosland was cool on the whole idea, Jenkins inserted a warning note: 'you and I', he said, 'could destroy each other.'[21] Crosland told his wife that he would not join the group partly because of pride and vanity, though he liked to think this was not the main reason. Rather 'their idea of a Labour Party is not mine. Roy has come actually to dislike socialism.' On that basis they could not and should not win over the party. 'The most that would happen,' Crosland added, 'is that the Party would be split for a generation.'[22] The Europe debate thus left deep scars, with a combination of policy and personality clashes occasioning a division that had been on the cards since 1967. Crosland and Jenkins had parted company irrevocably.

In personal reflections written over Christmas, Crosland admitted that 1971 had been a 'bad year'. His work as shadow Environment Secretary, increased attendance at conferences and his writing had all been eclipsed, he lamented, by a reputation for dithering and a lack of consistency that came from the Europe episode. In the year ahead, he resolved, he would try to stay on good terms with individuals but would resume his determination to 'widen base to anti-European Right + Centre'. This meant continuing his move away from the 1963 Club, which he remained convinced was 'elitist' and also 'wholly Royite . . . being No. 2 intolerable'. Generally, he concluded:

> don't fuss, fret, worry, dither, calculate, appear petulant especially don't think so much about personal tactics

after all, don't desperately want to be Leader – probably lack ruthlessness
to be it anyway, not v. good tactician! . . . therefore do your own thing!
– don't lose case, as did with 63 Club – v. bad
And won't do much better till Europe out of way.[23]

Europe gradually receded as the dominant issue on the political
agenda, but for Crosland its legacy lived on. The Jenkinsites had held
back in the shadow Cabinet elections, waiting to see if Crosland
would belatedly be won over. When he refused to co-operate, the
gloves could come off; in 1972 there would be a chance to exact
revenge.

19

The European Legacy, 1972–4

Reflecting on the events of the previous twelve months, the *Guardian* commented that 1971 had not been a good year for the Labour opposition. Harold Wilson no longer seemed an inspiring figure, and his leadership was secure only because none of his rivals had come to the fore. Callaghan lacked distinctiveness; Jenkins had not convinced the movement of his radicalism; Healey and Benn each had only a narrow appeal. Of the rest, Crosland had offended many of his old allies over Europe, but he remained the most significant 'font of radical thinking in the Labour leadership. . . . It is a pity he does not stand nearer the throne, in case Mr Wilson should falter.'[1]

In 1972 Crosland urged the need for a fresh start. The majority of the party, he said, were sick of 'unprofitable wrangling' and wanted to move on to a more constructive phase of opposition. It was time to leave behind the disagreements over Europe and to stop raking over the ashes of the last Labour government, whose record was looking better when set against Heath's difficulties with soaring inflation, rising unemployment and industrial unrest.[2] The pleas went unheeded. Throughout 1972–3, the opposition looked incapable of exploiting Conservative unpopularity. Labour made only one by-election gain and found support ebbing away to the Liberals and the Scottish Nationalists. Instead of turning outwards in an effort to inspire public opinion, factional in-fighting intensified, as Crosland was to discover to his cost.

With the backing of a newly appointed research assistant, David Lipsey, Crosland did his best to develop a programme for change as shadow Environment Secretary. He surprised some colleagues by his tenacity in resisting the government's Housing Finance Bill early in 1972. During one of the longest committee stages in post-war politics, Crosland was frequently found leading a small band of Labour MPs through gruelling all-night sessions at the House. He took the fight direct to the Prime Minister, calling on him to withdraw the measure, and midway through the committee proceedings two Tory ministers were moved away to other areas of responsibility.[3] By the time the bill received its third reading in the summer, Crosland claimed that the opposition had forced crucial concessions and that rent rises were not likely to be as crippling as at first seemed likely. From the *Guardian* he won the acclaim that he had 'enhanced his standing in the party by showing more talent for . . . hard political slog than some had given him credit for'.[4] He also set about addressing what he regarded as the central question in housing policy: how was it possible to reduce inequality by giving everyone a minimum standard of quality, comfort and privacy? During 1972-3 he outlined the basis for a Labour programme in office. He pledged to repeal policies that he said were causing inflationary rent increases. Efforts would be made to boost the low number of council house completions by the Tories and to prevent the land speculator from making 'outrageous fortunes at the expense of the house buyer'. If serious housing problems could not be solved overnight, Labour would nevertheless make a 'very, very much better go at it than this lot are doing now'.[5]

There was still the problem, which Crosland publicly acknowledged, that the party as a whole continued to lack a unifying theme. Modernisation had been all-important a decade earlier. 'Today, we have no similarly clear message.'[6] Instead, left-right divisions continued over domestic policy, and Crosland got caught up in renewed arguments over Europe. With Heath set to push the European Communities Bill through parliament, Wilson made a fresh effort in April 1972 to clarify Labour's position. The shadow Cabinet voted by the narrowest of margins, eight votes to six, to hold a referendum on Britain's continued membership of the Common Market in the event of Labour returning to power. Crosland voted against the proposal, arguing that it would needlessly reopen an issue that looked to have been settled.[7] On this occasion he found himself in the same camp as Roy Jenkins, but the decisive vote in favour of a referendum came from Edward Short, who like Crosland had abstained in the European vote of October 1971. The left were delighted, but pro-Marketeers saw the decision as an act of retribution for their defiance. After considering his options, Jenkins along with two colleagues – Harold Lever and George Thomson – resigned in protest from the shadow Cabinet. In the long run, this gravely weakened the Labour right and was to mark the effective end of any serious challenge for the leadership by Jenkins, though at the time his followers hoped he would only stand aside temporarily. Within days, attention was turning to the scramble to fill the responsibilities Jenkins had vacated, including the shadow Chancellorship.

When during the Easter recess news of the resignations broke, Crosland was in Japan attending a conference on the environment. He phoned Wilson to state unequivocally that he wanted to become shadow Chancellor and believed he was the best equipped candidate. Wilson, however, he found 'at his worst, evasive, rattled, all over the shop'. This evasiveness Crosland later attributed to the fact that others on the spot were in a stronger position to press their claims. The shadow Chancellorship went to Denis Healey; Callaghan filled the Foreign Affairs portfolio vacated by Healey; and Shirley Williams replaced Callaghan as shadow Home Secretary. The outcome may not have been due simply to Crosland's absence abroad at a critical moment. As one of his friends told him, Wilson had just seen the back of one potential leader of the centre-right and might not have wished to promote another with a similar pedigree. The Jenkinsites had fallen out with Crosland, but they would never back someone like Healey who had voted with the anti-Marketeers. For Wilson, Healey's action in the October vote was in his favour: he was being rewarded in part for loyalty to the party line. Crosland – as Callaghan warned him at the time – was suffering for abstaining rather than going the whole way and voting with the Labour mainstream.[8]

There was no time to dwell on the disappointment of being passed over again for the key economic post. After delivering his conference speech, Crosland took the first available flight back to Britain, contemplating on the journey his chances of securing the other major position made available by Jenkins' resignation – that of the party's deputy leader. One of those advising Crosland was the historian David Carlton, whose wife was parliamentary aide to another Labour MP, John Silkin. Carlton urged that there was little alternative but to stand, especially as the shadow Chancellorship had been decided in Crosland's absence:

> If you go on playing a waiting game you are likely to become an almost forgotten figure. You surely cannot afford to allow Mrs Williams or Roy Hattersley to draw level with you in stature, which they may rapidly do if you refuse to stand. It was the same kind of consideration that led Harold Wilson to run against Gaitskell in 1960 and . . . to stand for Deputy in 1962. He lost both contests but effectively blocked the

prospects of Greenwood, Crossman and Castle as standard-bearers of his wing of the Party. Hence you should not mind defeat by Michael Foot provided you are runner up. . . . But what if you should be defeated in the present contest not only by Michael Foot but also by some other figure on the Right? The only serious possibility is Edward Short. . . . You are in a better position than I to judge Short's chances. But unless it is absolutely certain that he will defeat you, I think you should run. After all, what have you to lose?[9]

Crosland learnt that he might well be defeated by Ted Short. He discovered that the Jenkinsites were intending to throw their weight behind Short as the man best placed to defeat Michael Foot, the candidate of the left. This, he believed, was meant not simply as a form of punishment for his behaviour over Europe. With one eye on the future, Short could be regarded as a stop-gap figure, whereas Crosland was not likely to stand aside obligingly if Jenkins decided to return to the fray. Crosland was scornful when some MPs resorted to the claim that only Short could act as a brake against the advances of the left. He teased David Owen, a rising star among the Jenkinsites, about his support for the man whose vote tipped the balance in favour of a referendum in the shadow Cabinet – so triggering Roy's resignation. Put on the spot, Owen changed tack. 'We think that on balance Ted behaved better than you,' he said, though Crosland rebutted this by pointing out that Short, like himself, had abstained in the October vote on Europe. Owen then took the line, which he elaborated upon in a lengthy letter justifying his position, that it was essential to remove Wilson; this might be possible with Short as deputy leader, whereas Crosland would strengthen the existing leadership. In his memoirs Owen regretted that he did not simply say he felt bound by group solidarity, with the majority of Jenkinsites firm in their view. His letter, he said, was treated with the contempt it deserved and his friendship with Crosland took several years to recover.[10]

If anything was needed to tip the balance, evidence of what he called the 'gang mentality' of the Jenkinsites persuaded Crosland to throw his hat into the ring. He issued a statement which included a sideswipe at his detractors:

I am not running in order to keep someone else out. I am running to win – on a non-sectarian ticket. I am standing because many of my

Parliamentary colleagues – both Right and Left, pro-European and anti-European – share my view that time is running out. . . . It is desperately urgent to re-create Party unity on the basis of a radical, egalitarian socialist programme.[11]

Crosland relied on a small team of supporters led by his PPS Dick Leonard to sound out backbench opinion, though he realised it was an uphill struggle. 'If Bill Rodgers could see our organisation', he quipped, 'he would fall out of bed laughing.' Callaghan told him to expect about fifty votes, and his own estimates varied from a disastrously low thirty-five to a respectable sixty-plus.[12] In the event Ted Short was elected deputy leader, defeating Michael Foot after Crosland was eliminated on the first ballot, trailing in third place with sixty-one votes.

His backers put the best possible gloss on the result. David Carlton told him that his solid showing compared with Callaghan's performance in 1963. It put down a marker and attracted some favourable newspaper coverage, with the *Guardian* especially talking about Crosland for the first time as a possible future leader. 'So far as I can judge,' Carlton added, 'you are still rising and well on course for a senior leadership bid in about five years' time.'[13] The short-term effect, however, was a further souring of relations with old friends. Roy Jenkins later told Dick Leonard that he had prevented Crosland from becoming deputy leader by swinging forty votes to Ted Short. He justified this on the grounds that Crosland had undermined his prospects of succeeding Wilson by refusing to join with his group. Jenkins had clearly not given up his leadership ambitions after resigning in April 1972. He wrote in his memoirs that if he had been going to succeed, it would have been necessary for Wilson to lose the next election and for there to be no alternative leader emerging on the 'reformist/internationalist' wing of the party while he was temporarily out of the running. 'This last consideration', he went on, 'no doubt played some part in prompting me and those closely associated with me to vote for Ted Short', though he did confess to some unease on the grounds that 'Crosland was a potential leader and . . . Short was not'.[14]

Any doubts about how far the two old friends had drifted apart were dispelled by a dinner held to commemorate the tenth anniversary of the death of Hugh Gaitskell in 1973. Crosland was annoyed that he was not initially asked to speak. It was eventually agreed that he should and he followed a lengthy contribution by Jenkins, giving what one person present called a 'beautifully delivered' speech, 'graceful and with . . . no emotion in the wrong place or overdone'.[15] Crosland was amused that he had 'routed' Roy, who chose the venue and set up the dinner. After press reports appeared saying the two men were no longer on speaking terms, a frosty encounter took place in which Crosland chided Jenkins for not speaking to him beforehand about the Gaitskell dinner and for a recent speech berating Labour leaders for giving way to the left. There was 'intense irritation', Tony said, among those like him who attended endless committee meetings to fight the left while others sat on the sidelines writing 'elegant biographical pieces for *The Times* for a fat fee'. Roy countered with accusations that Tony was to blame for his resignation in April 1972, when he dismissed the referendum decision with the claim that he was off to Japan to study urban planning, which was far more important. Susan Crosland, who was present at the scene, said it was like watching 'two dogs with a bone'.[16]

References to fighting the left underlined the implications of the dispute between Crosland and Jenkins. Fragmentation on the Labour right helped to open the way for the left to make much of the running inside the party. After the election defeat of 1970, disenchantment with the leadership developed steadily among rank-and-file activists, making it difficult for the likes of Crosland to secure election to the constituency section of the NEC. For the first time since the days of Bevan, left-wingers in the local parties found a national figurehead to identify with. In the words of Phillip Whitehead: 'There came out to join them Tony Benn, once the youthful technocrat of the first Wilson era, now a born-again socialist radicalised by the experience of workers in struggle.'[17] Benn was instrumental in pushing for the adoption of *Labour's Programme 1973*, a policy document narrowly carried by the NEC which called for major extensions of public ownership and greater state planning to reverse the tide of growing unemployment.

Crosland was accused by his detractors of not doing enough to counter the growing influence of the left and it was certainly the case that he retained an affection for his former Oxford pupil which others did not share. 'Won't hear a word said against him. I'm devoted to Tony Benn,' Crosland could be found saying in private. 'Nothing the matter with him except he's a bit cracked.' At the

167

Lincoln by-election of 1973, under pressure to act in a neighbouring seat to Grimsby, Crosland reluctantly spoke out against his ally of CDS days Dick Taverne, who stood as an independent after constituency workers refused to re-adopt him. On a platform opposed to Labour 'extremism', Taverne easily defeated the party's official candidate. Philip Williams wrote to say he was saddened to see Crosland 'lending respectability' to Labour's campaign at Lincoln, where the issue was one of bullying activists taking control away from the PLP. Disillusionment was growing, Williams warned, not only among 'Eurofanatics' but among many supporters of the original CDS campaign.[18]

On the other hand, many on the Labour right were in no position to criticise. Dick Taverne believed that the Jenkinsite group as a whole was no longer able to resist the left. Roy's attitude, he felt, was to keep his head down until such time as Labour lost the next election and came to its senses, turning to him for leadership.[19] In contrast, Crosland was so strident at meetings of the party's industrial policy committee that Tony Benn thought he was angling to take the Trade and Industry portfolio in a future government. At a joint meeting of the shadow Cabinet and NEC in May 1973, Crosland vigorously attacked the party's draft statement on policy, saying it would be foolish to make promises on public ownership that could not be kept. In withering tones he enquired: 'Why don't we nationalise Marks and Spencer to make it as efficient as the Co-op?' The mood of the country, he claimed, was towards the centre not the left, and Labour would do well to highlight traditional goals such as equality and the redistribution of wealth.[20] He countered accusations that he was not prepared to speak out publicly for fear of antagonising the left by describing the proposal to nationalise twenty-five top companies as 'half-baked'. Returning to an argument he thought had been won in the past, he repeated his view that socialist ends could be achieved by a variety of means; the 'blanket threat' approach to nationalisation, he said, was overshadowing good policies that were being developed in other areas. The *Observer* said this outspoken speech marked the first concerted attack on the left's growing influence. Not before time, the moderate majority on the shadow Cabinet was taking the initiative in resisting 'doctrinaire' proposals which it was feared might lose Labour the next election.[21]

Labour's public face of opposition thus continued to be one of dissent and confusion. Wilson found himself saddled with proposals in which he had no faith, and announced that he would veto the idea of taking a controlling interest in 25 of Britain's largest manufacturing companies. At the heart of Labour's difficulties were unresolved tensions between the political and industrial wings of the movement stretching back to *In Place of Strife*. By 1973 a new 'compact' went some way towards restoring harmony by pledging the party to price controls and repeal of Heath's hated Industrial Relations Act. But union leaders refused to commit themselves to formal wage restraint, and left and right remained at loggerheads over how to react to rising industrial unrest. Tony Benn, after his first social contact with Crosland for some time, noted in his diary that he had drifted a long way apart from his old friend. Crosland he said was in favour of a 'consumer-oriented Swedish type of socialism', arguing that Labour's problem was not Marxist militancy but whether the party should be so closely linked with the unions. Crosland had been among the first of Labour's senior figures after the 1970 election defeat to advocate a prices and incomes policy, claiming that this was essential in order to secure higher growth. For Benn, the most important change in his thinking since 1970 was his view that workers' rights needed to be defended and that this could only be done by a close alliance of the party and the unions. 'If we turn on the trade unions in the hope that we will be popular with . . . *Guardian* readers,' said Benn, 'we are sunk.'[22]

The two years after the fateful Europe vote had seen a small improvement in Crosland's political standing. He had scored some successes as shadow Environment Secretary, notably in helping to scupper government proposals for an airport-cum-seaport at Maplin, which he pilloried as 'Heathograd'. His name was being mentioned as one among several possible successors to Wilson, and Roy Jenkins discovered in the autumn of 1973 that he was no longer assured of an easy ascendancy over Crosland. In the annual round of shadow Cabinet elections held among MPs Crosland came in fourth, one place ahead of Jenkins. On the other hand, detachment from the hard-line Euro-enthusiasts came at a price. Jenkins still commanded the loyalty of an important minority of backbenchers, one capable of blocking efforts to secure for Crosland the position of Party Treasurer.[23] In an atmosphere of bickering between left and right, it was difficult for Crosland to make much headway with the strategy he had adopted after 1970 of appealing to the middle ground. He complained to one journalist that most lobby correspondents knew only ten MPs, half on the left and the other half Jenkinsites, failing to recognise that there was a 'centre' of the party.[24] His frustration was reflected in occasional signals to friends that he might leave politics if Labour lost again. Wilfred Beckerman, who continued to advise Crosland on economic issues after working with him at the Board of Trade, agreed that staying on would involve further sacrifices for little apparent result, though he urged him to continue 'as long as there is a chance that you might be the successor'.[25]

In the event, the fear of another long spell in opposition was unrealised. At Christmas 1973 Crosland travelled to North America, where he gave away his stepdaughter Sheila in marriage, returning to find that Edward Heath was calling a snap election in the wake of a deteriorating economic situation, compounded by the second miners' strike in two years. The Prime Minister posed the question: 'Who Governs?' Should the nation be led by its elected representatives or 'held to ransom' by the miners was Heath's election challenge. With the Labour Party's poor showing since 1970, Labour hopes were not high as the campaign began, and sections of the press launched fierce attacks on a manifesto which included calls for wider public ownership, a new wealth tax and sweeping extensions of welfare services. In Grimsby, Crosland gave prominence to his own individual priorities: food subsidies to keep down prices, higher old-age pensions and more resources for housing. Gradually Wilson made ground by chipping away at Heath's record on unemployment and inflation, while Callaghan – 'the keeper of the cloth cap' – made the case that only Labour could deal with the unions and bring industrial peace.

When the results were announced, Labour emerged as the largest party with four more seats than Tories, though in the first hung parliament since 1929 the balance of power rested with the minor parties. It was hardly a ringing endorsement: Labour polled fewer votes than in 1970, and its 37 per cent of total votes cast was low by post-war standards. But after Heath failed to reach terms with the Liberals, Wilson returned to Downing Street as Prime Minister early in March 1974. Rather to his surprise, Tony Crosland found himself back in government.

20

Socialism Now, 1974

Wilson resolutely ignored talk of possible deals to keep his minority government in office. Instead he appointed a Cabinet in which the centre-right again dominated, with Callaghan as Foreign Secretary, Jenkins at the Home Office and Denis Healey as Chancellor. This was balanced by the inclusion of left-wingers in the middle-ranks, notably Barbara Castle at Social Services, Tony Benn as Industry Secretary and Michael Foot entering the Cabinet for the first time as Employment Secretary, charged with handling relations with the unions. Within days, the Prime Minister had settled the miners' strike and brought to an end the official state of emergency. In spite of this promising start, no one doubted that the task ahead was more daunting than in 1964. Wilson had to demonstrate that he had some means of tackling both run-away levels of inflation – fuelled by a fourfold increase in world oil prices after the Arab–Israeli war – and the scars left by months of industrial unrest. Crosland, who went to a remodelled Department of the Environment (DOE), was asked by his wife if it was worth winning when it meant having to inherit such a mess. He replied that there were always things that could be done, though he did admit to a strange lack of exhilaration. This he attributed to the outcome of the election, which made it impossible to contemplate radical change and made inevitable another contest in the near future.[1] Before long, however, Crosland was enjoying his return to the corridors of power. Part of the reason for this was that he found himself in the headlines; Labour's return to office coincided with the publication of his most important work since *The Conservative Enemy* twelve years earlier.

The title of what was to be Crosland's final book, *Socialism Now*, was suggested by his PPS Dick Leonard, who felt something along such lines would 'maximise the extension of your appeal leftwards across the Party'.[2] After a fifty-page introduction, the remaining nineteen chapters were articles or speeches that had appeared in journals and newspapers over a period of years, mostly reflecting work in opposition since 1970 but some stretching back to 1966–67, with the emphasis on those areas of policy that had been of most concern to Crosland: housing, the environment and education. Dick Leonard struck a defensive note in the foreword he contributed as editor. *The Future of Socialism*, he said, had been produced at a time when Crosland had greater leisure to read and research. In 1956 he was not an MP and held no official position in the party; but from 1965 to 1970 he had been in Cabinet and since then had been a busy shadow minister. Crosland therefore no longer had the time or freedom to range as broadly as he might, with the result that the book concentrated on those issues that most preoccupied him in preparing for a return to power. On the other hand, Leonard pointed out, Crosland in the 1970s was able to speak not as a theoretician but as an experienced minister, one whose reputation in Whitehall had been built up through a combination of administrative skill and innovative ideas. The book reflected, in other words, the thoughts of 'a committed politician, yet one who has not ceased to think deeply and creatively about the problems with which he has been concerned'.[3]

Crosland's introductory essay, drafted in the autumn of 1973, was similarly defensive when compared with his earlier writings. The first half of the 12,000-word chapter was devoted to the issue of whether the 'revisionist thesis' which he helped to advance in the 1950s and 1960s was in need of a complete overhaul. He had no qualms in sticking to the view that socialism was essentially about equality. For the 1970s politician, there were 'plenty of harsh, specific and unmerited inequalities to combat in the next ten years; and a decade is my time-span, not eternity'. Yet it had to be recognised that several developments over recent years – not least deepening recession – had tested the revisionist claim that greater equality was attainable within the framework of a mixed economy. In Britain, he conceded again that the 1964–70 Labour government was viewed as a disappointment. There were successes that had gone largely unrecognised: education, health and social security all increased their share of national product, compared with a decline in defence; and a modest redistribution of wealth had taken place through the benefits system. These advances had been overshadowed, however, by economic failure. In 1970 unemployment and inflation were higher and growth slower than in 1964. Many revisionist proposals, such as public ownership of land and a full-scale national superannuation scheme, had never been put into effect, and Labour Britain was still 'conspicuous for its persistent and glaring class inequalities'. The exacerbation of inequalities since 1970 also posed unforeseen challenges. Heath's dismal record had caused a mood of public despair, with high inflation redistributing income from poor to rich and inciting a destructive struggle between organised groups to protect their own living standards.[4]

Crosland agreed there was a case to answer. Did the events of the past decade, with the economy in a state of semi-permanent crisis, invalidate revisionism? He began his answer to the question by arguing that it remained more coherent and persuasive than other creeds on offer, either the divisive dogmatism of the Tories or the revived 'semi-Marxist thought' favoured by some on the Labour left. The middle part of his essay laid out his case against those who asserted that Britain's crisis of capitalism could only be resolved by a massive programme of public ownership. He agreed that the poor image of private enterprise in recent years owed much to behaviour which led Heath to speak of the 'unacceptable face of capitalism', such as the corporate meanness of Distillers over 'thalidomide children'. However, nationalised industries did not have flawless records on safety, pollution or corruption, and the government itself was the largest employer of low-wage workers in the country. Public ownership to Crosland remained what it always had been: one of a number of means of achieving socialist ends. He favoured action himself in areas such as land, private rented housing, and parts of the construction and insurance industries. Yet none of this meant that the origins of the failures of the last decade lay in patterns of ownership. Other countries with similar mixed economies had moved ahead faster and there was no evidence to show how a massive transfer of ownership would help to achieve the objective of greater equality.[5]

What then was needed? Not, he said, a move to Clause Four socialism but rather 'a sharper delineation of fundamental objectives, a greater clarity about egalitarian policies and a stronger determination to achieve them'. All priorities should be costed and carefully planned to ensure they were part of a coherent strategy and not isolated achievements, as was the case when Labour was last in office. His own list of priorities included: the reduction of poverty ('the overriding moral imperative for a Labour government'); the provision of decent homes; the nationalisation of development land;

the redistribution of capital wealth; elimination of selection in secondary schools; and the extension of industrial democracy.[6] Crosland summed up that in a climate of pessimism it was important not to create excessive expectations or to delude anyone into thinking that reform could come about painlessly. Socialists should nonetheless be unrepentant in certain respects: in asserting that hard times made it more not less essential to strive for a more equal society, and in insisting that change would require higher taxes among the better-off, including workers such as dockers and printers who instinctively favoured pay differentials in place of equality. The whole edifice, he concluded, required agreement across the board on prices and incomes and faster growth, though no panacea for crisis-free growth appeared to be in sight:

> But whatever the rate of growth, we can, and must, mount a determined attack on specific social evils and specific inequalities. . . . We must prepare in advance a limited programme of radical measures which do not promise more than we can actually perform, which are closely related to the needs and aspirations of ordinary people, and yet which constitute a coherent egalitarian strategy instead of a muddle of bits and pieces.[7]

Crosland was lucky in the timing of his book. Appearing only weeks after Labour's return to power, it attracted widespread publicity. London bookshops were sold out on the day of publication and the *Sunday Times* carried lengthy extracts, saying that instead of a treatise for opposition, the book carried the argument between Labour's left and right 'into the heart of government'.[8] Some reviewers were warm, even lavish, in their praise. For the political scientist Anthony King, Crosland was 'probably the most important socialist writer Britain has produced'; he had Tawney's moral vision but also a greater command of the social sciences.[9] The timing did no harm in raising Crosland's personal profile, and some commented on its importance in furthering his credentials as a possible contender for the Labour leadership. From the political right there was grudging respect. One Tory opponent described Crosland as almost the only person in the last parliament who seemed capable of articulating what a modern Labour Party might look like. He had produced another thought-provoking and easy to read book, marked by a brevity of expression that many of his colleagues would do well to emulate.

1 The young Tony Crosland, around the time he was sent abroad to recover from a serious illness.

2 Crosland as a teenager with family friends, the Southwells, at Charmouth in Dorset.

3 *Below:* The dashing army officer, in the uniform of the Royal Welch Fusiliers, 1941.

4 *Right:* Arthur Jenkins (Labour MP and father of Roy) – a key figure in Crosland's political development.

5 Hugh Dalton (seated second right), another crucial influence on the early career of Crosland (far left). Also pictured here are the economists Nicholas Davenport (second left) and Ian Little (far right), with Little's wife, Dobs.

6 *Above:* Addressing
undergraduates as
President of the
Oxford Union, 1946.

7 *Left:* Crosland the
Oxford don, in his
rooms at Trinity, 1947.

8 *Top:* With constituency workers after being adopted as Labour candidate for South Gloucestershire, 1949.

9 *Above:* Crosland and his first wife, Hilary Sarson, whom he had met in Oxford after the war, on their wedding day in 1952.

10 *Top:* Electioneering with Roy Jenkins in the Grimsby constituency where Crosland won by the narrowest of margins at the 1959 election.

11 *Above:* With his mentor Hugh Gaitskell, addressing party workers in Grimsby, 1961.

12 Crosland married his second wife, Susan Catling, in February 1964. Also pictured are Susan's children from her first marriage, Sheila and Ellen-Craig.

13 *Below:* Tony and Susan relaxing together at their home in Lansdowne Road, 1969.

14 *Above:* The newly appointed Secretary of State for the Environment, 1974.

15 *Left:* Crosland at a Labour Party press conference, looking less than thrilled at the prospect of a second general election within ten months, September 1974.

16 *Top:* Crosland as Foreign Secretary in June 1976, refusing to wear the formal dress favoured by Prime Minister Callaghan and Home Secretary Roy Jenkins in awaiting the arrival of the French President at Victoria Station.

17 *Above:* The Croslands with American Secretary of State Dr Henry Kissinger, December 1976.

The *Economist* wished for more voices of such clarity and honesty; when Crosland spoke, it said, the cries of the Benns, Heffers and Skinners died away and Labour almost – though not quite – seemed worthy of becoming a majority government.[10]

Tony Benn was annoyed that the moderates in the government had been allowed to claim the initiative. Crosland, he felt, was being built up by Fleet Street as 'the hero', set against himself as 'the villain'.[11] Yet, on closer inspection, the balance of opinion was more critical of Crosland's work than it had been in the past. While several national newspapers and journals were sympathetic, others were more sceptical, pointing out that *Socialism Now* had no fresh remedies to propose for securing higher growth.[12] Some of Crosland's own friends, whom he asked to look at the manuscript in advance, thought that he quibbled too much in places, for example on the question of defining equality and describing how much change was required before an egalitarian society could be said to exist. On this Crosland would only say that he did not have 'the competence to write a new philosophical treatise' on conceptual issues such as the key causes of continued inequality; adding with an air of impatience that he was not 'cerebrating in a monastery' but attempting to tackle glaring problems. As for one of his central aims, that of reducing poverty levels, *Socialism Now* remained hazy on specific methods of achieving this, and Crosland admitted he was not 'competent' to judge which proposals were best suited to replacing the existing 'rag-bag' of benefits. This reticence was picked up by Wilfred Beckerman, who said it was all 'a bit vague . . . your admirers will have expected a new lead and insights into the events of the last twenty years. I rather fear they will be disappointed'.[13]

The book also failed to win many converts among newcomers emerging in Labour ranks. Crosland was brutal in his dismissal of the thesis propounded by some on the left, notably Stuart Holland, that capitalism was characterised by increasing monopolisation and a massive shift of power to private corporations. In private he dismissed Holland's ideas as 'bogus intellectualism', and in *Socialism Now* he claimed that industrial policy was not a first-order priority; weaknesses in the economy could be corrected by appropriate fiscal policies without the need to 'intervene all over the place'.[14] Crosland's attachment to the line that past failures were due to wrong choices and a lack of will power, rather than to misguided strategy, was also a concern for some on the Labour right. One of the sharpest critiques came from Giles Radice, who pointed out that no time had been spent in asking why the better off in society should favour egalitarianism, nor how public expenditure could be increased without further hiking up inflation. There was still room, Radice believed, for a book updating notions of equality and the relevance of socialism in the 1970s; scope, in other words, for a *Future of Socialism* mark II: 'As he himself admits, Mr Crosland has not written it. But that does not mean that it does not need to be done.'[15] Crosland's inflexibility, combined with the unrepentant tone of his writing, indicated to his critics that they had hit a raw nerve in asking him to revise *The Future of Socialism*. When pressed about why he was not systematically re-thinking his whole philosophy, he retorted at one point: 'Keynes didn't write another General Theory.' More bluntly still, he said he was 'too bloody busy'.[16]

He was certainly busy in his role as Secretary of State for the Environment. His responsibilities ranged over wide areas of policy stretching from local government to housing and transport. Within a week, officials at his huge Marsham Street office were implementing Crosland's request to freeze rent levels, and by the second week a programme to increase council house building was under way. At Easter 1974 he reflected in private notes on a surprisingly satisfactory return to government. One reason for this was his belief, shared by many others, that Wilson was 'much improved', and had so far displayed 'faultless political judgement'. The Prime Minister's tactical skills were put to best use with the government trying to survive on a day-to-day basis; these circumstances also helped ministers to pull together instead of encouraging talk of challenges to the leader's authority. Crosland described the Cabinet as one of 'exceptional quality', adding that 'only Barbara talks too much'. He also admitted that, like the Prime Minister, he was more relaxed this time round, partly because he was older and more experienced, but crucially because he had spent four years working on the issues and so came in 'knowing a lot', having a broad idea of what he wanted to do. He was not overwhelmed 'by ignorance' as in his early months at previous departments such as the Board of Trade. The return of an official car, he believed, improved his efficiency, and it was also 'nice not worrying about money'.[17]

The honeymoon period did not last long. In the absence of a parliamentary majority, it was widely assumed that Wilson would need to call another election in the autumn. This meant ministers were expected to set in motion all their major departmental plans before the summer recess. Crosland devoted much of his time to ensuring the repeal of the 1972 Housing Finance Act and to preparing a White Paper on the public ownership of development land. He also discovered that with a large team of nine junior ministers, it was necessary to engage in much 'psychiatric work – comforting those who thought they ought to be in the Cabinet'.[18] During his August holiday in France, Crosland noted how his relaxed feelings at Easter had been eroded because of the pressure to do in two months what would normally take two years. Working on the land White Paper had been 'Hellish & not enjoyable'. In addition, the government's precarious parliamentary position required almost continuous attendance at the House in order to stave off the danger of losing a snap parliamentary vote. As for what had been achieved, he believed the land White Paper was worth all the hard work, but admitted nothing had been done on transport and that housing reforms had been planned well in advance. This record did not sound much, but perhaps the main thing had been to preside over a vast and politically sensitive department while avoiding major 'cock-ups'. His most controversial proposal had been to shift the balance in the distribution of the Rate Support Grant, a move not welcomed by many Labour MPs. The policy, he reflected, was 'morally & socially absolutely right, but politically definitely wrong'.[19]

Around the Cabinet table, Crosland cut a more impressive figure than he had in the late 1960s. No longer feeling himself to be in the shadow of Roy Jenkins, who by 1974 was not regarded as the only crown prince, Crosland contributed to several key areas of discussion. He was prominent in criticising Tony Benn's proposed industry White Paper, and was also to the fore in lengthy Cabinet sessions called to discuss Chancellor Healey's requests for a tight rein on public expenditure. Barbara Castle made the first of what Joel Barnett – Healey's deputy as Chief Secretary to the Treasury – called 'many long harangues' on the need for social security to have an increased allocation of funds. Barnett continued that:

> . . . much the most effective contribution to the discussion came from Tony Crosland, another major spending Minister. But Tony did not only speak up for more public expenditure then, he also did so later as Foreign Secretary, when his own programme was not in the firing line, other than for the odd few million pounds. This quality of objectivity

combined with his knowledge, experience and considerable ability, made him the Minister who had the greatest impact on Cabinet decisions on most issues.[20]

As in the past, the Prime Minister was less generous in his appraisal. When Wilson gave a special end–of–session speech to the PLP, Shirley Williams and Callaghan were singled out for special praise. Crosland muttered to Barbara Castle, sitting next to him: 'Shirley 3, Jim 2, Barbara 1, poor Tony nought.'[21]

In mid–September 1974 Wilson called the expected election. His reasoning was that the government had, temporarily at least, steadied the economy. Heath's policy of compulsory wage restraint had been replaced by a 'Social Contract' which involved voluntary agreements with the unions. By holding inflation to reasonable levels, the government could claim modest improvements in living standards. In addition, the Prime Minister realised that little more in the way of legislation could be pushed through, and so opted to end the shortest parliament since the 1680s. Two elections in the same year did little to stimulate voter interest: the turnout in October 1974 was to slump by more than two million from the February level. Many of the faces dominating the campaign were familiar ones, though Crosland was given a higher profile at Labour's national press conferences. His appearances, noted *Socialist Commentary*, were 'invariably stunning – striped shirts, cigarellos, flamboyant yellow braces, and that unique mix of olympian intellect and seething passion'.[22] A swing of two per cent was enough to give Labour a slender overall majority of just three seats. Wilson could celebrate a unique four election victories from five contests as leader, though the party's share of the poll was the lowest for any majority government since the 1920s. For Crosland, it set the seal on a good year. During 1974, one journalist noted, he had emerged as a more substantial figure in Labour's senior hierarchy, yet without 'having very much compromised himself, without having very much trimmed or conceded. It's an impressive performance, in a way a triumph of man over manner.'[23] Even so, the outlook was far from rosy. Economic recovery remained fragile and steady support for the Liberals, combined with the low election turnout, suggested that confidence in the government was not high. The going was set to get rough.

21

'The Party's Over', 1974-6

Wilson made few changes in the composition of his government. Crosland continued at the DOE, though only after being teased by Tony Benn as they went into Downing Street about being appointed to Defence:

> 'What?', Crosland exclaimed. 'Defence,' I repeated. 'After all, a paratrooper, wartime record, an obvious appointment . . .'
> 'I just don't believe it.'
> I said, 'For heaven's sake, don't tell Harold I've told you when you go in and see him.' I absolutely had him.
> Then he said, 'Do you mean it?'
> I said, 'Of course I don't.' And all of a sudden he was very relaxed.[1]

Crosland was reconciled to remaining at the same middle-ranking level of the Cabinet for as long as Wilson was in charge: 'He can't give me anything less, though he'll be damned if he'll give me anything more.'[2] When ministers reassembled for the first Cabinet meeting after the election, the mood was downbeat. According to Tony Benn, Callaghan poured cold water on proceedings by highlighting the difficulties ahead. In addition to Labour's wafer-thin majority, there was great unease among the middle classes and somehow the Social Contract had to be made to work. Crosland too was 'gloomy', saying nationalisation was irrelevant to the poor state of the economy, which he feared would make difficult his task as a spending minister.[3]

The Secretary of State had a tough time with the first issue on his desk when he returned to the DOE. Conservative housing legislation in 1972 had required local councils to adopt a rigid timetable for increasing rents. Those who defied the law were threatened with automatic disqualification from council service and a fine of £6000. Public attention focused on the angry protests of Labour councillors at Clay Cross in Derbyshire, and the party's 1973 conference had passed a resolution pledging support for councillors who defied the law. In office Crosland proposed a general amnesty on disqualification for those late in implementing the law, but the fine was to remain. In November 1974 he secured final approval from the Cabinet for his preferred solution. Benn noted in his diary: 'Tony said he found it distasteful but he hoped to present it to the House in such a way that Dennis Skinner would not walk out of the Chamber.'[4] Crosland's reputation within the PLP did not sink as much as he feared, though it proved a difficult line to tread between observing the law and respecting party feeling. Clay Cross, he wrote in private notes, had been a 'wretched bore: but someone had to do it – only option was to resign.'[5] On a broader front, the government got off to a brighter start than some of its own members anticipated. Labour had won over forty more seats than the Tories, and the parties on the opposition benches showed little sign of working together to pressurise the new administration. This helps to explain how the Prime Minister emerged unscathed from the issue which dominated the political agenda in the first half of 1975 – the referendum on Britain's continued membership of the EC.

In line with the party's manifesto commitment, Wilson and his Foreign Secretary, Jim Callaghan, set about negotiating new terms for British membership. These fell short of what many party activists sought, but with Cabinet approval the Prime Minister recommended acceptance of the terms in a referendum. In an effort to pacify anti-market sentiment, Wilson took the unusual step of removing the Cabinet obligation to accept collective responsibility. As a result Tony Benn was free to give a lead to the cross-party 'Britain out' movement. In Cabinet, Crosland described himself as an agnostic who thought there was a strong case for staying in. Otherwise 'we would go back to a sort of Churchillian myth that we were the greatest and most important country in the world'.[6] He was determined to avoid the errors of 1971 and so made his position as clear as possible in public speeches. Taking the pragmatic line that things had moved on since British entry, he appeared on Labour Committee for Europe platforms, a party-based grouping for those who did not wish to associate themselves with the broader 'Britain in Europe' organisation. Crosland's words were not much reported in comparison with those of Jenkins, whose supporters pressed hard in what Dick Leonard called an effort to 'put Roy back in the political race'. In early June the referendum produced a two-to-one majority for staying in the Community. Most accolades went not to Jenkins but to Wilson, who was praised for his statesmanship in maintaining party unity over a highly divisive issue. Crosland, relieved that the European minefield had been safely negotiated, regarded this as one of Wilson's main achievements, a triumph which had eluded Peel over the Corn Laws and Gladstone over Ireland.[7]

By the spring of 1975, however, fresh clouds were gathering on the economic horizon. Over the winter the Chancellor had maintained a strategy of relying on the Social Contract to ensure 'sensible' wage bargaining in return for extended welfare benefits, paid for by redistributive taxation and large-scale borrowing. But as the world recession deepened British exports suffered, growth fell sharply, unemployment rose and inflation at over 20 per cent seemed to be veering out of control. Healey came to the view that it was time to take his foot off the accelerator and apply the brake. In March 1975 he proposed a tough budget which raised income tax and slashed spending programmes by one billion pounds. 'As ever', Joel Barnett recalled, 'the most powerful alternative criticism came from Tony Crosland.'[8] Crosland had hitherto admired Healey's handling of the economy. The two men were never close, but each respected the other's intellectual and administrative abilities, and Crosland did not suffer from the jealousy that led him to make life difficult for Jenkins in the late 1960s. But as Environment Secretary he felt it was important to speak out. He protested that there 'was a smell of 1966', adding that the political impact would be 'traumatic' and that 'half the Manifesto would go down the drain', including his own departmental concerns such as rent controls, transport subsidies and land policy.[9] Nevertheless, with Wilson's backing, the Chancellor won the day. Large reductions were agreed in several areas under Crosland's jurisdiction, notably roads, water and sewerage. Some Whitehall insiders believed more hardship would be needed, since half the cuts entailed curtailing future rather than current projects.[10]

Healey was in no mood to relent, and was soon urging upon colleagues the need for further reductions. Crosland found some support from the left in resisting Treasury thinking. On 14 July Barbara Castle spoke of 'another grim morning milling round our economic miseries'. The Chancellor began by noting that public expenditure had grown from 42 per cent of GDP to 58 per cent over the last twenty years. 'As usual', Castle continued, 'Harold called Tony C. – the Chancellor-in-waiting – next, and as usual, we got a mixture of brilliant analysis and suspended action.'[11] Senior Treasury officials regarded Crosland as the most heavyweight opponent of Healey's policy, but took comfort from the absence of any detailed alternative strategy, either from him or from the left. The best the Chancellor's opponents could manage was to play for time and to suggest the formulation of a more coherent approach to making cuts. In early August ministers gathered at Chequers with the intention of achieving a consensus on priorities for reduced expenditure; but despite Wilson's best efforts the meeting focused on general issues. According to Barbara Castle, Healey's 'guns had been spiked by a paper put in by Tony Crosland giving international comparisons of the percentage of GDP spent by different countries on public services. . . . It showed that we were far from lavish in public expenditure; other countries did more than we did in this field.' Joel Barnett described the meeting as wholly inconclusive, with several ministers either not listening or refusing to face up to the scale of Britain's economic difficulties.[12]

By the middle of 1975 internal party divisions were again resurfacing. The Tribune group of left-wing MPs complained of a betrayal of the manifesto. Tony Benn was demoted from Industry to Energy after the failure of the 'Britain out' campaign in the European referendum; any prospect of an industrial strategy along the lines of the *1973 Programme* receded, and the government abandoned the faltering Social Contract in favour of a formal pay policy, attempting to hold down wages across the board. On his annual summer holiday, Crosland reflected that he was not surprised by Benn's demotion or by the retreat from the style of the manifesto. It was a 'myth', he said, that the party at the top had moved sharply to the left, and it was predictable that rhetoric about an 'irreversible shift' in power had turned out to be half-baked. The great danger was that confidence in the government was sinking so fast that, as in the late 1960s, political recovery would prove impossible. It was vital therefore to 'create sense that [we] still have a *vision* despite constraints'.[13] This was the thrust of a speech Crosland made after returning from his holiday. Faced with the first real decline in living standards for a generation, it was imperative that Labour maintained a 'sense of purpose', setting out limited priorities then pursuing them with total commitment.[14]

During the autumn he tried to bring this approach to the heart of the decision-making process, setting out for the Prime Minister his own priorities for public expenditure. It was essential, he said, to bring the debate into the open, and to do so in a non-departmental frame of mind. To the annoyance of his own officials, he spelt out how two of the three main spending areas of the DOE were in his estimation low priority. His personal list of less important areas included aid to industry ('much of this is a horrible waste of money'); transport (must keep decent system, but subsidies to rail often help better off); and other environmental services (much crucial to well being, such as sewerage, but extravagant in some directions, such as leisure services). In the middling category he placed the NHS (lower proportion of GNP than elsewhere). His high priorities were overseas aid ('test of a Labour Government's conscience'); urban renewal (a 'shambles because uncoordinated'); social service cash benefits; and housing (should seek to reduce subsidies but increase investment).[15] Other ministers refused to adopt the same approach. Barbara Castle was frequently critical of Crosland's 'oratorical gestures', saying that he failed to follow through complaints; to his annoyance, her practice was to defend her departmental budget down to the last penny. Joel Barnett noted that Crosland was the only minister in bilateral discussions with the Treasury who offered to sacrifice a low priority for a high one.[16]

In spite of their differences, Crosland and Castle worked together when in November 1975 the Chancellor requested a further massive cut of £3.75 billion from public expenditure. Healey said unless a balance-of-payments surplus could be reached by 1978, any gains from the arrival of North Sea oil would be wiped out. Crosland's counter-proposal for cuts of only £2 billion he described as a 'recipe for disaster'.[17] Amidst whispers that Healey would resign unless he secured Cabinet backing, the dissenters were only narrowly beaten. Crosland noted that Healey had a built-in majority, with two 'pompous' ex-Chancellors (Callaghan and Jenkins) parading their wounds from past battles and several others 'too dim or too timid' to resist.[18] The Crosland–Castle alliance did not last long. When ministers in detailed discussion offered less than the target figure, Healey insisted the remainder must come from the biggest spending departments, including environment and social security. Barbara Castle recorded Crosland's statement that his department was responsible for 17 per cent of expenditure but had accepted 38 per cent of the cuts; if others had been as helpful ('another dig at me'), any difficulties would be resolved. Crosland decided it was time to draw a line in the sand. He managed to stave off the worst by slamming his papers together in a gesture of resignation which alarmed the Prime Minister; the proposed cut in housing investment he described as his first 'near' resigning issue since 1964.[19]

These recurrent economic crises inevitably overshadowed Crosland's work as a departmental minister. As the battles in Cabinet indicated, housing was his major concern, and many hours were spent working on a comprehensive housing review which he established under his own leadership. Some of those working with Crosland believed the review served to shelve highly sensitive issues, such as the effects on the housing market of mortgage interest tax relief, but when the review was completed (after Crosland left the DOE) it did propose wide-ranging solutions, particularly in the area of council housing.[20] The most painful part of the minister's task was the need to persuade local authorities to curtail their spending plans, which had risen sharply since the reorganisation of local government carried out by Heath's government. In a speech at Manchester during May 1975 he told local government that Britain was facing a grim economic outlook unless urgent action was taken. 'We have to come to terms with the harsh reality of the situation which we inherited. The party's over.' One of Crosland's junior ministers at the DOE, Gordon Oakes, wryly told his boss that if the party was over, he was the 'poor bloody barman', charged with the task of going round 'collecting the glasses': persuading reluctant Labour authorities to rein in spending.[21]

Crosland's reputation as a writer was also affected by what looked like a re-run of the mid-1960s, with a return to deflation, the introduction of 'cash limits' on public spending and ministers drifting from one crisis measure to the next. In December 1975 he struck a defiant note in a Fabian pamphlet entitled *Social Democracy in Europe*, based upon a lecture given at an international conference in Central America. He acknowledged that his brand of revisionism was under attack not only from resurgent left-wing thinking but also from 'anti-egalitarians' on the political right, emerging in Britain over the past year with support from leading Tories. He questioned Keith Joseph's plea that businessmen should have greater rewards as they were 'the people who give themselves ulcers', asking why incentives were only thought necessary for the middle class when the incidence of ulcers was twice as high among manual workers. He also stuck to his guns on the need for growth and high public spending, though he further modified his view about the need to prioritise by declaring that preference should be given to social expenditure which was 'unambiguously progressive', while restraining that which sustained large bureaucracies of middle-class professionals.[22] However, the reception given to the pamphlet was cool. Hitherto sympathetic commentators expressed frustration that Crosland could suggest no new means by which to translate his desire for greater equality into practice. And claiming that the high priest of equality was on the run, right-wing newspapers suggested he should spend less time attacking others and more asking why his 'collectivist, know-nothing' government was faring so badly.[23]

In spite of the government's growing unpopularity, Crosland was not downcast. One reason was his ability to detach himself from Cabinet and departmental worries. As one of his officials at the DOE put it, he had many 'corners'. He had no interest in 'social life: he'd been through that', but there was his writing, Grimsby, football and an 'immense preoccupation with family . . . never overtly mentioned: it was just evident'.[24] In 1975 Crosland and his wife purchased for £45,000 a country cottage at Adderbury, three miles south of Banbury in Oxfordshire, and he told the journalist John Cole that he found himself thinking about his next holiday more often than before. He confirmed to Cole that as a minister he was in a happier frame of mind than he had been in the late 1960s, because he was older and had experienced present difficulties before. He was also becoming, over a decade on, more appreciative of Wilson's leadership and he was not unduly worried about the state of the party. Marxist infiltrators at local level needed to be watched, but he remained adamant that 'Bennery' was dead in the Cabinet since Tony Benn had fallen from favour. The press, he believed, exaggerated stories about infiltrators because this made better copy than the fact that left–right divides were a permanent feature of Labour politics.[25]

Crosland's standing inside the Cabinet had also been consolidated during 1975. His ability to contribute to broad areas of discussion was admired by Michael Foot on the left and by Joel Barnett on the right. The Chief Secretary to the Treasury noted how Crosland – though unable to avoid his share of the cuts which all ministers suffered – had at least ensured that he and not Treasury officials determined where the axe should fall. For Barnett, a careful observer of all the key players in Cabinet, Crosland's stature was on a par with that of Callaghan and Healey, and he had put himself back in the running as the obvious choice to go the Treasury whenever the Chancellorship became available.[26] There were indications, though similar signs had proved false in 1967, that Wilson was recognising the logic of such a move.[27] Underpinning Crosland's confidence in his own position was a realisation that the star of his old rival, Roy Jenkins, was no longer in the ascendant. According to one of the Prime Minister's advisers, Jenkins spoke infrequently in Cabinet and seemed 'to be awaiting the unfolding of some scenario of nemesis'.[28] At one meeting Crosland enjoyed watching Barbara Castle attacking Roy for his claim that high public expenditure was a threat to democracy. British spending on social services was below the European average, she pointed out, asking if democracy was disintegrating in Europe. 'Roy smiled rather sourly,' she noted, and Crosland said to her: 'That was very funny.'[29]

Over the Christmas period in 1975 Crosland began to immerse himself in the transport review established at the DOE some eighteen months earlier. In the past he had proclaimed 'transport is a great bore'. As he settled down to finalise the details of a lengthy study intended to lead to a White Paper, he told his wife: 'Had forgotten Transport is so interesting.'[30] The review was later called Crosland's 'last will and testament as Environment Secretary', a document bearing all the cohesion and forcefulness one would expect from its author.[31] Labour policy, it noted, should not lose sight of the need to provide good public transport for the diminishing but still substantial numbers − approximately thirty per cent of the population − who had no car. As a result, priority should be given to greater investment in coach and bus services, with less attention for motorways and commuter-driven rail networks, whatever the political consequences.[32] The document was widely praised as 'sensible Socialism' when it was published shortly after Crosland left the DOE, though Alan Watkins noted that it threw Labour MPs into some confusion. The party line had always been: trains good, cars and lorries bad. Now it seemed trains were bad all the time because they were used mainly by the middle class. Cars were still wicked but buses 'are virtuous because they are used by the working classes'.[33] Crosland completed his work on the transport review in mid−March 1976, and went to bed on Monday 15 March assuming that as Environment Secretary he would soon be steering transport reform through the Cabinet and the PLP. The following day his assumptions were overturned by remarkable news: Harold Wilson had resigned.

22

The Battle of the
Crown Princes, 1976

Wilson's long tenure as leader of the Labour Party was due in part to the lack of an agreed successor. In private conversation over the winter of 1975-6 he commented that there were six crown princes. This, he noted, was a more secure position for the incumbent than facing one or two powerful rivals, as he had in the late 1960s.[1] As on most matters of Labour politics, Wilson proved to be spot on. In the leadership contest that followed his resignation, six members of the Cabinet threw their hats into the ring, though only after recovering from the shock of Wilson's unexpected bombshell. Jim Callaghan had been given advance warning a few days earlier, on Wilson's sixtieth birthday, and Denis Healey was told in a lavatory shortly before the Cabinet convened on the morning of the resignation, 16 March. Most ministers were 'flabbergasted'. Tony Benn wrote that nearly everyone around the Cabinet table was 'stunned', with only Callaghan – finding it hard to conceal his excitement – showing sufficient composure to respond with an immediate tribute to the Prime Minister.[2] The sense of surprise in Downing Street was shared by ministers on duty elsewhere. Callaghan's deputy at the Foreign Office, Roy Hattersley, was listening to the Bulgarian national anthem at Sofia airport when the British ambassador whispered to him that the Premier had resigned. Hattersley was convinced he had missed an unexpected development in Bulgarian politics. 'Not their Prime Minister,' clarified the ambassador as the music played on, 'our Prime Minister.'[3] Tony Crosland, like several of his colleagues, suddenly had to confront the question: should he stand for the Labour leadership?

Newspaper speculation on the morning of Wednesday 17 March was feverish. Was it possible to accept at face value Wilson's statement that he had long planned to retire at the age of sixty, or were darker forces at work? Was the Prime Minister expecting a sudden economic crisis or a scandal linked to a security services plot?

And who would inherit the crown? Wilson was to remain as premier until a successor emerged from a hastily convened ballot of Labour MPs; the keys to No. 10 Downing Street were in the hands of 317 members of the PLP. Before the day was out five contenders had declared themselves. The front-runner from the outset was Callaghan, by virtue of his experience, his wide contacts in the Labour movement and his popularity with the general public. There were strong suspicions that the timing of Wilson's resignation was designed to maximise Callaghan's chances. Relations between the Prime Minister and his Foreign Secretary had recovered a long way from the low point of *In Place of Strife*, and since Labour returned to power in 1974 Callaghan had been – in practice if not in name – Wilson's 'inner Cabinet and Deputy Prime Minister rolled into one'.[4] For Roy Jenkins, this was the moment he had been waiting for since 1968. After listening to Wilson's resignation statement, Jenkins went off to meet close allies for a pre-arranged lunch which turned into a planning meeting. The mood among his followers was that victory was within reach, though it would be a tough struggle.[5] On the Labour left Michael Foot, urged by friends to pick up the mantle of Nye Bevan, quickly decided to put his name forward. So did Tony Benn: to 'establish a power base', with a view to winning a future contest, and 'to get an alternative policy across'.[6]

Crosland's was the fifth name to come forward, all within thirty-six hours of Wilson's announcement. As with many of his decisions, there was much agonising to be gone through first. Like his colleagues, he knew that the premiership was something of a poisoned chalice. Labour's prospects were far from rosy, with sterling weak, unemployment and inflation high, and the government's slim majority in the House of Commons looking ever more insecure. Allied to his desire not to give up further time with his family, it was no surprise that Crosland was found telling friends, 'I'm not sure I even *want* to be Prime Minister.' Nor was he likely to benefit from the agreed ballot procedure. Voting was to be under an 'exhaustive' system, with the candidate gaining fewest votes at each stage being eliminated until one name emerged with an absolute majority. Crosland's PPS, by now Peter Hardy, MP for Rother Valley, told him he was a natural second choice for many MPs, but would not attract many first preferences. The same reasoning explains why Roy Hattersley in Sofia desperately tried to get through to the DOE on the telephone. He wanted to warn Crosland against standing: 'a derisory result', he felt, 'would ruin both his prospects and his reputation.' The minister, Hattersley was told, had already left for Buckingham Palace; not, however, to kiss hands with the Queen, but rather to deputise at an official function.[7]

Hattersley's pessimism was not shared in all quarters. Crosland found some encouragement from press commentators. The *Guardian* said it was essential to move beyond Wilson's 'politics of pragmatism', and Peter Jenkins wrote that Crosland had many of the necessary qualities, as well as a 'cloth-cap Grimbarian style' in recent years which made him acceptable to a broad section of the party. From a more unexpected quarter, George Gale in the *Daily Express* described Crosland as a viable compromise figure with fewer enemies than several of the contenders; he was 'possibly the best equipped of all the candidates'.[8] When Crosland met with a small band of supporters at the House of Commons early on Wednesday, the mood was cautious. His decision was finely balanced: was it worth seeking to put down a marker, or would a humiliating exit on the first ballot blight his future prospects? Jim Callaghan, he knew, had prospered after coming last in 1963, but not in a field of five contenders. Peter Hardy and others were dispatched to take soundings around the bars and tea-rooms, but by mid-afternoon Crosland had decided to take the plunge. He went on television to describe himself as a radical moderate; he would, he claimed, draw support from the 'common ground which unites Left and Right' in the party. The final decision rested on a feeling that he might regret never having tested himself, whatever the consequences. According to his wife, he was swayed by a mixture of pride, recklessness and stubborness.[9]

With a week to go before polling, the campaign teams and candidates quickly swung into action. Confident of success, Callaghan opted for Olympian detachment, sticking to his busy schedule as Foreign Secretary and declining to give interviews. Fellow MPs, he said, were not likely to be impressed by pictures of him on their TV screens dressed in a striped apron and 'pretending to wash up in the kitchen' – a snipe at William Whitelaw's conduct during the Tory leadership contest won by Mrs Thatcher the previous year.[10] Callaghan did, however, let it be known that his backers included several Cabinet colleagues and junior ministers. The trusty lieutenants of Roy Jenkins, such as Bill Rodgers – bloodied in the battles over Europe of the early 1970s – were seen around Westminister meticulously noting down voting intentions. Tony Benn broke Cabinet ranks to publicise his case for industrial democracy and open government. 'I jumped through the burning hoop and I came out the other side' was his melodramatic diary description. 'It was amazing. I am a free man.'[11] On all sides black propaganda was the order of the day. Michael Foot's backers claimed that at least ninety votes were in the bag, while the Callaghan and Jenkins camps both produced impressive lists of would-be supporters, partly in order to deter a sixth contender, Denis Healey, from entering the race. The Chancellor held back, fearing a poor result in the aftermath of a bruising encounter with left-wing MPs critical of his policy. But Treasury colleagues exploited Healey's dislike of being seen to be running away; by late afternoon on Thursday he too was officially a candidate. Before long Healey supporters were claiming that at least 180 MPs were of the view that they would 'rather die' than vote for Roy Jenkins.[12]

Crosland, in the meantime, had to rely on a tiny band of followers including Gordon Oakes (MP for Widnes), his PPS Peter Hardy, Bruce Douglas-Mann (Merton), and the Tribunite Bruce Grocott (Lichfield). Although this indicated an ability to attract support from a broad spectrum of party opinion, no one in Crosland's team was a household name, and it was therefore vital to make a direct appeal to MPs with a full statement of policy aims. This Crosland did in typically robust fashion, summarising what he said was his consistently distinctive brand of democratic socialism. The essence of his programme was a belief in a dynamic mixed economy, based on full employment, a workable incomes policy, a more equal society and a high priority on public spending for social services:

> In present circumstances, the economy must come first, however harsh the measures needed to put it right. But the Party must retain a clear vision of its ideals. . . . We need to get inflation properly under control. . . . Then, more fairness. . . . We shall not get a dynamic economy while some people inherit more than others earn in a lifetime. We must introduce a Wealth Tax to supplement the new Capital Transfer Tax. Finally, public spending. Public spending is not just a matter of flushing pounds down a Whitehall sink. Public spending is pensions; public spending is decent housing; public spending is hospitals, schools, public transport. I believe that people want these services. We must improve them just as soon as our economic situation allows. That, then, is what I stand for. I always have and I always will.[13]

What all the other campaign teams agreed upon was that Crosland was bringing up the rear. His supporters reconvened on Wednesday evening to report that soundings around the Commons confirmed the likelihood of elimination on the first ballot, with only about a dozen confirmed backers.[14] Even close friends could not be counted on to pledge their support. Some felt it necessary to explain why in person. Roy Hattersley went straight to the DOE from Heathrow after arriving back from Bulgaria and Crosland greeted him with the news that he was a declared leadership contender. Hattersley announced that he would be voting for Callaghan on the grounds that Michael Foot, for all his virtues, would not make a credible Prime Minister. 'Then fuck off,' Crosland retorted. Hattersley did, making a swift exit, only to be called back by a porter saying that the minister would like a word. 'I told him that the Secretary of State had already had two, and pushed the swing doors.' He was though prevailed upon to return, where Crosland had a whisky at the ready and promptly invited Hattersley to lunch at the weekend. When the Hattersleys arrived for pre-lunch drinks, Crosland made a formal introduction: 'This is Roy Hattersley. He's going to vote for Callaghan and is going round forcing people to listen to the hard truth as if he were a member of the Oxford Movement.'[15] By this stage, with other MPs declaring that they would not back Crosland – whatever their admiration for him – it became necessary to issue a statement denying any intention to withdraw from the race.[16]

Weekend press coverage underlined the daunting task facing Crosland. His name was barely mentioned in the surveys among Labour MPs and the public carried out by Sunday broadsheets. Most attention was focused elsewhere: on Callaghan's strong showing among Labour voters in the country; on the possibility of Michael Foot topping the first ballot; and on the issue of whether Roy Jenkins could mount an effective challenge by picking up votes from Healey and Crosland, both of whom it was assumed would be eliminated early on. Seventy to eighty votes for Jenkins, it was agreed, would put him seriously in the running for the second or third ballots that seemed inevitable with so many candidates. For Crosland there were only crumbs of comfort. He was portrayed as someone who could command respect but not votes. In the opinion of the *Sunday Times*, he was a serious thinker about Labour's role in modern society, and he was neither narrow nor envious; but his lack of 'dedicated personal support' meant he was unlikely to figure when the results were made known the following Thursday.[17] The *Observer* agreed about Crosland's probable fate, which it regarded with some regret:

> Mr Crosland has a genuine social democratic vision and a reforming zeal. He is one of those rare intellects who can conceive and propagate new political ideas. Yet despite a (not wholly undeserved) reputation for personal arrogance, he has the political sense to understand the need for compromise. He would know how to follow sensible policies and hold the Labour Party together simultaneously. In missing Crosland, at least this time, Labour is missing the kind of radical and reformist leadership it needs.[18]

The final few days of the campaign were uncomfortable ones for Crosland. Jim Callaghan was unaware that some of his supporters relayed a menacing message shortly before nominations for the contest closed. It was no use Crosland offering support at a later stage; if he could not be relied upon, 'Jim had not the slightest interest in him.' The effect was counter-productive. Crosland's stubborn resolve not to stand aside was stiffened.[19] Even so, his sense of isolation was reinforced when he was ignored in a BBC Panorama special screened on Monday evening. In frustration he complained to the Director-General, accusing the BBC of 'arrogantly' assuming the right to pick and choose between candidates in the leadership contest. News of this complaint reached the *Daily Telegraph*, which spoke of a lack of proportion, especially from someone known for his sophisticated detachment from everyday politics. The 'party which is over', it insisted, 'is his.'[20] Last-minute efforts to win over support from the Jenkins camp met with little success. Several MPs, including Betty Boothroyd, had warm words for Crosland but insisted they were sticking with Roy.[21] On the evening before the results were announced, Crosland was asked by his wife how many votes he would consider to be reasonable. He summed up: 'Ten to fifteen: disaster. Fifteen to twenty: very bad. Twenty to twenty-five: tolerable. Twenty-five to thirty: good. Thirty to thirty-five: very good. Anything over thirty-five: sensational.'[22]

'It's very bad' was his terse verdict the following day. At 6 o'clock on 25 March Labour MPs squeezed into a committee room at the House to hear the outcome. The fears of the Crosland team were realised as the figures were read out:

The Battle of the Crown Princes, 1976

Michael Foot	90
Jim Callaghan	84
Roy Jenkins	56
Tony Benn	37
Denis Healey	30
Tony Crosland	17

Reactions varied. Foot and Callaghan could look forward to a final ballot showdown between left and right. Tony Benn was delighted to have won more support than the Chancellor, and before MPs dispersed he announced his withdrawal from the contest, urging his backers to rally behind Michael Foot.[23] Healey decided not to quit, despite claims that he might split the centre-right vote and so bolster Foot's chances. He was, in Barbara Castle's phrase, a 'pugilist, not a patrician'.[24] This was a jibe at Roy Jenkins, whose poor showing and decision to stand aside attracted widespread comment. The result confirmed the extent to which Jenkins, since his resignation from the deputy leadership, had become detached from mainstream party opinion. A story circulated after the contest that a Yorkshire MP, approached in the Tea Room and asked if he would be backing Jenkins in the leadership contest, replied. 'No, lad, we're all Labour here.'[25] Even his base among pro-Europeans had shrunk. One estimate suggested he won the backing of fewer than fifty of the ninety MPs said to be strong Marketeers.[26] In public Crosland's supporters put on a brave face. 'We were out to establish a position in the centre of the party,' commented Peter Hardy, 'and 17 is a pretty good total to start with.' Yet it was a crushing moment. At the bottom of the pile, Crosland was not in a position like other contenders to consider his options; he was automatically eliminated.

Why had he fared so badly? Crosland's poor showing was partly due to forces beyond his control. His campaign team, in reporting back conversations with Labour MPs, emphasised that in many eyes he lacked credibility having never held one of the three major offices of state – the Foreign Office, the Treasury or the Home Office. Environment was not considered a 'glamorous' department and, as Clay Cross demonstrated, meant incurring unpopularity among Labour councillors. Although Crosland had won plaudits for his ministerial performance on housing, this was often from left-wingers who would never back him in a leadership battle.[27] The credibility

Cummings, *Daily Express*, 28 March 1976 (© Express Newspapers, London 1976)

problem was compounded by Crosland's low profile among the public and party activists. One opinion poll during the contest found that only 2 per cent of voters thought he would make the best Prime Minister; indeed only one in four Labour supporters could name him from his photograph.[28] Callaghan, Jenkins and Healey had, of course, all occupied front-line Cabinet posts. In a contest where the centre ground was crowded, it was hardly surprising that the least experienced candidate suffered, especially as some of his views did not fit neatly with the simple left–right labels favoured by backbenchers. Establishing a clear identity was difficult for a 'radical moderate'; one analysis found that Crosland drew less support from the right than from the 'non-Tribunite left' of the party.[29] The timing of the contest was also unhelpful. Whether by accident or design, Wilson's decision to go in 1976 did no favours to several of the crown princes, especially Denis Healey, of whom it was said after his recent encounter with the left that he was incapable of torturing his victims without leaving a mark. Crosland also suffered, commenting that the contest was 'a year too soon for Denis. Four years too late for Roy.

Five years too soon for Tony [Benn]. Two years and one job too soon for me.'[30]

Crosland's own shortcomings were likewise important in explaining why he trailed so badly. Over the years he had spurned advice that he should 'gather troops' in anticipation of a leadership change. He had few trade union links and, unlike other contenders, he never spent time at Westminster cultivating a personal following. His attitude was such that even his supporters said he gave the impression he 'didn't care whether he got to No. 10 or not'.[31] If his views were not clearly understood within the PLP, let alone outside, then this too was Crosland's responsibility. He had largely avoided the television studios and was reluctant to accept that many newspapers favoured brief summaries rather than elaborate argument. 'We tend to assume', his adviser David Lipsey told him, 'that people read books/articles more closely than they do.'[32] Perhaps the major stumbling block, however, was the legacy of his detachment from the pro-Marketeers since the early 1970s. The *Sunday Times* noted that the supporters of Crosland and Jenkins reserved their most vitriolic language for one another. Jenkins was depicted as a coalitionist, the worst form of Labour heresy; whereas Crosland's 'treachery' over Europe was an example of his 'wobbliness'. Healey had been 'cold bloodedly shitty' in 1971, 'but at least he was decisive'.[33] Crosland had not gone out of his way to heal these old wounds. His close ally Dick Leonard candidly told him that some of the younger Jenkinsites, such as Giles Radice, were trying to build bridges by promoting new definitions of socialism appropriate for the 1970s; yet they found Crosland dismissive on the grounds that none of this new thinking matched his own work.[34] He had, in other words, alienated many of his former allies but failed to build up an alternative power base. While Europhiles remained cool, many other Labour MPs still took the view, rightly or wrongly, that Crosland was a 'minor Roy Jenkins'.[35] Roy Hattersley's warning appeared to have been vindicated. A derisory result seemed to have done nothing for Crosland's 'prospects and his reputation'. Once again he had failed to step out of the shadow of his great rival among the post-Gaitskell generation on the Labour right. Yet the following fortnight witnessed a remarkable transformation in fortunes.

In the second ballot, Callaghan emerged as front-runner with 141 votes to Foot's 133, with Gordon Oakes attempting to ensure that all seventeen Crosland votes were switched to Callaghan. Denis Healey maintained his level of support at thirty-eight votes, but was obliged to concede, leaving the way clear for Callaghan to defeat Foot by 176 votes to 137 in a third contest. The elementary school boy had triumphed over five Oxford graduates. In early April Callaghan accepted the Queen's invitation to form a new administration, a task he set about with vigour, making several changes to Wilson's outgoing Cabinet. Among those removed or who retired were Barbara Castle – a long-standing antagonist on the left – and Ted Short, who had triumphed over Crosland in the 1972 deputy leadership contest. Promotions among younger aspirants included Shirley Williams, who added the portfolio of Paymaster-General to her job as Prices Secretary, thereby becoming a 'deputy deputy Prime Minister' after Michael Foot.[36] But the greatest surprise came in the senior ranks. Only weeks after coming last in the leadership election, Crosland was appointed Foreign Secretary.

Callaghan later explained his reasoning in his memoirs. Denis Healey, he maintained, was a sheet anchor in the Cabinet; it was therefore easy to accommodate his preference for staying at the Treasury. As for the Foreign Office, there was no disputing the credentials of Roy Jenkins for the job, but his identification with the pro-European case would have led to grave suspicions among anti-Marketeers in the party. Callaghan said he had no wish to upset the 'uneasy truce' on Europe within Labour ranks, especially as another suitable candidate was available. Crosland's record made him better equipped to carry through those decisions that would inevitably bind Britain more closely to the European community. According to the new Prime Minister, Jenkins was given the reasonable option of remaining as Home Secretary, and it was a matter of regret when he chose instead to leave British politics to take up the Presidency of the European Commission.[37] This explanation tells only part of the story. Jenkins remained bitter that Callaghan, at a tense meeting on 6 April, refused to say why he was not being offered the one post that might keep him in London; nor was he told who was in the frame.[38] Crosland was hardly the most obvious choice as Foreign Secretary on past experience. Despite a reputation among socialist intellectuals in Europe, he had never – in the words of *Observer* columnist Alan Watkins – been greatly attached to 'foreigners as a class'. There was now a risk of diplomatic crises arising from the need to transmit *Match of the Day* to remote parts of the globe. Like Ernest Bevin in 1945, Crosland would start with very little detailed knowledge of foreign policy.[39]

Callaghan's thinking went much deeper. On one level there were personal considerations. Tensions during the leadership campaign had not eradicated his regard for Crosland, who had first backed him in the leadership contest of 1963. By contrast, Callaghan's relationship with Jenkins had never been close, and as we have seen Crosland was his preferred successor when Jenkins was made Chancellor in 1967. In addition, the new Prime Minister carefully weighed up how best to balance party factions inside the Cabinet. After his strong showing in all three ballots, Michael Foot had met with Callaghan to press various demands. One was that the Foreign Office should not go to Jenkins, regarded by Foot's supporters as the unacceptable face of the Labour right. Foot's success was not repeated when he tried to save Barbara Castle, as she recorded in her diary:

> Clearly Mike had been preoccupied with three things: first to get the leadership of the House himself; secondly, to stop Jenkins getting the Foreign Secretaryship; thirdly, to get Albert Booth as his own successor at Employment. He obviously thought that a score of three out of four was satisfactory.[40]

Pride and honour were thus kept intact on both wings of the party. Foot and the left had been given some reward, but the major portfolios remained in the hands of a new centre-right triumvirate led by Callaghan, Healey and Crosland. The concordat, ensuring no early resumption of factional in-fighting, had been bought at the cost of two sacrificial victims: Castle and Jenkins.

This represented, in personal terms, a profound reversal of prospects. The decision of Jenkins to go to Brussels made it unlikely that he would challenge again for the Labour leadership. Callaghan, with a ruthlessness that belied his avuncular 'Sunny Jim' image, had in effect removed Jenkins from the ranks of the senior Labour hierarchy. As Tony Benn remarked, the leadership contest had been as much of 'a death for him as Herbert Morrison's execution at the hands of Gaitskell in 1955'.[41] Crosland, by contrast, had finally made the breakthrough to the highest ranks. The humiliation of 25 March was suddenly a thing of the past. After accepting Callaghan's offer he left a telephone message drily telling his wife that he was 'fairly cheerful' about the outcome. The decision to stand in the leadership contest, far from seeming a blunder, was fully vindicated; indeed, without it, his claim on one of the three great offices of state could

197

Anthony Crosland

have been more easily ignored. There was, moreover, the prospect of further advancement to come. Callaghan told lobby correspondents that Healey and Crosland would probably switch posts in the next eighteen months; both men would be well suited to the change. Newspapers reported that for Crosland the Foreign Office was a 'waiting room for the Treasury'; ten years after being snubbed by Wilson, he might finally get the economic portfolio he had sought for so long.[42]

Speculation about the longer-term knew no bounds. At sixty-four, Callaghan's age made it unlikely that he would stay much beyond the next general election, whatever the outcome. In looking forward to a time when the Labour leadership would again be up for grabs, there was every reason to think Crosland would be a more serious contender than he had been in 1976. Advisers such as Dick Leonard underlined what he hardly needed to be told: that the future held out possibilities unthinkable only weeks before. The problem of a low profile among activists and the public would be overcome by tenure of the Foreign Office, and even more the Chancellorship. On the assumption that the party would continue to choose its leader from the centre-right, the only rival seriously in the frame was likely to be Healey, although Leonard pointed out that he would be a 'formidable competitor'. The strategy to win a future contest was clear, and needed to be acted upon without delay. Crosland, he wrote, would need to win about half of those who this time voted for Callaghan and Jenkins. Even if Foot didn't stand again, most votes of left-wing MPs would go to Benn: Crosland could only hope to pick up sufficient support to cancel out Healey's lead on the 1976 ballot. Hence the need to gain new ground among moderate backbenchers. The Callaghan supporters could not be regarded as a cohesive group like the Europhiles; the best chance here was not a display of intellectual quality, but evidence of ministerial and parliamentary competence. As for the Jenkinsites, some were already flirting with Healey and they would require renewed courting, perhaps by meeting with the 1963 Club on a regular basis. None of this could be left until another contest came up. Leonard's parting shot was that Crosland should resolve to visit the Tea Room every time he was in the House. Instead of having a drink, 'have a cup of tea instead (good for your health and your image!)'.[43]

Much of this gazing into the crystal ball was, of course, conditional on the uncertain fate of Callaghan's administration. Before another leadership contest could be contemplated there were likely to be more pressing concerns ahead. Would a government mired in economic crisis and faced with a dwindling majority be able to survive? The new Prime Minister, like his predecessor, had started by putting in place a centre-right alliance at the top; but unlike Wilson in 1963 he was faced with an alarming growth of militant sentiment among rank-and-file activists. It was not clear that the new leadership would be any more successful than the old in turning back the left-wing tide in the constituencies. Unless efforts were made to build up a stronger base away from Westminster, some commentators suggested, the writing would be on the wall for Croslandite social democracy. With the benefit of hindsight, the events of April 1976 were a catalyst in the decade-long process of Labour fragmentation: for Roy Jenkins the road from Brussels was to lead inexorably to a complete breakaway from Labour and the formation of the SDP in the early 1980s. At the time, however, things looked different. For Tony Crosland it was a moment to cherish: cast for so long in the role of useful support actor, he was at last moving centre stage. If 1967 had been on Jim Callaghan's conscience then he had more than redressed the balance. He had signalled that the future belonged not to six but to 'two crown princes – Mr Healey and Mr Crosland'.[44]

23

Foreign Secretary

In the past Tony Crosland had not enjoyed the first weeks in new ministerial posts, and the Foreign Office was no different. His understanding of international socialism gave him some basis from which to work, but he was conscious that there was much to learn. Whereas his predecessor Callaghan had shadowed foreign affairs in opposition, Crosland – in the words of one of his advisers – was 'dropped from the skies into the FO'.[1] As well as trying to think his way into the major issues of policy, there were the usual distractions of a new department, notably the need to get to know a large team of officials led by the Permanent Secretary, Sir Michael Palliser. In addition, he had to fulfil commitments to overseas visits made by Callaghan, and faced the problem of adjusting to the ethos and physical setting of the Foreign Office, with its huge and elegant rooms. Despite his promotion to the highest ranks, Crosland stuck to his habit of refusing to comment until he felt in command of the topic under discussion. Tony Benn recorded the events of Callaghan's first Cabinet as Prime Minister: 'When Foreign Affairs came up, Tony Crosland just said, "Nil". His idea of being clever is to pretend there is nothing that should be brought to the Cabinet.'[2] In June, Benn lunched with the Foreign Secretary in his office and found he was gradually warming to the task:

> Anyone working there would be quite paralysed and incapable of challenging the existing authority in any way. He had his jacket off and was in his blue-and-white striped shirt with his shoes off, his specs on his nose and a cigar. . . . He is enjoying it enormously though he says it is a bore to go abroad so much.[3]

However, tensions persisted beyond a few weeks. Some civil servants resented the minister's tendency to rely on outside advisers such as David Lipsey in preference to his reading official briefs. He in turn struggled to conceal his dislike of what he considered to be endless, time-wasting meetings and functions with foreign ambassadors. 'What's the point,' he asked his wife rhetorically on one occasion, 'when I don't know what to say to him or understand what he's saying to me?' His temper was not helped by the intrusiveness of having detectives watching over him for the first time – 'absurd waste of taxpayers' money', he complained. But the greatest problems of protocol came over the dress code expected of a Foreign Secretary. The Prime Minister was incensed when Crosland turned up in a charcoal-grey suit to greet the arrival in London of the French President, Giscard d'Estaing, while Callaghan and other dignitaries were all wearing morning dress. The Foreign Secretary remained unrepentant, and during a trip to the United States accompanying the Queen he went to great lengths to secure agreement that he could attend dinners at the White House and the British Embassy in his own preferred suit. His wife described his attitude to dress code as a mixture of ideology, self-indulgence and 'perversity', though it also owed something to a disdain for middle-class conventions arising from his early life.[4]

Difficulties between the Foreign Secretary and his officials were exacerbated by matters of substance as well as style. At previous departments, notably Education and Environment, Crosland had arrived with a clear sense of his priorities. Foreign Office officials were sympathetic to the main concerns which the minister set out, which he summarised as maintaining national security, lessening tension between east and west in Europe, reducing the risk of war elsewhere in the world, assisting with human rights and protecting British citizens abroad.[5] But there were clashes in areas where civil servants had strong views, notably on free trade and on the EC, on which some officials had 'the evangelists' faith' in contrast to Crosland's more agnostic approach.[6] What helped a gradual pulling together within the department, however, was the pressing need to tackle two issues that forced their way to the top of the agenda early in 1976. The first was the 'Cod War'.

Crosland's arrival at the Foreign Office coincided with in-creasingly frequent and acrimonious clashes between British trawlers and Icelandic gun-boats. In spite of pressure from fishing interests in his own constituency and elsewhere, Crosland backed a compromise solution worked out in agreement with EC ministers in June. There was inevitable disappointment among Grimsby fishermen, but the minister went some way towards winning a reputation for statesmanship. John Killick, Britain's permanent representative at NATO, wrote to say that the Icelanders were full of praise in private for his handling of negotiations. They did not regard him as a soft touch but rather respected his serious commitment to finding a settlement. It might be of some consolation, Killick wrote, at a time when brick-bats were being thrown from many quarters, to know of 'your high standing with your NATO colleagues'.[7]

'When I pop off', he said to the Prime Minister, 'and they cut open my heart, on it will be engraved "Fish" and "Rhodesia".'[8] During the spring of 1976 the American Secretary of State Dr Henry Kissinger launched a major new initiative in southern Africa. This inevitably drew the USA into the problem of Rhodesia, which Britain had been grappling with for more than a decade since the Rhodesian leader Ian Smith had made his unilateral declaration of independence (UDI). Kissinger decided to consult the British *en route* to visiting Africa. He hoped to be briefed at Heathrow, but was told that the Foreign Secretary, only two weeks into his job, was insisting on a dawn meeting in Grimsby. Crosland gradually de-veloped a good relationship with Kissinger, but their friendship did not get off to the best of starts. At their early morning meeting the Foreign Secretary showed more interest in securing Kissinger's help in preventing American shipyards from selling gunboats to Iceland than he did in Rhodesia. Journalists also got the impression that Grimsby's home match against Gillingham was as important as any-thing else. Crosland shared the view of his officials that Kissinger was barging into an area of policy where British knowledge was superior, and his fears were only partially allayed when the Americans stepped up the tempo. He welcomed American support for the principle of majority rule in Rhodesia, but he was less enthusiastic about Kissinger's determination to pressurise Ian Smith into making an early deal.[9]

The strains between Britain and America intensified during the autumn. The Foreign Office was convinced that any lasting settle-ment would not be possible without the endorsement of other 'front-line' states bordering Rhodesia. To Crosland's annoyance, Kissinger freely used a private discussion paper given to him as if it represented settled British policy. Crosland wrote to say that while welcoming his 'courageous' initiative, it needed to be understood that the British government had not endorsed any detailed proposals.[10] In late September the Foreign Secretary told Cabinet colleagues that Kissinger had worked out the basis for terms which Ian Smith would announce, though these had not been accepted by all the front-line presidents in Africa. Several ministers were sceptical about whether progress could be made and were reluctant to get too embroiled after Britain's repeated failures to secure a settlement. Tony Benn said it was all very well speaking of majority rule within two years, but felt Crosland could not answer his point that Britain would appear to be endorsing the Smith regime in the interim period.[11] When Smith made a broadcast the following day declaring his acceptance of 'the British plan' there was consternation that Kissinger – whether by accident or design – had gone beyond his brief in interpreting what constituted British approval. Crosland exchanged sharp words with his American counterpart, and before long ministerial doubts were proving to be justified. Smith started to backtrack on what was acceptable to whites in Rhodesia and the front-line presidents in Africa began to denounce publicly the terms on offer.

At the Labour Party's annual conference, the Foreign Secretary made a brief speech in which he tried to regain the initiative. Britain, he said, had taken the lead in convening a conference in Geneva aimed at producing a solution grounded in 'black majority rule and so in justice and equality'. In private, he remained less optimistic. In spite of Kissinger's urgings, he decided not to attend the Geneva talks at the outset; rather he held himself back in the unlikely event of progress being made.[12] The talks began in late October but after a couple of months ground to a halt. The American presidential election in November brought a change of administration which left Kissinger with only weeks to serve. Foreign Office officials were not too upset to see the back of him, believing that Crosland and his junior minister, Ted Rowlands, had a better grasp of the whole Rhodesian problem. Over the months, however, the Foreign Secretary had developed a high regard for Kissinger's dry wit and wide knowledge of international affairs, whatever their difficulties over Rhodesia. Kissinger too had come to think that if Crosland was an 'acquired taste' he was aquiring it.[13] When the American Secretary of State left office, Crosland wrote him a warm personal letter, saying that it was unusual to make a new friendship giving so much pleasure comparatively late in life, adding humour to the sometimes bleak world of foreign affairs. He also praised Kissinger's devotion to the task at hand and his conceptual grasp: 'much of what I now understand about international matters I have learnt from you.'[14]

The demands of the Foreign Office gave Crosland little time to dwell on the government's renewed economic difficulties. During the spring of 1976 Healey made vigorous efforts to persuade the financial markets of his prudence. He introduced a tight budget shortly after Callaghan took over as Prime Minister, and followed this up with a new stage in the voluntary incomes policy. But sterling remained under pressure, not helped by a bungled Treasury attempt to engineer a controlled devaluation as a means of boosting British exports. By the summer it was clear that the Chancellor wanted another package of cuts to maintain confidence in the pound. According to his wife, Crosland had his 'fenced-in look', bemoaning the fact that being away so much 'for months I've not had time to think properly about economics'.[15] In July the Cabinet reluctantly endorsed Healey's demand to raise interest rates and cut public expenditure by one billion pounds, not a huge sum in relation to total spending but unwelcome enough to many in Labour ranks who were dejected by the Chancellor's emphasis on fiscal rectitude. Crosland missed several of the meetings held to determine where the axe should fall. When he did appear he upset the Prime Minister by supporting his successor at the DOE, Peter Shore, in resisting transport cuts. Callaghan asked tartly what he might give up from the Foreign Office budget instead, and his annoyance was intensified when Crosland made further interventions on behalf of housing. As in the past, Healey benefited from a lack of unity between Cabinet dissenters. Tony Benn noted how Crosland's rearguard action on behalf of some spending areas was accompanied by 'a great attack on how many long-haired social workers there were. It was disgusting.'[16]

During his two-week August holiday in France, Crosland reflected on this latest 'relapse into total ec. orthodoxy'. It had happened, he felt, for a variety of reasons. Press backing was growing stronger for the tightening of public spending; the Cabinet was 'v. orthodox' in its thinking; and as Foreign Secretary he was 'away and muzzled'. Within the PLP, he believed the left was rudderless and unable to provide much resistance now that 'the absurd Benn–Holland–Bish strategy' – his way of describing the left's industrial policy – 'is dead as a dodo'. The price of the latest crisis, he wrote, was the 'demoralisation of decent rank and file' and a halfway return to the mood of 1968-9. It also meant the collapse of his attempt to stick to agreed priorities in hard times: 'Now no sense of direction & no priorities: only pragmatism, empiricism, safety first, £ supreme.'[17] There were strong grounds for Crosland's note of despair. In many ways Healey had got the worst of all worlds. He had alienated backbenchers, especially those he described as 'out of their tiny Chinese minds', and he had angered Cabinet colleagues who felt bounced into accepting an additional National Insurance surcharge which the Chancellor announced. Ministers resolved in future to scrutinise more carefully Treasury demands for cutbacks. Their opportunity to do so would not be long delayed for, most worrying of all, Healey had failed to restore City confidence. 'The markets wanted blood', recalled one Whitehall insider, and the July package 'didn't look like blood'.[18]

Crosland's punishing schedule as Foreign Secretary also gave him little time to contemplate the change in his own standing. His supporters were agreed that it was an important promotion. One of his few friends among Conservatives, Edward Boyle, wrote to say that the Foreign Office was still a key position in any government and that it was a delight to 'see you *at last* worthily powerful'.[19] As one of the three senior members of Callaghan's team, Crosland became the subject of greater press attention than in the past. Several lengthy profiles appeared, some of them concentrating on the character of the 'distinguished–looking man with a somewhat world-weary expression' who had been made Foreign Secretary: 'Mr Crosland is seen as a complicated man, his personality embracing a bundle of contradictions. One writer called him a fascinating blend of elitist, democrat and inverted snob. He has been described as alternately engaging and prickly.'[20]

It was also noted that Crosland's early dissenting background could still be traced in his attitude to working long hours and in his use of language. His preferred adjective of approval was 'serious' – a serious person, book or argument – whereas his disapproval was usually summed up in the term 'frivolous'. His short-term political sights, it was concluded, were still set on the Treasury, and it remained difficult to say what his chances might be in any future leadership contest.[21]

Press stories continued to appear hinting at the likelihood of Crosland and Healey swapping posts in the not too distant future.[22] This possibility had not been diminished in spite Crosland's differences with the Prime Minister, over dress code and over the

July cuts. Callaghan had long experience of Crosland as an awkward customer, but though the two rarely met socially, their working relationship was sufficiently strong to survive occasional disagreements. Crosland's closest advisers were keen to ensure that he continued to figure in the Prime Minister's mind when it came to any calculations about future ministerial changes. Soon after Crosland had taken over at the Foreign Office, David Lipsey was giving him advice on how to consolidate his political position. There would, he noted, be press opportunities of a new type – 'front page rather than page 4' – but care would have to be taken to ensure coverage was 'positive and political, requiring an active policy and a Socialist philosophy'. In the meantime, it was also important to work on trade union contacts and to have a post-mortem with key supporters from the leadership election once a pre-arranged visit to China was out of the way.[23]

Throughout the summer of 1976 a small group of MPs, including Oakes, Hardy, Grocott, Douglas-Mann and others who had voted for him in March, met to discuss how to further Crosland's interests. There was much discussion of whether Crosland should stand again for the NEC, having fallen from ninth place in 1973 to twelfth in 1975. The progress of other potential leaders was also tracked, and it was noted that Shirley Williams was becoming the standard-bearer of some former Jenkinsites.[24] Crosland's view was that there was all to play for. Unlike in the past, he had a dedicated team of backers to promote his interests, and on his summer holiday he reflected that with Roy 'out' and himself occupying one of the major offices, the test would come in the next two years.[25] An unexpected test for the Labour administration as a whole came sooner than he expected, however; in late 1976 ministers became embroiled in what was soon being called 'the IMF crisis'.

24

The IMF Crisis

Crosland returned to work in September 1976, refreshed after holidaying alone in France over the summer. For a short while, the political situation appeared to be settling down. David Lipsey told him that with the backing of union leaders, the party had accepted the latest round of cuts surprisingly well, and public opinion had not turned against the government as much as had been feared.[1] The Foreign Secretary decided it was time to mend some fences. After the disagreements over the July measures, he 'kissed and made up' with the Prime Minister, and was pleased to find that Callaghan accepted his advice to bring Roy Hattersley into the Cabinet as part of an autumn reshuffle. In addition, Crosland enjoyed an amicable lunch with Roy Jenkins. With their period of intense rivalry behind them, the mood was more relaxed than for some years past and they agreed it would be good to meet more socially.[2] The Foreign Secretary also tried to look on the bright side in a lecture he gave on the theme of 'Equality in Hard Times'. He acknowledged that economic difficulties imposed limitations on any movement towards a more equal society, but 'we can and must continue to make significant progress'. To his concern for an improved sense of priorities in spending he added the case for Labour introducing inexpensive but important reforms: industrial democracy; moves to outlaw racial and sexual inequality; a fairer tax system; devolution in order to disperse political power; and a renewed commitment to internationalism. Economic problems should on no account force Britain into 'brooding isolationism. After all, we are still one of the richest nations . . . on earth.'[3]

But in the autumn of 1976 'brooding isolationism' came closer as sterling continued its relentless slide. In an atmosphere of mounting crisis, with Britain's currency reserves ebbing away in frantic efforts to prop up the pound, the Chancellor decided that Britain must apply to the International Monetary Fund (IMF) for assistance. This, he believed, was the only viable means of repaying a six-month standby loan agreed with world banks in the summer. Delegates to Labour's annual conference endorsed a programme which included calls for extending welfare benefits, and were in no mood to listen to the Chancellor's tough words on the need for realism. Tony Benn called Healey's speech 'vulgar and abusive', and he was not alone in fearing that an IMF loan would be conditional upon further dis-inflation.[4] In October the economic crisis threatened to turn into a full-blown political crisis. Callaghan and Healey were at odds over the raising of interest rates to a record high, and press leaks appeared of growing tension between the two senior figures in the govern-ment. The Prime Minister had backed the Chancellor at Labour's conference, but he was fearful of the consequences of yet more cuts. Healey recollected that Callaghan was 'badly bruised' by the recep-tion he received from Labour delegates and was uncertain whether it was economically right or politically possible to go for greater cuts, which unlike any of the periodic reductions since 1964 looked set to make serious inroads into public expenditure as a proportion of GDP.[5] Crosland's view was that enough medicine had been administered in July for the economy to make a recovery, given time. He told the journalist John Cole that he was against the idea of further 'slashing cuts' to satisfy the financial markets, but he could see the logic of going just far enough to stabilise the position of sterling.[6]

During November, with the IMF team of negotiators arriving in London to lay down terms for a loan, Callaghan resolved upon his strategy. He would try to get the best possible terms for the loan, to prepare the country for further hardships ahead, and to keep the party together and so avoid resignations that might lead to the break-up of the government. He was determined to eliminate what his policy advisers called 'the suicidal extremism of the Treasury and the protectionist extremism of Mr Benn'.[7] On 18 November he told Cabinet colleagues that the administration was entering a critical stage of its life. The Chancellor, he said, would accept no agreement with the IMF until securing Cabinet approval, and ministers would be allowed to bring forward any proposals of their own. Callaghan's view was that he could best maintain unity by allowing extensive discussion; no one would be able to claim that all avenues had not been explored.[8] The same evening Crosland attended a private meeting called by the Prime Minister, with the Chancellor in attendance. Also present was Edmund Dell, the Trade Secretary, who said the purpose was to ascertain whether there could be any meeting of minds among the 'main contenders'. Crosland argued that there was no economic case for further cuts, and that everything was in place for recovery. Dell replied that if this were true – which could not be known at the time – the scepticism of the markets could undermine and possibly bring down the government before Labour reaped any rewards.[9] The scene was set for an exhaustive series of Cabinet meetings that would resolve the issue.

By Monday 22 November press leaks were rife about the IMF seeking to impose deflationary measures on the government, and groups of ministers were hastily arranging meetings to decide on tactics. Resistance to the Chancellor, as in the summer, was likely from several sources. Peter Shore was an advocate of selective import controls, while others on the left led by Tony Benn were determined to press their 'alternative economic strategy' of greater protectionism and planning. In addition there were several 'social democratic' or centre-right dissenters, led by Crosland. When these met on the evening of 22 November, it became apparent that there were differing motives among those present. Shirley Williams and David Ennals were keen to defend their departmental budgets at Education and Social Services, whereas Harold Lever and Roy Hattersley were more concerned that the whole exercise was unnecessarily de-flationary. The Foreign Secretary was unable to get to the meeting, preoccupied as he had been throughout October with the Rhodesian question, but he was pessimistic about winning many concessions. He told his wife that Callaghan was likely to inform Labour MPs they could either have the cuts or Mrs Thatcher. He bemoaned what he called 'the most right-wing Labour Government we've had for years'. More cutbacks, he said, would make 'pointless' all he had done on housing and transport, and all Barbara Castle and others had achieved for the social services. 'There must be a better alter-native,' he added, resolving to work something out.[10]

The following day Healey outlined the initial bargaining position of the IMF to the Cabinet: in return for a $3.9 billion loan, the government had to cut some £3 billion from the Public Sector Borrowing Requirement (PSBR) during 1977-8, sell off £500 million of BP shares and ensure strict control of the money supply. Crosland was called next to put the case for rejecting the terms. He began by outlining why he felt there was no economic case for the IMF package. Not only were Treasury forecasts for the PSBR unreliable, but deep cuts would add to unemployment, meaning lower tax revenue and an increase to the borrowing requirement. The only serious argument for the cuts was the need to restore international confidence. If this was the case, Crosland continued, the government's best course was to look for cosmetic cuts of one billion pounds, half from the sale of shares, warning the IMF that further demands would be met by the winding down of defence commitments and the introduction of a siege economy. The key was for the government to keep its nerve: 'we must stop paying "Danegeld"'. The Foreign Secretary was followed by a succession of speakers equally alarmed by the IMF terms. Peter Shore commented to the effect that 'we're being asked to bite the bullet but in fact we'll blow our political brains out'.[11] The only strong support for the Chancellor came from Dell and Reg Prentice who, in the eyes of anti–deflationists, took a 'Healier-than-thou attitude to cuts'.[12] Crosland's delight was compounded when the Prime Minister reserved his position rather than weighing in behind Healey, as he had implied the previous day. The first round had gone to the Cabinet dissidents.

The Chancellor still had reason to think he would ultimately prevail. His opponents had not put the flesh on the bones of any realistic alternative, and showed little inclination to combine their efforts. On Wednesday 24 November Tony Benn met with left-wing critics and it was agreed to 'rally round' Crosland's position of securing cosmetic cuts; but soundings amongst advisers suggested the left did not want to form any firm alliance, still hoping to push their own 'alternative strategy'.[13] The next day the Chancellor was sub-dued in repeating his case. Crosland spent some time urging an import deposits scheme he had worked on with Roy Hattersley. The scheme was designed as a 'shrewd way of turning the flank of the Treasury', aiming at reducing the PSBR while appealing to both sets of Cabinet critics.[14] Once again no firm decisions were taken. It was agreed that time should be spent listening to the detailed proposals of Benn and Shore, but the Cabinet was not due to meet until the following Wednesday, as Callaghan and Crosland had to attend a European Council meeting in The Hague. In the interim, the Prime Minister finally decided to swing his weight behind the Chancellor. Flying home from the Hague, Callaghan said other European leaders would not offer the type of unconditional assistance he had been pressing for and that he would now make clear his support for Healey. He believed negotiations had produced the lowest cuts package the IMF would accept – almost half the level originally demanded – while still maintaining credibility in the markets; it was time to 'settle'.[15]

By the time the Cabinet reconvened on 1 December the tide was turning. Neither Shore nor Benn made much headway in outlining their preferred solutions. Benn in particular received a mauling from the Chancellor; he admitted in his diary that he had been 'teased and hounded'. Several ministers who had yet to declare said they would back the wishes of the Prime Minister, and the Defence Secretary, Roy Mason, praised Healey for his courage and turned on the critics. The nation could not survive as an isolated siege economy along the lines Benn was suggesting, while Shore and Crosland, he said, were 'looking for a painless way out'.[16] That evening Crosland told his wife that if it became known that Jim had been beaten in Cabinet there would be 'murder'; the Prime Minister was the government's strongest asset. As a result, he said he would probably concede when ministers met again next morning. Support among the 'social democratic' dissenters was in any case ebbing away. Harold Lever had voiced concern that the import deposits scheme was too protectionist for his liking; Shirley Williams and David Ennals were confident of saving some of their departmental plans. Callaghan had asked Crosland to keep his intention to back Healey confidential, but the Foreign Secretary did warn his sole remaining supporter Roy Hattersley in order to persuade him to fall into line; it was, he said, 'no time for heroics'. Before going home for the night, Crosland went to the Prime Minister's room at the House, confirming his intention to give his reluctant support.[17]

The Cabinet meeting of Thursday 2 December thus marked the point at which the IMF terms were accepted in principle. Healey began by repeating that unless the PSBR was cut the IMF would not offer a loan and Britain would be unable to borrow abroad. The Cabinet must accept the modified terms: cuts of £1 billion for 1977–8 and £1.5 bn. for 1978–9. Callaghan spoke up to support the Chancellor, offering to consider further the import deposits scheme but insisting that rejection of the package could lead to the break-up of the government. Crosland intervened to say that in his view the Prime Minister's statement fundamentally changed the situation:

> He thought it was wrong economically and socially, destructive of what he had believed in all his life. . . . 'But the new factor is your view,

Prime Minister. What would be the consequence of rejecting the Prime Minister? The unity of the Party depends upon sustaining the Prime Minister and the effect on sterling of rejecting the Prime Minister would be to destroy our capacity. Therefore I support the Prime Minister and the Chancellor'.[18]

Roy Hattersley followed suit, though others continued to protest. Peter Shore attacked Crosland for backing something he openly said was wrong, and Tony Benn repeated his view – strongly rebutted by Callaghan – that this looked like a re-run of 1931: 'It will be the death warrant of the Labour Government if we accept this.' The meeting ended in confusion over what exactly had been agreed, but the die had been cast. The best Benn and Foot could do was to secure approval that the Cabinet minutes would say that a 'majority agrees', not that the Cabinet 'noted with approval' the Chancellor's policy.[19]

On 7 December ministers started the process of determining where to make the required cuts. As discussions dragged on over the next few days, Callaghan lost his temper and said he would take his own package to the Commons; dissenting ministers should resign if they must. Crosland was depressed that the Treasury had got even half the cuts originally demanded, and to the dismay of his own officials he took the line that if hard choices were unavoidable cuts should be made in defence rather than housing. In the event reductions were widely shared though welfare benefits were protected.[20] On 14 December Healey had a rough ride when he requested approval for the government's 'Letter of Intent' to the IMF. In response to a question from Crosland, Callaghan confirmed that import deposits were ruled out altogether. In what Joel Barnett called a 'long and unhappy discussion', the Chancellor's opponents were determined to make one last assault upon his handling of policy.[21] The following day there was worse to come. In the House of Commons Labour MPs listened in sullen silence as Healey announced the IMF terms. At a low ebb, the Chancellor was loudly jeered by the opposition and vulnerable to an assault from his Tory shadow; fortunately, Geoffrey Howe let him off the hook. Even so, it was impossible to conceal the scale of the humiliation. Tony Benn wrote in his diary on 16 December ('the first time Crosland had admitted there were foreign affairs for a long time') that press reaction was overwhelmingly hostile to the idea of the nation being 'in hock' to foreign financiers, with tabloid headlines such as 'Britain's Shame'.[22]

Crosland's behaviour during the IMF crisis has been criticised from two main perspectives, the first that of the Labour left. In the days that followed the Chancellor's announcement, left-wing MPs were scornful of talk that Crosland had been leading opposition in the Cabinet. When it came to the crunch, one said, 'he collapsed like a pack of cards'.[23] The Foreign Secretary was convinced, however, that if he had not yielded at the decisive moment the consequences would have been disastrous. He had tried to create a unifying position for all Cabinet dissidents, but Roy Hattersley recalled that approaches by his own adviser, David Hill, to the left were rejected 'point blank. The Bennites could see no advantages in making common cause with the Croslandites'.[24] Resignations were rumoured at various points, but Crosland like his colleagues on the left knew this would be immensely destabilising. One minister told a reporter early in December: 'Every one of us knew that the Government would be destroyed if anyone pushed his disagreement to the point of resignation.'[25] Crosland may therefore, as Peter Shore said, have endorsed something with which he disagreed, but it was in the belief that to cause the defeat of the Prime Minister after he had declared his hand would lead to chaos on the currency markets and the break-up of the government in circumstances that would almost certainly have brought the Conservatives to power. In his memoirs Callaghan refers to his gratitude and relief at hearing of Crosland's switch, saying it meant he could proceed 'without the necessity of delivering an ultimatum to the Cabinet, for although I was not prepared to continue if the Cabinet had failed to back me, no one except Tony Crosland knew this'.[26]

The other strand of opinion critical of the Foreign Secretary comes from Healey's staunchest ally in 1976, Edmund Dell. In his later writings on the IMF crisis, Dell contrasts the courage and fortitude of the Chancellor with Crosland's lack of realism. Britain had a debt, he claims, which could not be discharged without IMF assistance. To complain about faulty Treasury forecasts was irrelevant, since Crosland could not know if his own forecasts for the PSBR were any better; even if all was in place for economic recovery, everything could be undone by 'market disbelief'. According to Dell, Crosland tried to claim the intellectual high ground by leaking his case to sympathetic journalists, but his 'exercise in self-deception' was exposed when he capitulated in the 'pantomime' performance on 2 December. Britain had no choice but to accept the IMF loan and, providing Callaghan gave a firm lead, the government was unlikely to fall. 'In short', Dell concludes, 'the argument was for overkill. If it proved to be overkill, we could always add back.'[27] Some of Dell's case has been conceded by Crosland supporters. Roy Hattersley later acknowledged that the crisis was essentially about the mysterious concept 'international confidence', but agreed it was no less real for that. On the other hand, Hattersley shared Crosland's view that it was not easy to 'add back' political support once jeopardised; the experience of 1968-9 had demonstrated this.[28]

Other colleagues were more impressed by the stand Crosland took. Both the Prime Minister and the Chancellor may have been exasperated by Crosland at times, but they recognised him as a 'formidable' critic, one whose attitude was consistent with a determination to resist Treasury orthodoxy that had been evident throughout the previous decade.[29] Healey was more tolerant than Dell in part because – as his memoirs later stated – he too had doubts about some of the advice he was receiving from Treasury officials, based upon figures which did indeed prove to be wrong. It was bad enough that the PSBR in 1976-7 turned out to be £8.5 billion, rather than the £10.5 billion Treasury forecast upon which the Cabinet was obliged to act. What was worse, Healey explained, was the probability that 'Treasury officials deliberately overstated public spending in order to put pressure on governments which were reluctant to cut it'.[30] In the view of Roy Hattersley, Crosland fought a 'scintillating' intellectual case, especially in view of the demands of the Foreign Office. He could call on little assistance in his efforts to rebut the combined weight of the Chancellor, the Trade Secretary and the whole Treasury apparatus. He was right to question the 'absurdly variable' PSBR and right to concede when he did to Callaghan, recognising that to fight a Prime Minister who backed his Chancellor was a recipe for political catastrophe. Crosland had not only fought 'a dashing rearguard action'; he also achieved some victories whenever the battle turned into 'hand to hand combat'.[31]

How significant were any such victories? Crosland's critics on both the left and right of the party believe that he was decisively defeated. One left-winger called his change of course in Cabinet 'the day Croslandism died. He said to me: "This is nonsense, but we must do it." He knew it meant the abandonment of his position as a revisionist theorist. . . . It was tormenting for him. I watched him, torturing himself.'[32] In response to Susan Crosland's assertion that the outcome was a draw between the Treasury and the Foreign Secretary, Edmund Dell likens this to a cricketer claiming he was not out because two stumps remained after his middle one had been removed. 'The truth was that he had been out-argued by Healey and demolished by the facts.'[33] Colleagues such as Shirley Williams believe this ignores the hard politics of the struggle and underrates what Crosland did achieve. Cabinet dissenters, she notes, helped to produce a final outcome significantly different from what was originally demanded; it was unusual for the IMF to be pushed so far in modifying its terms, and Crosland's resistance helped to make this possible.[34]

He was of course dismayed to see further cutbacks, but in many respects the 1976 crisis was simply a re-run of developments he'd had no option but to accept in the late 1960s and over the previous eighteen months. In his private notebook, Crosland wrote at the end of the year that almost everything he said about the July package could be rewritten about the December cuts. There were a few differences, notably Healey being given a harder time in Cabinet, but otherwise there was the same sense of 'depressing inevitability' and – fortunately – the same relatively easy ride with the party and the unions. 'Surely now so much deflation . . . & wage restraint that *must* work.'[35]

The IMF medicine did indeed work rapidly. Those who regard the crisis as the 'last nail in the coffin of Croslandism' generally depict the events of 1976 as a great watershed in British politics: the moment when the post-war welfare state finally hit the buffers, signalling the collapse of old-style Labourism.[36] However, this arguably succumbs to retrospective judgements coloured by Labour's collapse after the 'winter of discontent' in 1979. The government did pay a high political price for the IMF cuts, falling futher behind in the polls and losing its overall majority in the Commons after two by-election defeats in quick succession. Yet Callaghan averted a worst-case scenario. His battered administration remained united and in office; there had been no 1931-style party split or attack on social benefits; and the calming of the financial markets and the ending of world recession provided the basis for economic recovery in 1977. Interest rates fell, sterling recovered and Healey never had to draw on more than half the available loan. Earlier than anticipated he was celebrating 'Sod off Day' – the moment when Britain became free of IMF control.[37] The most detailed assessment of the IMF crisis concludes that while it did help to legitimise post-1979 Thatcherite monetarism it did not lead to any major change of philosophy in Labour ranks. Healey sought to restore many of the cuts when it seemed safe to do so and allowed the PSBR to rise above the level that generated such alarm in 1976. 'Apart from the continued issue of monetary targets (which were rarely hit),' note Kathy Burk and Alec Cairncross, 'economic policy in the last years of the Labour government differed little from what it had been before the arrival of the IMF'.[38]

Croslandism thus survived the IMF crisis, more battered than at any stage in recent years but at least able to fight another day. Indeed outside the Cabinet, within the PLP and among press commentators, Crosland's reputation at the time was less damaged than that of his two most senior colleagues. The Prime Minister received credit for holding the government and party together, just as Wilson had over Europe, but for several months he had to take responsibility for Labour's steep decline in popularity. Crosland's change of course on 2 December may have angered the Labour left, but this was nothing compared with the charges of betrayal laid at the door of the Chancellor. Healey's longer-term prospects of becoming party leader had been severely dented by the tone of his unrelenting criticism of left-wing MPs, many of whom accused him of happily doing the dirty work of the Treasury and the IMF. By contrast, Crosland was credited in some quarters with at least attempting a damage limitation exercise. 'His standing in Cabinet', wrote the Observer, 'has been improved by his part in the IMF debate.'[39] It continued to be assumed that Crosland and Healey would switch posts, possibly after the next budget but no later than the autumn of 1977. A weary Denis Healey told the TUC they would not have to argue with him for much longer. The Chancellor was keen to move to the Foreign Office as soon as economic circumstances allowed, while the Foreign Secretary still hoped it was possible to 'do better' at the Treasury, despite inevitable constraints in the aftermath of the IMF episode.[40] Crosland's most long-standing political ambition appeared tantalisingly close.

25

The Final Weeks, 1976-7

As the dust settled on the IMF crisis, Crosland returned with some relief to his departmental concerns at the Foreign Office. In December 1976 he told his wife that he was getting to grips with the job. He laughed at himself for saying he was not interested in foreign policy: 'It was a silly, childish remark for me to make.'[1] In contrast to his early months, he felt confident in facing the major issues, and he began to make preparations for Britain's presidency of the EC during the first half of 1977. In a detailed article published in *Socialist Commentary* he set out his thinking on Europe. Having been one of the more sceptical pro-Marketeers, he said, he was not suffering the same disillusionment as others over the development of the community. He also claimed that his earlier stance had been vindicated: economic arguments about British membership were proving 'inaccurate or irrelevant', whereas the political case for staying in remained compelling.[2] Foreign Office officials who preferred a stronger pro-European line realised that Crosland's firm style of chairmanship was at least likely to prevent discussion at Brussels dragging on interminably without agreement. Civil servants were also of the view that with Kissinger out of the way Crosland would be able to make progress in Rhodesia, and work began on a fresh British initiative to be launched in the new year. David Lipsey told Crosland with satisfaction that relations between the Foreign Office and the party are 'by all accounts, far better than they were in the PM's day'.[3]

For the first time the Croslands spent Christmas at their country home in Oxfordshire. The Foreign Secretary's holiday reading included looking at a draft of the biography of Hugh Gaitskell which his friend Philip Williams had been working on for several years. In spite of the recent trauma of the IMF episode, Crosland was in a positive frame of mind. In part this was due to his enjoyment of holiday seclusion. 'Think I like Adderbury best of all in winter' he said to Susan. 'Gives an even greater sense of our being alone together.' He was also looking forward to the new year, not only to the challenges ahead at the Foreign Office but also to the probability that he would soon become Chancellor. He told his wife: 'it would be marvellous to get Rhodesia settled before I go to the Treasury.' He agreed that six months travelling backwards and forwards to Brussels would be a 'bore', but he thought Susan would enjoy accompanying him on a trip to Washington to meet the new American President, Jimmy Carter. 'He lit a cheroot. "*Phyfft, phyftt.* Hope Jim doesn't change his mind and swop Denis and me before August. Now that I'm in my stride I've rather taken to this job",' wrote Susan.[4] Crosland's upbeat mood continued into January when he made a confident TV appearance on the BBC *Panorama* programme, ranging across numerous aspects of foreign policy including Europe, Rhodesia and human rights. When questioned by David Dimbleby about whether he would welcome a move to the Treasury, he gave a suitably diplomatic answer: 'No, I am enjoying myself. I am enjoying myself.'[5]

He was 'enjoying himself' despite a gruelling schedule which included regular engagements in his constituency, all-night sittings of parliament and attendance at Cabinet meetings, as well as the demands of his office. Early in February some welcome respite came with a weekend spent at Dorneywood, the Foreign Secretary's official residence. The red boxes on Rhodesia were an inevitable accompaniment, but there was also time for relaxation with guests such as Roy Hattersley. Strolling through the winter parkland wearing his red-leather carpet slippers, Crosland talked with Hattersley about the need for a new book on the theme of 'Socialism in a Cold Climate'. Hattersley, he chided, would not be up to writing it, and he himself was too busy, but he remained hopeful that someone would come forward to emulate *The Future of Socialism* by adapting revisionism to the new economic circumstances of the mid-1970s.[6] It was essential, he argued, to get across the point that the Labour left were not the only theorists: 'The Centre must remember and keep reminding people that we are ideologists too.' Crosland then attempted a simple definition of socialism. 'Socialism', the Foreign Secretary said, 'is about the pursuit of equality and the protection of freedom – in the knowledge that until we are truly equal we will not be truly free.'[7]

The week after the Dorneywood visit was one of Crosland's busiest since going to the Foreign Office. After a morning meeting on Monday 7 February he boarded an RAF plane bound for Brussels, where he was due to chair a meeting of the Council of Ministers; this was his eleventh trip abroad in three months. A marathon session of EC ministers began at 10 a.m. on Tuesday morning and continued until 5 a.m. the following morning, with Crosland insistent on staying put until an agreement had been reached on the fishing industry. After two hours sleep on Wednesday morning he returned to Downing Street for a Cabinet committee which lasted until lunchtime. In the evening he addressed a PLP group on Rhodesia and made a speech at a farewell dinner arranged for the departing American ambassador to Britain. On Thursday a morning Cabinet session was followed by lunch with the Governor of the Bank of England, an afternoon spent answering letters from constituents, and evening meetings on foreign affairs, followed by three votes in the House. Friday 11 February saw several morning engagements, including meeting new ambassadors; lunch with Dick Leonard – who was helping him work on a new paper on Rhodesia; and an afternoon trip to Oxford. Here he visited Philip Williams, in hospital recovering from a stroke, before going on to address the Oxford Democratic Labour Club at St John's College. With gin and tonic in hand and cigar in mouth, his theme was the danger of the left taking over the Labour Party and how it could be resisted.[8]

It was fitting that this talk – on an issue which had preoccupied him over the years and in the place where his political ambitions had taken shape nearly forty years earlier – should be Crosland's last public address. Leaving Oxford, Crosland went to his country home where he and wife were celebrating their thirteenth wedding anniversary. On Saturday he spent more time working on Rhodesia. The following day, Sunday 13 February, he returned from buying newspapers. 'Adderbury is an absolutely ravishing village,' he said. 'This is an "ultimate" weekend.' But as he settled down to more work on the Rhodesian papers, he suddenly said, 'Something has happened . . . I can't feel my right side.' The severity of what had happened was not immediately clear. With Crosland's speech deteriorating, a local GP arrived to say he thought it was a twenty-four hour spasm which should allow a full recovery. A consultant was then called and advised that the Foreign Secretary would be more comfortable in the Radcliffe Infirmary where he could be fully checked. Susan Crosland was soon being told that it was not a short-lived spasm but a more severe stroke that might leave him permanently paralysed on one side. By 10 o'clock on Sunday evening he was entering a comatose state, and the following day the hospital issued a bulletin stating that Crosland was dangerously ill. Susan asked David Lipsey to tell the children that he was not going to recover.[9]

Over the following days and nights Susan Crosland remained at the Radcliffe Infirmary. She was accompanied by Ellen–Craig while her eldest daughter – married as Mrs Sheila Conroy – eventually arrived from overseas with her husband and baby. Much of the time 'the room was still, just the two of us'.[10] Away from the hospital, politicians came to terms with the news. The Prime Minister in a telephone conversation praised Mrs Crosland for her bravery, and David Owen – a junior minister at the Foreign Office – spoke of his shock at hearing the news. 'His lifestyle, the long hours, good food, little exercise, alcohol and cigars could not have helped. It was hard to accept that a life so full should now be ebbing away.'[11] This explanation of the stroke was to be frequently repeated in the weeks ahead; few made the point that Crosland's father had been struck down in a similar way at a comparable age. After six nights and five days at the hospital, Crosland died early on the morning of Saturday 19 February, aged 58, with his wife and two stepdaughters at his side. Roy Jenkins, whose relationship with his old friend had continued to improve in the last few months, was in Rome:

> I awoke about 6.30, having had a vivid dream about Tony being present and his saying in an absolutely unmistakable, clear, rather calm voice, 'No, I am perfectly all right. I am going to die, but I'm perfectly all right.' Then, at about 8 o'clock we had a telephone call from the BBC saying that he had died that morning . . . at almost exactly the same moment that I awoke from my dream about him.[12]

Epilogue

The Prime Minister led the tributes to his Foreign Secretary in the House of Commons on Monday 21 February 1977. In a packed chamber, Callaghan made a moving speech, describing Crosland as 'gifted beyond the reach of many of us', a man who combined 'physical courage, mental toughness and great personal charm'. William Whitelaw followed for the Conservatives and the Liberal leader, David Steel, lamented that public life had been deprived of a figure of 'exceptional quality'.[1] The sense of loss was obvious even among those in Labour ranks with whom Crosland had not always been on the best of terms. After the intense disagreements over Europe at the beginning of the decade, friendships with Jenkinsites such as David Owen were gradually being restored. With Denis Healey deeply involved in preparing his next budget, and regarded by Callaghan as essential at the Treasury to provide continuity, it was Owen who was chosen to replace Crosland at the Foreign Office. The House was deeply moved, Owen recalled, by the manner of Crosland's death, and like many others he was greatly saddened by the loss of someone so 'intellectually honest and fundamentally decent'.[2] On the Labour left, Tony Benn wrote affectionately in his diary that under 'that gruff and arrogant exterior he really had a heart of gold'. In spite of their strong political differences, especially since 1970, Benn agreed that Crosland did have a 'profound influence' as the 'high priest of revisionism or social democracy in the Labour Party for a generation'.[3]

Tony Benn also noted that for a couple of days the newspapers were packed with obituaries of Crosland, most of which went into 'an emotional spasm about him'. The tone adopted by some journalists came as no surprise. The verdict of Crosland's friend Alan Watkins was that he had been the outstanding socialist theoretician since the Second World War; a successful minister; an assiduous constituency MP; and beneath his brusque exterior a kind and considerate man.[4] Dick Leonard, as a former PPS of Crosland's, wrote of his place being assured among 'the upper – if not the top – ranks of Labour politicians', and his local Labour party issued a statement saying that the Foreign Secretary and his wife had been 'true friends' of Grimsby; his was an 'incalculable loss' to the town and to the Labour movement.[5] There were also warm tributes from more unexpected sources, with several Conservative-supporting newspapers praising Crosland's moderation and good sense. The *Daily Mail* could not resist suggesting that time was running out for the government. Labour since 1974 had already lost the services of Harold Wilson, Roy Jenkins and Barbara Castle. In the aftermath of Crosland's death, Callaghan's team looked 'tired and no longer flushed with talent'.[6] David Watt in the *Financial Times* wrote of the combination of the 'personal tragedy' and the 'major public calamity'. It was not only poignant to see a figure of vitality robbed of the Exchequer prize he most wanted. Crosland's death would also accelerate the process of Labour becoming a party 'without a doctrine . . . It is like the first frost of winter'.[7]

On a wintry day in early March Mrs Crosland scattered her husband's ashes in the Humber off Grimsby, the small boat battling against atrocious conditions, and three days later a memorial service was held at Westminster Abbey. Tony Benn described it as a tremendous event, with the Abbey packed. Cabinet members were in the choir stalls on one side; other ministers and ambassadors opposite. There were three former Prime Ministers in attendance, and some of the dignitaries were surprised to find that prominent seats had been reserved for a coachload of party workers from Grimsby.[8] Dick Leonard read a lesson which included passages from *The Future of Socialism* and Jack Donaldson referred to some of Crosland's personal qualities: his genuine socialist temperament and – in his final years especially since his marriage to Susan – his 'capacity to love'.[9] The esteem in which Crosland was held by his constituents was underlined when the writ was subsequently moved for the Grimsby by-election. With the government deeply unpopular following the IMF crisis, a massive Labour majority of 23,000 was overturned at Ashfield on the same day. In Grimsby, where the Labour majority was less than 7,000, Crosland's replacement as Labour candidate, Austin Mitchell, clung on by the margin of 520 votes. Political pundits were baffled; constituency workers in Grimsby had no doubt that it was the memory of Crosland which secured the victory.[10]

The outpourings of respect and affection for Crosland in the weeks after his death have led some to claim that he was one of the 'lost leaders' of post-war politics. Various admirers compared him with Iain Macleod: a figure who had reached the senior ranks and whose loss at a relatively young age was a vital blow to his party. If he had lived long enough to go the Treasury, it has been claimed, Crosland's leadership potential would have been further enhanced. His profile would have been raised by having held two great offices of state, and he would have been able to develop his whole 'political personality', so underlining his credibility as a possible successor to Callaghan.[11] Crosland's chances might also have been helped by his conscious appeal to mainstream party opinion and by the dearth of alternative candidates on the centre-right. Roy Jenkins was no longer in the race and Denis Healey had antagonised many MPs outside the ranks of the left, as became clear when he failed to defeat Michael Foot in the leadership contest that followed Callaghan's resignation in 1980. 'Since Healey got within ten votes of defeating Foot for the leadership,' Noel Annan has argued, 'Crosland would have won it.'[12] This view is shared by Jenkins and David Owen, the latter believing it would have had profound consequences for politics in the 1980s. With the backing of his long-time friend Callaghan, Owen claims, Crosland could have secured the leadership and in so doing forestalled the breakaway of backbenchers who left Labour to form the SDP.[13]

Others, however, doubt whether he can be described as a lost leader. 'He would have been no good at it,' wrote his old friend Woodrow Wyatt: 'He lacked the wiles of Harold Wilson and had insufficient robustness.'[14] Some of his supporters admit that if Crosland did want to be leader he had a strange way of going about it, refusing to accept the conventional niceties of political behaviour. Aside from being 'famously rude and difficult', he had no real power base in the Labour Party because, as Noel Annan remarked, he could not be bothered to build one. His contacts with trade unions were minimal and he had only a small band of dedicated followers in the PLP. He never willingly embraced the medium of television, feeling that his accent was a handicap, and his support in the newspaper press was limited, in part due to his reluctance to reduce the subtlety of his position to the left–right simplicities favoured by headline writers. Critics add that Crosland did not have some of the essential attributes of a leader. He was not a particularly strong orator, making it difficult for him to capture the hearts and minds of the party faithful; and he lacked the 'coarseness' or 'hard edge' of a type that Gaitskell, Wilson and Callaghan all possessed.[15] A few of the obituary notices of Crosland picked up on these themes, claiming that the 'odour of the armchair strategist' always clung to him and that he had not a 'ghost's chance' of becoming leader.[16]

The question of whether Crosland could have led the Labour Party remains, of course, impossible to answer; we can only guess how he might have fared in the 1980 contest against Foot and Healey. The outcome of that leadership struggle did underline the point that luck and timing often play a critical role in determining who comes out on top. Jim Callaghan, who greatly benefited from the timing of Wilson's decision to retire in 1976, later gave a guarded judgement on whether Crosland might have been his successor. He had long since come to the conclusion, he said, that 'nothing can be ruled out in politics'.[17] There is more agreement with the view that Crosland was, if not a 'lost leader', then a 'lost Chancellor'. Callaghan had advised that Crosland should go to the Exchequer in 1967 because he would have brought a 'dash of imagination' to the post. His supporters believe he would have made an excellent Chancellor, bringing a radicalism, lack of reverence for orthodoxy and sense of direction that had not been seen since the days of his early mentor, Hugh Dalton.[18] But asking 'What if?' is to play 'virtual history'. Crosland's career must be judged against what happened in his lifetime not on the basis of what might have been. The flattering tributes paid in the immediate aftermath of his death came to be challenged in time by more sober assessments and the questioning of Crosland's significance and legacy started.

By the late 1970s the revisionist tradition which Crosland epitomised was under fierce assault from both ends of the political spectrum. On behalf of the Labour left, which continued to gain ground among party activists, the writer Anthony Arblaster articulated the view that Crosland had been too complacent about the possibility of securing continuous growth. The disappointment of his expectations was the product of the 'wrongness of his analysis', notably his inability to recognise the continuing resilience of capitalism and the consequent need to take control of the economy via public ownership. 'His survivors do not merely have no alternative strategy to offer,' concluded Arblaster: 'They show little sign of realising that the strategy which he consistently advocated has already failed.'[19] Crosland's death also encouraged the political right in their efforts to seize the intellectual high ground. Colin Welch, deputy editor of the *Daily Telegraph*, launched a trenchant critique during the 'winter of discontent' in which he defended inequality and attacked the assumption that higher spending led to better public services. There was, Welch lamented, an enormous contrast between Crosland's 1956 vision of open-air cafés and the 'shabby, decaying slum, the haunted house, in which we have been condemned . . . by his egalitarian fervour to live. All around us we see frustration, failure, hopelessness.'[20]

After Labour's decisive defeat at the 1979 election, another line of attack was opened up: from within the revisionist tradition itself, which had been gravely weakened by the death of Crosland. David Marquand, who left British politics to follow Roy Jenkins to Brussels, argued that the basis of Crosland's political approach – economic growth, high spending and redistribution – had collapsed slowly during the course of the 1970s. Yet instead of rethinking its assumptions the Labour Party 'clung to them with increasing desperation the more obviously they needed revision'. Marquand was among those who joined Jenkins and other disillusioned moderates to form the SDP, convinced that Labour under Michael Foot no longer provided a vehicle for sensible social change. As part of the justification for creating a new centre force in British politics, dedicated to 'breaking the mould' of the two-party system, Marquand argued that by the mid-1970s Croslandism had exhausted itself. According to Marquand, Crosland must have known in his heart of hearts by the time of the IMF crisis that the 'revisionist game was up'. Croslandite reform, he reflected, had been too much a top-down process, failing to see that any vision of a fairer society could be realised only by 'communitarian ties', not by policies 'handed out from on high to a grateful society, like chocolate bars at a children's party'.[21]

These various charges were never systematically countered by Crosland's devotees. David Lipsey wrote in *The Socialist Agenda*, a collection of essays published in 1981, that it was not his intention to 'attempt any point by point rebuttal' of the various critics. Most of the essays in the book were devoted to showing how revisionism might be adapted to the testing circumstances of the early 1980s. 'May not', Lipsey asked, 'the humane and flexible vision of the democratic socialists . . . rise again from the ashes as the guide by which we conduct our affairs?'[22] This was not only unlikely at a time when Labour was veering to the left; it also conceded the point, by implication, that Crosland had remained stubbornly resistant to rethinking his own position, insisting to the end that the difficulties of successive Labour governments were due to wrong choices at particular moments rather than to flawed strategy. 'As Lady Bracknell might have said', one reviewer of *The Socialist Agenda* wrote, 'to be blown off course once is a misfortune; to be blown off course every time you take office suggests a lack of seaworthiness in the vessel'.[23] Susan Crosland's biography was published the following year, painting a unique personal portrait but not attempting a detailed response to her late husband's political critics.

There was a further reason why some of Crosland's detractors went unanswered. In his lifetime he had always attracted more admirers than followers, and with the creation of the SDP there were few in senior Labour ranks who were determined to keep the Croslandite flame burning. The one notable exception was Roy Hattersley, deputy leader of the party under Foot's successor, Neil Kinnock. Throughout the 1980s and beyond, Hattersley resolutely stuck to the view that Crosland provided 'the only theory of democratic socialism that we need'.[24] But Croslandite themes found little resonance in official policy as Kinnock painstakingly sought to return Labour to the centre ground of politics, and Crosland's rhetoric seemed even more remote under 'New Labour' as it evolved in the 1990s. Tony Blair's successful attempt as opposition leader to amend Clause Four of the party's constitution – removing the nationalisation objective – might be regarded as a retrospective victory for Crosland. In spite of a similar wish to 'modernise', however, the differences between the 1970s and the 1990s were more striking than the similarities. Many of the hallmarks of Crosland's politics were absent by the time Blair swept to power in 1997: the commitment to high public spending and redistribution, the concern for economic and social equality, the importance attached to libertarianism and the willingness to proclaim openly 'socialist' ambitions.[25] Croslandism, despite the best efforts of its adherents, had not managed to 'rise from the ashes'.

So where should Crosland's reputation stand more than twenty years after his death? There are strong reasons why it is inappropriate to conclude that he died a tragic figure, his 'project in ruins' and with little lasting impact on British politics. In the first place, as we saw in looking at the IMF crisis, Callaghan's government emerged bloodied but unbowed from the events of 1976, and was ahead again in the opinion polls within eighteen months. Far from there being terminal 'overload', public spending remained high as ministers redoubled their efforts to undo the damage caused by the IMF cuts. *At the time of his death*, in other words, it was not clear that the Foreign Secretary's 'project' was ruined beyond repair; the decisive damage to Labour as a governing party came later, in the first half of 1979.

The second reason that Crosland deserves an important place in Labour history is that, *looking backwards from 1977*, he could claim notable achievements, both in outlining a coherent political theory and in attempting to put that theory into effect. His contribution as a minister was all the more striking given that he was never in a position to make the key decisions in economic policy. In the early days of Wilson's 1964 government he complained to David Owen that 'it was just Harold and Jim fixing things between them'; his frustration on this score was felt even more acutely after Jenkins became Chancellor in 1967.[26] His own shortcomings may have played a part in denying him earlier promotion to the senior ranks, but so too did Harold Wilson, who consistently denied Crosland the key offices he needed to shape events. As David Reisman has written, it was only at the Treasury that Crosland would have been in a position to reshape the tax system, to propose alternatives to periodic deflation and to search for new ways of stimulating economic growth.[27]

'Croslandism' at no stage fully encapsulated Labour thinking. The terms Croslandism, revisionism and social democracy are often used without distinction, each being characterised by a commitment to neo-Keynesian economics and progressive social reform, but Croslandism, as we have seen, emphasised equality with a force and commitment that was not shared by many so-called revisionists or social democrats. In an interview during 1974 Crosland was asked what he meant by socialism:

> I've always thought that Socialism was fundamentally about greater equality, and by greater equality I don't mean simply more equality of opportunities so that the strong can get to the top more easily, I don't mean simply more equality of income, crucially important though that is. . . . I meant a wider social equality which would also cover the distribution of property, which would also cover the educational system

. . . would also cover relationships in industry. . . . I think to me that is what Socialism means, that we should have a more equal and more egalitarian, which I would consider a more just society.[28]

This overriding concern with equality was never made the corner-stone of Labour policy. In a party where competing visions overlapped, and where the temporary domination of one strand of thought did not eliminate others, there had been moves in a Croslandite direction during the period of Gaitskell's leadership, in spite of resistance from the left. John Vaizey has described Hugh Gaitskell as the 'political embodiment of what Crosland stood for'; but the prospect of egalitarianism becoming the 'big idea' of Labour policy in the 1960s disappeared with the death of Gaitskell. This, in Vaizey's words, relegated 'Crosland's brand of democratic socialism to the place of a theory rather than to that of a tested experiment'.[29] There were many reforms carried out under Wilson of which Crosland approved and which furthered his objectives, but he remained convinced that Wilson had no deep-seated attachment to egalitarianism. It was not simply confinement to middle-ranking posts that left Crosland disgruntled. As David Lipsey notes, he grew increasingly out of sorts with the 'conservative pragmatism of the post-Gaitskell Labour leadership'. In this light, Croslandism had 'not been tried'.[30]

Wilson's administrations did, however, encourage trends which Crosland's critics – writing against the troubled backcloth of the early Thatcher years – tend to overlook. In spite of the resistance he encountered to the type of strategy outlined in his writings, Crosland was able to claim that Britain in the 1970s was a more equal society than when he first went into politics. The exhaustive researches of a Royal Commission on the distribution of income and wealth, chaired by Lord Diamond, found that both in terms of post-tax income and capital wealth there had been steady and continuous redistribution since the war. The top 10 per cent of earners com-manded 21.4 per cent of total personal incomes in the mid-1970s, compared with 34.6 per cent in 1939.[31] Crosland was the first to accept that poverty and class inequalities remained, but in his eyes the 'evidence of increasing equality is surely undeniable'. It was reflected, he noted, in the improved social capital of the nation, such as better-equipped schools, new recreation facilities and local authority housing built to higher standards than before. Writing in 1975,

Crosland argued that the 'gloom and doom merchants' exaggerated their case. Surveys showed that the populace at large was no more discontented than in previous generations, and he could also point to progress on libertarian reform and cultural opportunities, if not on standards of architecture and urban planning. As John Vaizey noted at the time of Crosland's death, the average standard of living was 'emphatically higher' than anybody could have anticipated 'when the guns stopped firing in 1945'.[32]

Crosland not only played a pivotal role in helping to forge the intellectual climate which underpinned moves towards greater equality. He also made a lasting personal contribution to the cause he espoused, a contribution downplayed by his detractors. Crosland may not have been able to control economic policy as Chancellor, but his memory lives on in two key reforms he initiated as Secretary of State for Education. In the early 1970s he claimed that, in time, both comprehensive schools and polytechnics would increase opportunities in education and so enhance the drive towards social equality. A generation later these claims were being borne out at a time when the majority of children had access to comprehensive education, and the polytechnics were being awarded university status. An authoritative study based on 1500 comprehensive schools found that, with the injustices of the grammar–secondary-modern school divide removed, average standards had risen steadily since the late 1960s. In the polytechnics, numbers had grown fivefold since Crosland's time at the DES, with twice as many part-time students than at established universities and greater numbers of women and students from ethnic backgrounds.[33] Notwithstanding the endurance of these Croslandite legacies, there was no immutable law which dictated that Britain would always progress towards greater equality. At the end of a period of uninterrupted Conservative government under Margaret Thatcher and John Major, the Institute of Fiscal Studies reported in 1997 that Britain had become far more unequal over the previous two decades: a 'parade of dwarves and a few giants', in which the gap between the rich and the poor had widened sharply.[34]

With the benefit of hindsight, also, harsh assessments of his career and legacy now seem misplaced. In the light of key political developments in the late 1970s and 1980s, foreshadowed during Crosland's life, Croslandism has an enhanced appeal in relation to the rival creeds emerging towards the end of his life. He would certainly have been unimpressed by what occurred at opposite ends of the political spectrum after his death. In 1983 the Labour leader, Michael Foot, presented the electorate with a manifesto of a nature that Crosland had always resisted, including commitments to unilateral nuclear disarmament and extensive nationalisation. The result was the party's most crushing defeat since the Second World War, with a share of the vote that threatened Labour's prospects of remaining the main opposition force. Crosland, without question, would have been equally dismayed by the development of Thatcherism. As David Lipsey notes, he felt 'wholehearted disgust' for what he experienced as 'Heath, mark 1', and he would have 'loathed' the 1980s variety, with its 'concentration on the bourgeois virtues, its celebration of inequality . . . and its accompanying attitudes of intolerance, whether of blacks, "scroungers" or trade unionists'.[35]

Crosland would also have eschewed the erstwhile Labour revisionists who joined the Social Democratic Party. There is widespread agreement that, had he lived, Crosland would not have joined with those who left Labour to form the SDP. This was not simply a matter of his deep affection for the party, going back to his youth, or his suspicion – in David Lipsey's words – of the 'fluffy liberalism' of some of the disaffected moderates. It also reflected his belief that Conservatism could only be effectively opposed by a broad-based Labour coalition, led by a leadership which held the centre ground against the extremes of left and right in the party.[36] If the balance tilted too much in one direction, the answer was not to abandon the ship. Rather, it was to continue making the case from the inside for radical but sensible Labour policies – 'furious moderation', as it was once called – just as he had in the days of Gaitskell and was still attempting during the IMF crisis. Those who joined the SDP would dispute the claim, made by moderates such as Roy Hattersley who remained in Labour ranks, that it was the defectors who 'exposed Britain to a full decade of Thatcherism'. Despite the claims of the SDP, the mould of British politics was not broken. A generation later it was a Labour Prime Minister who sat in Downing Street, and Social Democrats – many of whom rejoined 'New Labour' – were left to reflect that they had failed to produce any comprehensive political theory such as Crosland had produced in his day.[37]

Judgements made about Crosland at the time of his death thus carry more weight than some of the later, more critical assessments.

'His was a unique career,' wrote his American friend Daniel Bell, 'a reflective mind of great intellectual power and curiosity who also lived the active life of the socialist politician.'[38] *The Future of Socialism* put him on a par with the leading left-wing writers of the twentieth century such as Tawney and Durbin. He had come closer than anyone in post-war politics to outlining a persuasive theory which combined 'liberty *as well* as equality, prosperity *and* fairness; individual freedom *together* with a sense of one community'.[39] As a minister, he had reached the highest rank below that of the premiership, with a status and reputation which equalled that of his old friends and rivals, Roy Jenkins and Denis Healey. When asked in the 1990s who was the best minister he had encountered, Gerald Kaufman, a veteran of the Wilson–Callaghan era replied without hesitation, 'Tony Crosland', describing him as the greatest loss to British politics in the past generation. Putting together his combined achievements – as a theoretician and as a minister – Crosland deserves to be remembered not only alongside those who died tragically young, such as Gaitskell and Macleod, but also among the ranks of those rare politicians like Bevan and Butler whose outstanding qualities were not diminished by their failure to become party leaders.[40]

Whatever the political problems of the mid-1970s, it is difficult to believe that Tony Crosland died a disappointed man. Confirmation of this came in the last interview he gave to a journalist, on 10 February 1977, only three days before his stroke. Crosland told Ivan Rowan of the *Sunday Telegraph* that he and his wife had agreed that if they were killed together in a plane crash they could have no regrets; it had been a 'marvellous life' and everything had been worthwhile. 'He sat facing me in his room at the House of Commons,' Rowan wrote, 'a long, thin black cigar in one hand, a glass of whisky in the other.' The journalist got the impression from casual references he made to colleagues that the Foreign Secretary did consider himself a leadership contender, especially if Denis Healey remained under a cloud following the IMF episode. Crosland insisted, however, that the leadership issue was not something that kept him awake at night, and David Lipsey rang Rowan the following day to add the thought that Crosland saw himself as a long-distance runner. Forty-eight hours later Crosland collapsed. The *Sunday Telegraph* article became an obituary notice rather than a consideration of the Foreign Secretary's future prospects. The journalist's own view was that Crosland would not have made it to the leadership; there was too much against him, including perhaps that he didn't want it quite enough. But, as Rowan concluded, this may have been no bad thing: 'He died, his wife at his bedside, less than ten minutes' walk from his old college, Trinity. What a marvellous life. What a graceful runner.'[41]

Notes

ABBREVIATIONS

TBD	Tony Benn Diary
ACD	Alec Cairncross Diary
BCD	Barbara Castle Diary
ACP	Anthony Crosland Papers
RCD	Richard Crossman Diary
HDD	Hugh Dalton Diary
PGWD	Patrick Gordon Walker Diary
RHD	Robert Hall Diary
CKD	Cecil King Diary
PRO	Public Record Office

For full references to the above material, including editors of diaries and volumes consulted, see Select Bibliography.

Introduction

1 David Lipsey and Dick Leonard (eds), *The Socialist Agenda. Crosland's Legacy* (London, 1981), p. 1.
2 e.g. Raymond Plant, 'Social Democracy', in David Marquand and Anthony Seldon (eds), *The Ideas that Shaped Post-War Britain* (London, 1996); David Reisman, *Anthony Crosland. The Mixed Economy* (London, 1997).
3 David Marquand, review of Reisman, *Times Literary Supplement*, 4 November 1997.
4 John Vaizey, *In Breach of Promise: Five Men who Shaped a Generation* (London, 1983), pp. 5-6.
5 David Marquand, *The Progressive Dilemma* (London, 1991), pp. 174-6; *Times Literary Supplement*, 4 November 1997.
6 Susan Crosland, *Tony Crosland* (London, 1982); John Campbell, review in *Political Quarterly*, 54 (1983), pp. 109-10.
7 Campbell review, *Political Quarterly*, pp. 109-10.
8 Ben Pimlott review of *Tony Crosland*, *New Society*, 3 June 1982.

Chapter 1 Highgate and Oxford, 1918-40

1 *Observer* profile, 25 July 1965; Susan Crosland, *Crosland*, pp. 3-4.
2 See T. Hinde, *Highgate School. A History* (London, 1993).
3 Susan Crosland, *Crosland*, p. 6.
4 Hinde, *Highgate School*, p. 91.
5 *Bristol Evening Post*, 17 October 1951.
6 *Daily Mail* profile, 23 May 1965; Susan Crosland, *Crosland*, p. 9.
7 Essays contained in Crosland papers (hereafter ACP), London School of Economics, 1/7.
8 B. Harrison, 'Oxford and the Labour Movement', *Twentieth Century British History*, 2, 3 (1991), pp. 226-71.
9 Richard Hillary, *The Last Enemy*, cited in *Observer*, 25 July 1965.
10 Letter by Philip Williams in *Daily Mail*, 10 December 1979; notes by Crosland on various books, ACP 1/11 and 2/17.
11 Denis Healey, *The Time of My Life* (London, 1989), p. 36.

12 *Oxford Viewpoint*, 2, 5, 1949.
13 *Oxford Magazine*, 23 November 1939; telephone interview with Lord Healey, 27 April 1998.
14 J. Campbell, *Roy Jenkins. A Biography* (London, 1983), p. 14.
15 Susan Crosland, *Crosland*, p. 10; Woodrow Wyatt, *Confessions of an Optimist* (London, 1985), p. 179.
16 Private information.
17 *Sunday Times*, 20 February 1977.
18 Roy Jenkins to Crosland, 22 March 1940, ACP 9/1.
19 'The Labour party and the war', January 1940, ACP 2/18.
20 Roy Jenkins, *A Life at the Centre* (London, 1991), p. 36.
21 Attlee to Crosland, 29 April 1940, ACP 9/1; Jenkins, *Life at Centre*, p. 37.
22 Arthur Jenkins to Crosland, 19 April 1940, ACP 9/1.
23 Crosland to Williams, 10 July 1940, ACP 3/26.
24 Vaizey, *In Breach of Promise*, p. 80.
25 Crosland to Williams, 13 March 1945, ACP 3/26.

Chapter 2 Socialist Subaltern, 1940–43
 1 Crosland to Jessie Crosland, July and Autumn 1940, ACP 3/21.
 2 Crosland to Williams, 23 September 1940, ACP 3/26.
 3 Crosland to Jessie Crosland, Autumn 1940, ACP 3/21.
 4 Crosland to Williams, August and September 1940, ACP 3/26.
 5 Crosland to Williams, 29 October 1940, ACP 3/26.
 6 Crosland to Jessie Crosland, n[o] d[ate], ACP 3/21.
 7 Crosland to Williams, December 1940, ACP 3/26; to Jessie Crosland, n/d, ACP 3/21.
 8 Crosland to Williams, 10 February 1941, ACP 3/26.
 9 Crosland to Williams, 19 February 1941, ACP 3/26.
10 Notes on Officer Cadet Training Unit, ACP 3/5.
11 Crosland to Jessie Crosland, n/d, ACP 3/21.
12 Crosland to Jessie Crosland, n/d, ACP 3/21.
13 Crosland to Williams, 15 July, 11 August and 14 September 1941, ACP 3/26.
14 Crosland to Williams, 1 May 1942, ACP 3/26.
15 Major N. Boys to author, 17 March 1997.
16 Crosland to Williams, July 1942, ACP 3/26.
17 Crosland to Jessie Crosland, n/d, ACP 3/21; to Williams, n/d, ACP 3/26.
18 Crosland to Williams, 9 September 1942 and 8 March 1943, ACP 3/26.
19 Susan Crosland, *Crosland*, pp. 20–1.

Chapter 3 On Active Service, 1943–5
 1 Crosland to Williams, 22 May and 24 June 1943, ACP 3/26.
 2 Crosland diary, 4 October 1943, cited Susan Crosland, *Crosland*, p. 23.
 3 Crosland diary, 18 September 1943, ACP 3/1.
 4 Crosland diary, 24 and 25 October 1943, ACP 3/1.
 5 Crosland diary, 8 November 1943, ACP 3/1.
 6 Crosland diary, 8-11 December 1943, cited Susan Crosland, *Crosland*, pp. 23-4.
 7 Crosland diary, 12 December 1943, cited Susan Crosland, *Crosland*, p. 25.
 8 Major Boys to author, 17 March 1997.
 9 Crosland diary, 17 December 1943, cited Susan Crosland, *Crosland*, pp. 25-7.
10 Crosland diary, 14 and 31 January 1944, cited Susan Crosland, *Crosland*, pp. 27-8.
11 Crosland to Williams, 12 February 1944, ACP 3/26.
12 Crosland to Williams, 12 February 1944, ACP 3/26.
13 Crosland to Jessie Crosland, 10 July 1944, ACP 3/21.
14 Cited Susan Crosland, *Crosland*, p. 31.
15 Crosland diary, 11 August 1944, ACP 3/1.
16 Crosland diary, 30 August 1944, ACP 3/1.
17 *Evening News*, 19 February 1977.
18 Crosland diary, 9 January 1945, ACP 3/1.
19 Major Boys to author, 17 March 1997; Susan Crosland, *Crosland*, pp. 35-6.

Notes

20 Cited Susan Crosland, *Crosland*, p. 37.
21 Crosland to Jessie Crosland, 2 and 15 June 1945, ACP 3/21.
22 Crosland to Jessie Crosland, 26 July 1945, ACP 3/21.
23 Crosland to Williams, 8 August 1945, ACP 3/26.
24 Cited Susan Crosland, *Crosland*, p. 40.
25 Crosland to Williams, 14 October 1945, ACP 3/26.
26 Crosland diary, 10 January 1945, ACP 3/1; Alan Neale to Crosland, 9 August 1945, ACP 9/1.

Chapter 4 From Oxford to Westminster, 1945–50

 1 Paper on Crosland by Edward Boyle, 3 August 1976: Lord Boyle papers, Brotherton Library, University of Leeds, MS 660/53625.
 2 Crosland diary, 2 April 1946, ACP 16/1.
 3 Crosland to Williams, 24 March 1946, ACP 3/27.
 4 J. R. H. Weaver (President of Trinity) to Crosland, 24 December 1946, ACP 9/3.
 5 Angus Ogilvy to Crosland, n/d, ACP 9/3; Sir Michael Butler to author, 14 February 1997.
 6 e.g. articles in *Socialist Commentary*, December 1947 and January 1949.
 7 Crosland notes and jottings on various subjects, n/d, ACP 13/21.
 8 Crosland diary, 4 September 1949, ACP 16/1.
 9 Crosland diary, 4 September 1949, ACP 16/1.
10 *Sunday Times*, 3 September 1967.
11 William Rodgers, *Daily Telegraph*, 5 June 1982.
12 This story was told in discussion with Shirley Williams, 13 May 1997. Baroness Williams did not wish the name of the woman in question, a friend of hers at the time, to be disclosed.
13 Susan Crosland, *Crosland*, p. 45.
14 Vaizey, *In Breach of Promise*, pp. 80-1; M. Kogan (ed.), *The Politics of Education* (Harmondsworth, 1971), p. 149.
15 James Callaghan, *Time and Chance* (London, 1987), p. 399.
16 Cited Reisman, *The Mixed Economy*, p. 8.
17 Crosland diary, 27 March 1946, ACP 16/1.
18 Crosland to Williams, 21 April 1946, ACP 3/27.
19 K. O. Morgan, *Labour People* (Oxford, 1987), p. 119.
20 B. Pimlott, *Hugh Dalton* (London, 1985), p. 424; Dalton to Crosland, 20 December 1946, ACP 9/1.
21 Nicholas Davenport, *Memoirs of a City Radical* (London, 1974), p. 171.
22 Crosland to Dalton, 18 November 1947: Dalton papers, London School Economics, 10/3.
23 Pimlott, *Dalton*, pp. 589-90; Davenport, *Memoirs*, p. 73.
24 Pimlott, *Dalton*, p. 589.
25 Dalton to Crosland, 29 September 1948, ACP 9/1.
26 TBD, 11 March 1949, pp. 129-30.
27 Crosland to Dalton, 23 August 1949 and Dalton to Crosland, 26 August 1949, ACP 9/1.
28 Dalton to Crosland, 17 November 1949, ACP 9/1.
29 Crosland to Jessie Crosland, 22 January 1950, ACP 10/1; Crosland diary, 2 February 1950, ACP 16/1.
30 Crosland's election address, 'Let Us Win Through Together', n/d, ACP 7/1.
31 Crosland diary, 3-7 February 1950, ACP 16/1.
32 Susan Crosland, *Crosland*, p. 50; Crosland diary, 15 February 1950, ACP 16/1.
33 Crosland diary, 21-22 February 1950, ACP 16/1.

Chapter 5 Entering the House of Commons, 1950–51

 1 HDD, 25-26 February 1950, pp. 470-1.
 2 Dalton to Crosland, 8 April 1950, ACP 10/2.
 3 Hansard, *House of Commons Debates*, 5th series, vol. 474, 19 April 1950, columns 184-5; RHD, 21 April 1950, p. 110.
 4 *New Statesman*, 16 December 1950.
 5 Dalton to Attlee, 1 September 1950, Dalton papers 9/9.
 6 Callaghan, *Time and Chance*, p. 82; Davenport to Crosland, 15 April 1976, ACP 5/11.

7 HDD, 5 November 1950, cited Susan Crosland, *Crosland*, p. 54.
8 Dalton to Crosland, 25 November 1950, cited Susan Crosland, *Crosland*, pp. 55–6.
9 Dalton to Crosland, 25 January 1951, cited Susan Crosland, *Crosland*, p. 56.
10 Dalton to Crosland, 6 February 1951, ACP 10/2.
11 Crosland diary, January 1951, ACP 16/1; 'The Greatness of Keynes', *Tribune*, 23 February 1951.
12 HDD, 10 April 1951, p. 523.
13 Jenkins, *Life at Centre*, p. 87.
14 HDD, 2 May 1951, p. 541.
15 *New Statesman*, 5 May 1951.
16 Cited Susan Crosland, *Crosland*, p. 57; A. Sisman, *A. J. P. Taylor. A Biography* (1994), p. 198.
17 Robert Boothby to Crosland, 27 May 1951, ACP 4/2.
18 Crosland's election address, 'First Peace, Then Plenty', n/d, ACP 7/2.
19 Lady Frances Donaldson to Crosland, 24 November 1962, ACP 10/3.
20 Cited Pimlott, *Dalton*, p. 588.
21 HDD, March 1951, p. 508.
22 Cited Roy Hattersley, *Guardian*, 23 December 1995.

Chapter 6 The New Fabian, 1951-5
1 Dalton to Crosland, 26 October 1950, Dalton papers 9/10.
2 R. H. S. Crossman (ed.), *New Fabian Essays* (London, 1952), pp. xii–xiii.
3 Crosland, 'The Transition from Capitalism', pp. 33–43.
4 Crosland, 'Transition', pp. 61–3.
5 Crosland, 'Transition', pp. 63–8.
6 *Evening Standard*, 23 May 1952.
7 *New Statesman*, 30 May 1952; 'Fabianism Revisited', *The Review of Economics and Statistics*, XXXV, 3, (1953).
8 *Manchester Guardian*, 23 May 1952; *The Times*, 26 June 1952.
9 J. Browaldh to Crosland, 14 October 1952, ACP 10/1, on favourable coverage for Crosland in Sweden.
10 Crosland, *Britain's Economic Problem* (London, 1953), pp. 5-6 and p. 75.
11 Crosland, *Economic Problem*, pp. 207–22.
12 HDD, 7 June 1953, cited Susan Crosland, *Crosland*, p. 61.
13 *Daily Herald*, 28 May 1953.
14 *Financial Times*, 1 June 1953; *The Economist*, 6 June 1953.
15 *The Listener*, 11 June 1953.
16 *Reynolds News*, 12 April 1953.
17 *Bristol Evening Post*, 26 May 1953.
18 Dalton to Lord Robinson, 14 August 1952, Dalton papers 9/25.
19 Jenkins, *Life at Centre*, p. 89.
20 Hansard, *House of Commons Debates*, 5th series, vol. 540, 20 April 1955, col. 1240–1. See also J. Peel-Yates, 'The Political Activities of Anthony Crosland 1950-64', unpublished University of Leeds MA (1995).
21 Paper by Boyle, 3 August 1976, Boyle papers, MS 660/53625.
22 HDD, 14 December 1951, p. 576.
23 Cited Susan Crosland, *Crosland*, pp. 64–5.
24 RHD, 11 December 1951, p. 188.
25 RCD, 3 December 1953, pp. 280–1.
26 Crosland, Jenkins and Wyatt to Gaitskell, 27 March 1955, ACP 6/1.
27 Roy Hattersley, *Who Goes Home? Scenes from a Political Life* (London, 1995), p. 188.
28 Wyatt, *Confessions*, pp. 178–9.
29 *Observer*, 25 July 1965.
30 Jenkins, *Life at Centre*, p. 103.
31 HDD, 8 January and 6 April 1955, pp. 643 and 662.
32 Dalton to Crosland, 3 May 1955, Dalton papers 9/28.
33 Telephone interview with Bob Mitchell, 8 March 1997.
34 Crosland's election address, 'Fair Shares of Plenty', n/d, ACP 7/3.

35 HDD, mid-October 1954, p. 634 and 28 February 1955, p. 645.

Chapter 7 *The Future of Socialism*, 1956
 1 *The Spectator*, 8 July 1955.
 2 *Observer*, 9 October 1955.
 3 *Bristol Evening Post*, October 1951; HDD, 18 March 1955, p. 653.
 4 Vaizey, *In Breach of Promise*, pp. 84–5.
 5 Dalton to Crosland, n/d, cited M. Francis, 'Mr Gaitskell's Ganymede? Reassessing Crosland's *The Future of Socialism*', *Contemporary British History*, 11, 2 (1997), p. 59. I am grateful to Dr Francis for allowing me to see a copy of this article prior to publication.
 6 C. A. R. Crosland, *The Future of Socialism* (London, 1956). Use of the initials C. A. R. was an Oxford habit that persisted for many years; only his last book in 1974 used the name Anthony Crosland.
 7 *Future of Socialism*, p. 116.
 8 *Future of Socialism*, pp. 216–17.
 9 *Future of Socialism*, pp. 495–7 and 515–17.
 10 *Future of Socialism*, pp. 520–4.
 11 *Daily Telegraph*, 1 October 1956; *Evening News*, 27 October 1956.
 12 *Tribune*, 5 October 1956.
 13 *New Statesman*, 6 October 1956.
 14 Alan Watkins, *Observer*, 22 March 1992.
 15 H. R. Greaves, *Political Quarterly*, 28, 1 (1957); Hugh Dalton, *High Tide and After* (London, 1962), p. 267; *Forward*, 5 October 1956.
 16 *Financial Times*, 1 October 1956; *The Spectator*, 12 October 1956.
 17 Transcript of review by William Pickles, European Service, 'General News Talk', n/d, copy ACP 13/9.
 18 *Fabian Journal*, November 1956, pp. 30–3.
 19 *Guardian*, 22 March 1974; paper by Boyle, 3 August 1976, Boyle papers, MS660/53625.
 20 Crosland, *The Future of Socialism* (London, 1964 edn), p. xi.
 21 *Socialist Commentary*, September 1959, pp. 5–7.
 22 B. Crick, 'Socialist Literature in the 1950s', *Political Quarterly*, 31 (1960), pp. 362–8.
 23 J. Campbell, *Nye Bevan and the Mirage of British Socialism* (London, 1987), p. 271.
 24 Crossman to Crosland, 23 October 1956, ACP 13/10.

Chapter 8 Marking Time, 1957–9
 1 HDD, 27 October 1956, p. 680.
 2 Papers on Co-operative Commission Report, ACP 14/1.
 3 *The Economist*, 10 May 1958.
 4 *Daily Telegraph*, 7 May 1958; *Tribune*, 9 May 1958.
 5 *Scottish Co-operator*, 8 November 1958.
 6 Wyatt, *Confessions*, p. 225.
 7 B. Brivati, *Hugh Gaitskell* (London, 1996), p. 304; interview with Peter Shore, 20 May 1997.
 8 RCD, 11 July 1958, p. 688.
 9 RCD, 21 April 1953, p. 315.
 10 Ian Aitken, *Guardian*, 27 October 1992.
 11 Crosland to Williams, 18 November 1957: Philip Williams papers, Nuffield College, Oxford, 5/3; RCD, 21 May 1958 and 13 August 1959, pp. 686 and 769.
 12 Roy Jenkins, *Sunday Times*, 20 February 1977; Dick Leonard, *The Economist*, 19 February 1977.
 13 Wyatt, *Confessions*, p. 178.
 14 Jenkins, *Sunday Times*, 20 February 1977; Wyatt, *Confessions*, p. 181.
 15 Marquand, *Progressive Dilemma*, p. 166.
 16 A. H. Halsey, *No Discouragement. An Autobiography* (London, 1996), p. 126.
 17 Susan Crosland, *Crosland*, p. 83.
 18 Ann Fleming to Crosland, n/d, ACP 10/3; A. Lycett, *Ian Fleming* (London, 1995).
 19 TBD, 25 May 1957, p. 237; see also Susan Crosland, *Crosland*, p. 85.
 20 Interview with Anthony Howard, 10 June 1997.

21 TBD 17 December 1958, pp. 294-5.
22 Halsey, *No Discouragement*, p. 131.
23 Kogan (ed.), *Politics of Education*, p. 149; Daniel Bell, 'Anthony Crosland and Socialism', *Encounter*, 49, 2 (1977).
24 RCD, 2 February 1959, p. 732.
25 Susan Crosland, *Crosland*, p. 90; *Sunday Times*, 3 September 1967.
26 Richard West, *Time and Tide*, 1 March 1962.
27 A. Thorpe, *A History of the British Labour Party* (London, 1997), p. 146.

Chapter 9 'Mr Gaitskell's Ganymede', 1959-63
 1 RHD, 14 October 1959, p. 215.
 2 TBD, 15 September 1959, p. 312.
 3 BBC radio interview, February 1964, reprinted in *The Listener*, 29 October 1964.
 4 HDD, 11 October 1959, pp. 694-5.
 5 Susan Crosland, *Crosland*, p. 93; Philip Williams, *Hugh Gaitskell* (London, 1979), p. 539.
 6 Crosland to Gaitskell, 4 May 1960, ACP 6/1.
 7 B. Brivati, 'The Campaign for Democratic Socialism, 1959-64', unpublished London University Ph.D (1992), pp. 106-8; Brivati, *Gaitskell*, pp. 362-3.
 8 Susan Crosland, *Crosland*, pp. 100-1; Brian Walden to Frank Pickstock, 18 May 1960, cited in Brivati, 'Campaign', p. 115.
 9 'A Manifesto addressed to the Labour Movement', October 1960, copy in ACP 6/1; interview with Dick Taverne, 20 May 1997.
10 *News Chronicle*, 11 January 1960.
11 *New Statesman*, 12 March 1960.
12 'The Future of the Left', *Encounter*, 14, 3 (March 1960).
13 *Can Labour Win?*, Fabian Tract 324 (May 1960).
14 Memorandum by JD (James Douglas), 17 May 1960: Conservative Party Archive, Bodleian Library, Oxford, 2/21/6. I am grateful to Professor Rodney Lowe for pointing out this source.
15 Crossman, 'The Spectre of Revisionism', *Encounter*, 14, 4 (April 1960); RCD, 28 April and 3 May 1960, pp. 838-40.
16 Michael Foot, *Encounter*, 15, 1 (July 1960).
17 Stuart Hall, *New Left Review* (March-April 1960).
18 'On the Left Again', *Encounter*, 15, 4 (October 1960).
19 Gaitskell to Crosland, 4 September 1960, ACP 6/1.
20 Crosland to Gaitskell, 21 October 1960, cited Susan Crosland, *Crosland*, p. 103.
21 B. Pimlott, *Harold Wilson* (London, 1992), p. 245.
22 Paper by Crosland, November 1960, ACP 6/1; Susan Crosland, *Crosland*, pp. 107-8.
23 RCD, 29 June 1961, p. 954.
24 Paper by Crosland, July 1961, ACP 6/1.
25 Ms notes by Crosland, 'Case for Britain joining', 1962, ACP 4/9.
26 Susan Crosland, *Crosland*, p. 112.
27 *The Conservative Enemy. A Programme of Radical Reform for the 1960s* (London, 1962), p. 7.
28 *Conservative Enemy*, pp. 28-40.
29 *Conservative Enemy*, pp. 174-82.
30 David Marquand, *Guardian*, 15 November 1962; William Pickles, *Political Quarterly*, October-December 1963.
31 Michael Shanks, *Financial Times*, 12 November 1962.
32 Colin Welch, *Daily Telegraph*, 23 November 1962.
33 *Guardian*, 7 December 1962; *Tribune*, 9 December 1962.
34 Michael Barratt Brown, *New Left Review*, March-April 1963.
35 Roy Mason MP, *Plebs* [monthly magazine], January 1963.
36 Cited Susan Crosland, *Crosland*, p. 187.
37 Marcia Williams, *Inside No. 10* (London, 1972), p.211; Davenport to Crosland, 15 April 1976, ACP 5/11.
38 Susan Crosland, *Crosland*, p. 108; *New Statesman*, 18 February 1977.
39 Daniel Bell to Crosland, n/d, ACP 10/1.

Notes

40 *Guardian*, 4 May 1960.
41 *Sunday Times*, 3 September 1967.

Chapter 10 Coming to terms with Harold Wilson, 1963-4

1 *Observer*, 17 February 1963.
2 P. Paterson, *Tired and Emotional. The Life of Lord George-Brown* (London, 1993), p. 124.
3 PGWD, 20 February 1963, p. 277.
4 P. Kellner and C. Hitchens, *Callaghan: The Road to No. 10* (London, 1976), pp. 40-2.
5 RCD, 5 March 1963, pp. 983-4.
6 Pimlott, *Wilson*, p. 267.
7 Susan Crosland, *Crosland*, p. 117; Jenkins, *Life at Centre*, pp. 148-9.
8 TBD, 10 May 1963, p. 16.
9 'Political Institutions and Economic Growth', August 1963, ACP 4/8.
10 RCD, 8 October 1963, pp. 1026-7.
11 Cited Campbell, *Jenkins*, p. 75.
12 TBD, 3 December 1963, p. 81.
13 TBD, 30 November 1963, p. 81.
14 K. O. Morgan, *Callaghan. A Life* (Oxford, 1997), pp. 173-6.
15 Interview with Peter Shore, 20 May 1997.
16 Callaghan, *Time and Chance*, p. 400.
17 George Brown, *In My Way* (Harmondsworth, 1971), p. 90.
18 Interview with Anthony Howard, 10 June 1997.
19 Susan Crosland, *Crosland*, pp. 97-9 and 117-19.
20 Susan Crosland, *Crosland*, pp. 119-20 and 133-5.
21 Interview with Shirley Williams, 13 May 1997.
22 Alan Watkins, *Brief Lives* (London, 1982), p. 33; *Observer*, 18 April 1976.
23 Watkins, *Brief Lives*, p. 34.
24 D. Reisman, 'Crosland's Future: the First Edition', *International Journal of Social Economics*, 23, 3 (1996), pp. 2-55.
25 *Time and Tide*, 1 March 1962.
26 Peel-Yates, 'Political Activities of Crosland', p. 9: the proportion rose from 4 per cent to 30 per cent.
27 'General Election 1964', Report of the Agent, n/d, ACP 7/5.
28 Report of Agent; Crosland's election address, 'Vote Labour for the New Britain', n/d, ACP 7/5.

Chapter 11 Into Government, 1964-5

1 Jenkins, *Life at Centre,* p. 156.
2 Susan Crosland, *Crosland*, p. 126; ACD, p. 2.
3 Jenkins, *Life at Centre*, p. 157.
4 Campbell, *Jenkins*, p. 79; interview with William Rodgers, 3 December 1997.
5 Jenkins, *Life at Centre*, p. 157; Susan Crosland, *Crosland*, pp. 127-8.
6 Susan Crosland, *Crosland*, pp. 128, 130 and 136.
7 Edward Short, *Whip to Wilson* (London, 1989); Susan Crosland, *Crosland*, p. 132.
8 Interview with William Rodgers, 3 December 1997.
9 RCD, 13 December 1964, p. 100.
10 Civil servant Tom Caulcott, cited Susan Crosland, *Crosland*, p. 131.
11 'Outlook for 1965' memorandum by Crosland, 14 January 1965, PRO EW 16/1.
12 Harold Wilson, *The Labour Government 1964-70: A Personal Record* (London, 1971), p. 66.
13 RCD, 22 January 1965, pp. 136-7.
14 Jenkins, *Life at Centre*, pp. 170-1.
15 Wyatt letter to author, 15 April 1997.
16 Brown, *In My Way*, p. 113. For the debate about whether the DEA was a misconception from the outset or a good idea that went wrong, see the witness seminar in *Contemporary British History*, 11, 2 (1997), pp. 117-42.
17 Alan Watkins, 'The New Model Educator', *The Spectator*, 29 January 1965.

Chapter 12 Secretary of State for Education, 1965–7

1 Christopher Price memoirs. I am grateful to Mr Price for allowing me to see an advance copy of parts of his memoirs relating to Crosland.
2 Private information.
3 Sir Herbert Andrew, *Times Educational Supplement*, 15 October 1971; Crosland to Wilson, 13 March 1966, PRO PREM 13/1027.
4 Denis Howell, *Made in Birmingham: the Memoirs of Denis Howell* (London, 1990), pp. 170 and 185; Howell letter to author, 17 March 1997.
5 Kogan (ed.), *Politics of Education*, pp. 152–3.
6 Susan Crosland, *Crosland*, p. 148; DES, Circular 10/65, *The Organisation of Secondary Education*, 12 July 1965.
7 *The Times*, 16 November 1965.
8 'Comprehensive Education', 7 January 1966, copy in ACP 5/2.
9 Wilma Harte on Labour's Comprehensive Policy, 1 September 1967, ACP 5/1.
10 Telephone interview with Bob Mitchell, 8 March 1997.
11 *Times Educational Supplement*, 1 September 1967.
12 Wilma Harte on Comprehensive Policy, ACP 5/1.
13 'Independent Schools', n/d, ACP 5/2.
14 'Public Schools', memorandum by Crosland, 19 November 1965, PRO CAB 128/39.
15 Debate in *Women's Journal*, January 1967; Susan Crosland, *Crosland*, pp.146 and 149.
16 Transcript of interview for 'People and Politics', Thames Television, April 1974, ACP 13/20.
17 Andrew, *Times Educational Supplement*, 15 October 1971.
18 TBD, 15 November 1965, p. 350; Wilma Harte on Comprehensive Policy, ACP 5/1.
19 Kogan (ed.), *Politics of Education*, p. 197.
20 Woolwich Polytechnic speech, 27 April 1965, copy in ACP 5/2.
21 Kogan (ed.), *Politics of Education*, p. 193; Christopher Price memoirs.
22 Susan Crosland, *Crosland*, p. 147.
23 Interview with Denis Howell, 7 May 1997. See also Patricia Hollis, *Jennie Lee. A Life* (Oxford, 1997).
24 Speech at Future of the Polytechnics Conference, 9 June 1972, ACP 5/2.
25 Tyrrell Burgess, *New Statesman*, 29 January 1971.
26 *Education*, 15 April 1966.
27 Halsey, *No Discouragement*, p. 131.
28 Brian Jackson, *New Statesman*, 12 November 1971.
29 Toby Weaver to Crosland, 11 June 1973, ACP 12/4.
30 BCD, 27 June and 20 July 1967, pp. 136 and 140: [page references from *The Castle Diaries 1964-76*, 1990 edn].
31 Interview with Shirley Williams, 13 May 1997; Christopher Price, *New Statesman*, 15 November 1968: 'We must keep up the momentum which Tony Crosland started'.
32 Short, *Whip to Wilson*, p. 163.

Chapter 13 Plots and Crises, 1965–7

1 *Observer*, 25 July 1965.
2 Susan Crosland, *Crosland*, pp. 135, 145, 169 and 205.
3 BCD, 6 February 1967, p. 110; 'Lessons of '66', n/d, ACP 7/6; Ms notes on smoking and drinking, n/d [on DES notepaper], ACP 16/10.
4 Susan Crosland, *Crosland*, p. 153; Crosland to Sir Hugh Carlton-Greene, 25 October 1967, ACP 11/1.
5 Susan Crosland, *Crosland*, p. 152; RCD, 18 April 1965, p. 204.
6 BCD, 27 July 1965, p. 27.
7 Susan Crosland, *Crosland*, p. 172; RCD, 4 August 1965, p. 300.
8 RCD, 12 July 1966, p. 567.
9 Record of lunch with Crosland at United University Club, 12 March 1970. I am grateful to Dr David Butler of Nuffield College, Oxford, for sending me a copy of this source.
10 BCD, 19 July 1966, p. 76.
11 Cited P. Whitehead, *The Writing on the Wall: Britain in the Seventies* (London, 1985), p. 7.
12 Marquand, *Progressive Dilemma*, p. 161.

Notes

13 BCD, 25 July 1976, p. 79.
14 TBD, 18 September 1966, p. 475.
15 RCD, 4 August 1966, p. 603.
16 CKD, 10 August 1966, p. 84.
17 Susan Crosland, *Crosland*, pp. 163–4.
18 Interview with Alan Watkins, 3 December 1997; Susan Crosland, *Crosland*, p. 154.
19 Interview with David Marquand, 27 May 1997; telephone interview with Bob Mitchell, 8 March 1997.
20 Interview with Dick Taverne, 20 May 1997.
21 Interviews with Anthony Howard, 10 June 1997 and William Rodgers, 3 December 1997; Hattersley, *Who Goes Home?*, pp. 55–8.
22 CKD, 20 December 1966, p. 99.
23 Susan Crosland, *Crosland*, p. 172; interview with Denis Howell, 7 May 1997.
24 TBD, 9 August 1966, pp. 467–8.
25 Price memoirs. Christopher Price adds that he thinks he was probably beyond the pale as far as Crosland was concerned after once asking who Bernstein was.
26 David Owen, *Personally Speaking to Kenneth Harris* (London, 1987), p. 39.
27 David Owen, *Time to Declare* (Harmondsworth, 1992 edn.), p. 105.
28 RCD, 17 July 1967, p. 428.
29 Alan Watkins, 'Mr Crosland's Clarion Call', *The Spectator*, 21 July 1967.
30 Watkins, 'Clarion Call'; Matthew Coady, 'The Future of Croslandism', *New Statesman*, 21 July 1967.
31 RCD, 8 June 1967, p. 373.

Chapter 14 Missing the Chancellorship, 1967

1 Susan Crosland, *Crosland*, pp. 166–7 and 181–2.
2 *Sunday Times*, 3 September 1967.
3 RCD, 5 September 1967, p. 462.
4 RCD, 5 September 1967, p. 464.
5 Callaghan to Crosland, 29 August 1967, ACP 5/3.
6 Susan Crosland, *Crosland*, p. 184.
7 Note to George Brown, 15 September 1967, ACP 5/15; RCD, 8 November 1967, p. 561.
8 Susan Crosland, *Crosland*, pp. 187–8; Callaghan, *Time and Chance*, p. 221.
9 Jenkins, *Life at Centre*, p. 214.
10 Susan Crosland, *Crosland*, pp. 188–9; Callaghan, *Time and Chance*, p. 222.
11 Jenkins, *Life at Centre*, p. 215.
12 Jenkins, *Life at Centre*, p. 217; Austin Mitchell and David Wiener (eds), *Last Time. Labour's Lessons from the Sixties* (London, 1997), p. 211.
13 ACD, 7 December 1967, p. 258; Alec Cairncross to author, 26 March 1997.
14 Jenkins, *Life at Centre*, p. 217.
15 Campbell, *Jenkins*, p. 104.
16 RCD, 3 November 1967, p. 552.
17 Pimlott, *Wilson*, p. 488, citing an anonymous interview.
18 Jenkins, *Life at Centre*, p. 218.
19 Interviews with John Cole, 28 August 1996 and Anthony Howard, 10 June 1997.
20 RCD, 30 April 1968, p. 36.
21 Marcia Williams, *Inside No. 10*, pp. 211–2.
22 Pimlott, *Wilson*, p. 488; RCD, 5 September 1968, p. 628.
23 Jenkins, *Life at Centre*, p. 217.

Chapter 15 Anchored at the Board of Trade, 1967–9

1 RCD, 4, 9 and 12 January 1968, pp. 635, 642 and 646; TBD, 12 January 1968, p. 12.
2 Cited Susan Crosland, *Crosland*, p. 194.
3 Jenkins, *Life at Centre*, p. 228.
4 Susan Crosland, *Crosland*, p. 194; TBD, 12 and 15 January 1968, pp. 15–16.
5 Edmund Dell, *The Chancellors* (London, 1996), p. 353.

6 Interview with David Marquand, 27 May 1997; interview with Anthony Howard, 10 June 1997.
7 TBD, 11 February 1968, pp. 34–5.
8 TBD, 14 March 1968, pp. 45–7.
9 RCD, 10 and 12 April 1968, pp. 772–3 and 779.
10 RCD, 30 April 1968, p. 36; TBD, 30 April 1968, p. 63.
11 PGWD, 17 June and 19 July 1968, pp. 322–4.
12 Paul Foot's *The Politics of Harold Wilson*, published 1968, notes by Crosland, n/d, ACP 16/7.
13 Interview with William Rodgers, 3 December 1997; Susan Crosland, *Crosland*, p. 192.
14 *Sunday Times*, 10 December 1967.
15 Interview with Gwyneth Dunwoody, 9 July 1997.
16 Wilfred Beckerman to author, 11 September 1997.
17 George Bull, *The Director*, August 1968, pp. 218–20.
18 Interview with Edmund Dell, 16 October 1997; 'Anna' to Crosland, 5 September 1969, ACP 11/1.
19 *Daily Telegraph*, 5 June 1982; interview with Gwyneth Dunwoody, 9 July 1997.
20 Wilfred Beckerman, *Growth, the Environment and the Distribution of Incomes* (London, 1995), pp. xxix–xxx.
21 Jenkins, *Life at Centre*, p. 261.
22 BCD, 23 October 1968, p. 269.
23 'Socialists in a Dangerous World', supplement to *Socialist Commentary*, November 1968.

Chapter 16 Strife, 1969–70
1 Ian Mikardo, *Backbencher* (London, 1988), p. 176.
2 'For Cabinet on Industrial Relations Bill', notes by Crosland, n/d, ACP 5/4.
3 RCD, 8 January 1969, p. 312.
4 A. Sked and C. Cook, *Post-War Britain. A Political History* (London, 1979 edn), p. 162.
5 BCD, 14 July 1969, p. 351.
6 RCD, 24 June 1969, p. 535.
7 Morgan, *Callaghan*, p. 339; Owen, *Time to Declare*, pp. 155–6.
8 Christopher Mayhew, *Time to Explain* (London, 1987), p. 186; Roy Hattersley, cited in P. Ziegler, *Harold Wilson* (London, 1993), p. 295.
9 Mayhew, *Time to Explain*, p. 187.
10 TBD, 24 July 1969, p. 193.
11 RCD, 2 July 1969, p. 545.
12 Jenkins to Crosland, 16 September 1969, ACP 5/4.
13 Crosland to Jenkins, 18 September 1969, ACP 5/4; Susan Crosland, *Crosland*, p. 206.
14 Crosland to Wilson, 22 September 1969, ACP 5/4.
15 Susan Crosland, *Crosland*, p. 207.
16 RCD, 5 October 1969, p. 666.
17 TBD, 5 and 26 October 1969, pp. 204 and 208.
18 BCD, 15 October 1969, p. 362.
19 'B o T 67–9', notes by Crosland, n/d, ACP 16/7.
20 Wilfred Brown to Roy Mason, 15 November 1969, copy in ACP 11/1.
21 Susan Crosland, *Crosland*, p. 208.
22 RCD, 9 October 1969, pp. 671–2.
23 William Plowden, 'Riding Two Horses: The Crosland Ministry', *New Society*, 1 January 1970.
24 RCD, 17 November 1969, pp. 733–4.
25 'L.G & R.P 69–70', notes by Crosland, n/d, ACP 16/7.
26 RCD, 5 February 1970, p. 806.
27 CKD, 11 May 1970, p. 324.
28 RCD, 8 March 1970, p. 649; Jenkins, *Life at Centre*, p. 298.
29 Whitehead, *Writing on the Wall*, p. 44.
30 Crosland's election address, 'Make Britain a Still Better Place to Live in', n/d, ACP 7/7.
31 Jenkins, *Life at Centre*, p. 300.
32 D. Butler and M. Pinto-Duschinsky, *The British General Election of 1970* (London, 1971), pp. 337–51.

33 RCD, 15 February 1970, p. 819; TBD, 8 April 1970, p. 260.
34 John Cole, *As It Seemed To Me* (London, 1995), pp. 76-7.

Chapter 17 'A Full-Time Politician', 1970–71
1 Comments on Wilson's *The Labour Government*, n/d, ACP 16/7.
2 Susan Crosland, *Crosland*, p. 210; TBD 24 June 1970, p. 298.
3 Jenkins, *Life at Centre*, pp. 309-10.
4 Susan Crosland, *Crosland*, p. 259; *Observer*, 18 April 1976.
5 Postcard from A. G. Orchard to Crosland, 19 August 1970, ACP 12/4.
6 Watkins, *Brief Lives*, p. 33.
7 Watkins, *Observer*, 20 February 1977.
8 Interview with Gwyneth Dunwoody, 9 July 1997; Marcia Falkender, *Downing Street in Perspective* (London, 1983), pp. 243-4.
9 Peter Jenkins, 'The Train to Crosland Road', *Guardian,* 21 January 1970; *Grimsby Evening Telegraph*, 19 February 1977.
10 TBD, 20 July 1970, p. 301.
11 *The Times*, 25 September 1970.
12 *Guardian*, 8 January 1971.
13 *A Social Democratic Britain*, Fabian Tract 404 (January 1971), p. 2.
14 *Social Democratic Britain*, p. 5.
15 David Lipsey, speaking on BBC Radio Programme, 'The Makers of Modern Politics' by Anthony Howard, 1995; taped recollections sent to author by Gordon Oakes MP, summer 1997.
16 *The Listener*, 11 February 1971; *New Statesman*, 29 January 1971.
17 *Tribune*, 15 January 1971.
18 Brian Walden to Crosland, 8 January 1971, ACP 13/13; *Observer*, 10 January 1971.
19 Susan Crosland, *Crosland*, pp. 212-16.
20 Owen, *Time to Declare*, p. 167; Marquand, *Progressive Dilemma*, pp. 174-5.
21 *Socialist Commentary*, November 1970, pp. 704-5.
22 *The Times*, 25 September 1970.
23 Kogan (ed.), *Politics of Education*, p. 159.
24 Crosland to Wilson, 10 November 1970, ACP 5/4.
25 *Towards a Labour Housing Policy*, Fabian Tract 410 (September 1971).
26 Note of press conference, 15 September 1971, ACP 13/25.

Chapter 18 The Common Market Debate, 1971
1 Ms notes on Europe, 1967, ACP 4/9.
2 Jenkins, *Life at Centre*, p. 318.
3 Ms notes by Crosland, c. May 1971, ACP 4/9.
4 Susan Crosland, *Crosland*, p. 219.
5 'The speech that was never delivered!, early July 1971 – after talking to Hatt, Owen, Leonard', ACP 4/9.
6 *Sunday Times*, 11 July 1971.
7 George Strauss to Crosland, 15 July 1971, ACP 4/9.
8 *The Economist*, 17 July 1971.
9 *Sunday Times*, 18 July 1971.
10 TBD, 17-19 July 1971, pp. 356-8.
11 Susan Crosland, *Crosland*, pp. 220-2; Ms note by Crosland on 1963 Club, 20 July 1971, ACP 4/9.
12 Bruce Douglas-Mann to author, 4 August 1997.
13 Ms note by Crosland, 'Me and Europe', September 1971, ACP 4/9.
14 Susan Crosland, *Crosland*, p. 224; Press statement by Crosland, 29 October 1971, copy in ACP 4/9.
15 Owen, *Time to Declare*, p. 179.
16 Susan Crosland, *Crosland*, p. 229.
17 Owen, *Time to Declare*, p. 178.
18 Susan Crosland, *Crosland*, p. 224.

19 Ms note, 'Me and Europe. Epilogue', December 1971, ACP 4/9.
20 *Sunday Times*, 31 October 1971.
21 Susan Crosland, *Crosland*, pp. 227–8; Ms note, 'Dinner with Roy', 18 November 1971, ACP 4/9.
22 Susan Crosland, *Crosland*, p. 229.
23 Ms notes, 'Thoughts at Salcombe, Xmas 1971', ACP 6/2.

Chapter 19 The European Legacy, 1972–4
1 *Guardian*, 31 December 1971.
2 Speech at Plymouth Polytechnic, 17 March 1972, copy ACP 13/24.
3 Susan Crosland, *Crosland*, pp. 234–5; Crosland and others to Heath, 7 March 1972, ACP 4/16.
4 Speech at meeting of Association of London Housing Estates, 13 May 1972, copy ACP 13/25; *Guardian*, 5 May 1972.
5 *Guardian*, 15 and 16 June 1972; Transcript of Party Political Broadcast, 27 November 1973, copy ACP 13/24.
6 *Daily Express*, 13 December 1972.
7 TBD, 29 March 1972, p. 420.
8 Susan Crosland, *Crosland*, pp. 239–40; David Carlton to Crosland, 12 April 1972, ACP 6/2; telephone interview with Dick Leonard, 18 April 1998.
9 'Memo on Deputy Leadership', enclosed with Carlton to Crosland, 12 April 1972, ACP 6/2.
10 Owen to Crosland, April 1972, ACP 6/2; Owen, *Time to Declare*, p. 205.
11 Press statement by Crosland, April 1972, copy ACP 13/25.
12 Susan Crosland, *Crosland*, p. 243; Ms note by Crosland, n/d, ACP 6/2.
13 Carlton to Crosland, 25 April 1972, ACP 6/2.
14 Susan Crosland, *Crosland*, p. 244; Jenkins, *Life at Centre*, pp. 352–3.
15 Noel Annan to Crosland, n/d, ACP 12/1.
16 Susan Crosland, *Crosland*, pp. 251–2.
17 Phillip Whitehead, cited P. Hennessy and A. Seldon (eds), *Ruling Performance* (Oxford, 1987), p. 283.
18 Susan Crosland, *Crosland*, p. 204; Williams to Crosland, 6 February 1973, ACP 12/4; Dick Leonard to author, 21 May 1988.
19 Taverne interview, cited R. Desai, *Intellectuals and Socialism* (London, 1994), p. 151.
20 TBD, 13–16 May 1973, pp. 32–5.
21 Speech to Rother Valley Labour party, 9 June 1973, copy ACP 13/24; *Observer*, 10 June 1973.
22 TBD, 26 August and 19 December 1973, pp. 61 and 80. See also Crosland, *Social Democratic Britain*, p. 7.
23 Note on talk with Bill Rodgers in Italy, [by Dick Leonard], 6 September 1973, ACP 6/2; telephone interview with Dick Leonard, 18 April 1998.
24 Cole, *As It Seemed*, p. 98.
25 Beckerman to Crosland, 24 February 1974, ACP 12/1.

Chapter 20 *Socialism Now*, 1974
1 Susan Crosland, *Crosland*, pp. 259–60.
2 Leonard to Crosland, 12 August 1972, ACP 13/15; telephone interview Dick Leonard, 18 April 1998.
3 Anthony Crosland, *Socialism Now and Other Essays* (London, 1974), edited by Dick Leonard, pp. 9–11.
4 *Socialism Now*, pp. 17–26.
5 *Socialism Now*, pp. 26–43.
6 *Socialism Now*, pp. 44–8.
7 *Socialism Now*, p. 58.
8 *Sunday Times*, 10 March 1974.
9 *New Society*, 4 April 1974.
10 J. H. Bready, *Baltimore Evening Sun*, 10 April 1974; Timothy Raison, *The Listener*, 21 March 1974; *The Economist*, 27 April 1974.

Notes

11 TBD, 10 March 1974, p. 118.
12 e.g. Peter Jay, *New Statesman*, 22 March 1974.
13 Ian Little to Crosland, n/d and Wilfred Beckerman to Crosland, 6 November 1973, ACP 13/17; interview with Edmund Dell, 16 October 1997.
14 Interview with David Lipsey, cited M. Wickham-Jones, *Economic Strategy and the Labour Party* (London, 1996), p. 86.
15 Giles Radice, 'Revisionism Re-visited', *Socialist Commentary*, May 1974, pp. 25-7.
16 Interview with David Marquand, 27 May 1997; interview with John Cole, 28 August 1996.
17 Notebook, Easter 1974, ACP 16/8.
18 TBD, 7 July 1974, p. 193.
19 'Aug. 74: reflections on Govt.', ACP 16/8.
20 Joel Barnett, *Inside the Treasury* (London, 1982), p. 47.
21 BCD, 30 July 1974, p. 160: [hereafter page references are from the longer extracts found in *The Castle Diaries 1974-76*, 1980 edn].
22 Cited Susan Crosland, *Crosland*, p. 279.
23 Transcript of interview between Crosland and George Gale, London Broadcasting Radio Programme, 'Feedback', 25 April 1974, copy ACP 13/20.

Chapter 21 'The Party's Over', 1974-6

1 TBD, 15 October 1974, pp. 238-9.
2 Susan Crosland, *Crosland*, p. 284.
3 TBD, 15 October 1974, pp. 239-40.
4 TBD, 5 November 1974, p. 258.
5 Cited Susan Crosland, *Crosland*, pp. 281-3.
6 TBD, 18 March 1975, p. 347.
7 Susan Crosland, *Crosland*, p. 291; Cole, *As It Seemed*, p. 126.
8 Barnett, *Inside the Treasury*, p. 64.
9 TBD, 25 March 1975, p. 356.
10 Bernard Donoughue, *Prime Minister. The Conduct of Policy under Harold Wilson and James Callaghan* (London, 1987), p. 62.
11 BCD, 14 July 1975, pp. 460-1.
12 BCD, 4 August 1975, p. 482; Barnett, *Inside the Treasury*, pp. 77-9.
13 'Aug. 75: Reflections on Govt.', ACP 16/8.
14 Speech to Richmond-on-Thames Fabian Society, 20 September 1975, copy ACP 13/24.
15 Crosland to Wilson, 31 October 1975, ACP 5/8.
16 BCD, 6 November 1975, pp. 542-3; Susan Crosland, *Crosland*, p. 307.
17 TBD, 13 November 1975, p. 461.
18 'Xmas 1975: Adderbury', notes by Crosland, ACP 16/8.
19 BCD, 14 December 1975, p. 596; 'Xmas 1975', ACP 16/8.
20 Bruce Douglas-Mann to author, 4 August 1997.
21 A. McConnell, 'The Recurring Crisis of Local Taxation in Post-War Britain', *Contemporary British History*, 11, 3 (1997), pp. 39-62; taped recollections sent to author by Gordon Oakes, summer 1997.
22 *Social Democracy in Europe*, Fabian Tract 438 (December 1975), pp. 6-9.
23 Peter Jenkins, *Guardian*, 26 and 27 November 1975; Joe Rogaly, *Financial Times*, 25 November 1975.
24 Cited Susan Crosland, *Crosland*, p. 310.
25 Cole, *As It Seemed*, pp. 142-4.
26 Interview with Michael Foot, 10 June 1997; Barnett, *Inside the Treasury*, p. 77.
27 Falkender, *Downing Street in Perspective*, p. 244: Crosland and Shirley Williams were the two names uppermost in Wilson's mind for the Treasury.
28 Donoughue, *Prime Minister*, p. 74.
29 BCD, 4 March 1976, p. 670.
30 Susan Crosland, *Crosland*, pp. 308-9.
31 *New Statesman*, 16 April 1976.
32 Draft of Crosland cover note, 12 February 1976, ACP 5/10.
33 *Observer*, 18 April 1976; *Evening Standard*, 14 April 1976.

Chapter 22 The Battle of the Crown Princes, 1976
1 Cole, *As It Seemed*, p. 146.
2 Healey, *Time of My Life*, p. 446; TBD, 16 March 1976, p. 535.
3 Hattersley, *Who Goes Home?*, p. 161.
4 Cole, *As It Seemed*, p. 146.
5 Jenkins, *Life at Centre*, p. 434.
6 TBD, 16 March 1976, pp. 536-7.
7 Susan Crosland, *Crosland*, pp. 313-14; Hattersley, *Who Goes Home?*, p. 161.
8 *Guardian*, 17 March 1976; *Daily Express*, 18 March 1976.
9 Press statement by Crosland, 17 March, ACP 6/3.
10 Callaghan, *Time and Chance*, p. 392.
11 TBD, 17 March 1976, p. 539.
12 Healey, *Time of My Life*, pp. 446-7; *Sunday Times*, 21 March 1976.
13 'Why I am Standing', note by Crosland, n/d, ACP 6/3.
14 Taped recollections sent to author by Gordon Oakes, summer 1997.
15 Hattersley, *Who Goes Home?*, p. 162; Susan Crosland, *Crosland*, p. 316.
16 *Daily Express*, 17 March 1976; *Daily Telegraph*, 20 March 1976.
17 *Sunday Times*, 21 March 1976.
18 *Observer*, 21 March 1976.
19 Susan Crosland, *Crosland*, p. 316.
20 Crosland to Sir Charles Curran, 22 March 1976 and Curran to Crosland, 22 March 1976, ACP 6/3; *Daily Telegraph*, 24 March 1976.
21 Boothroyd to Douglas-Mann, n/d, ACP 6/4.
22 Susan Crosland, *Crosland*, p. 318.
23 TBD, 25 March 1976, pp. 544-6.
24 BCD, 25 March 1976. p. 747.
25 Cited S. Haseler, *The Tragedy of Labour* (London, 1990), p. 119.
26 Kellner and Hitchens, *Callaghan*, pp. 170-2.
27 Lipsey to Crosland, 29 March 1976, ACP 5/10.
28 *Sunday Times*, 21 March 1976.
29 Peter Kellner, 'Anatomy of the Vote', *New Statesman*, 9 April 1976.
30 Cited *Sunday Times*, 28 March 1976. 'Aug. 76', notebook, ACP 16/8: all 'my vague fears/hopes' were based on assumption that election would only come when Callaghan was too old.
31 Interview with Denis Howell, 7 May 1997; Susan Crosland, *Crosland*, p. 311.
32 Lipsey to Crosland, 29 March 1976, ACP 5/10.
33 *Sunday Times*, 21 March 1976.
34 Dick Leonard, 'Memo on Leadership Election and its Implications for the Future', 1 June 1976, ACP 6/4.
35 *Daily Mirror*, 24 March 1976; *Observer*, 21 March 1976.
36 *Guardian*, 9 April 1976.
37 Callaghan, *Time and Chance*, p. 399.
38 Jenkins, *Life at Centre*, p. 442.
39 Alan Watkins, *Observer*, 11 April 1976.
40 BCD, 8 April 1976, p. 761.
41 TBD, 5 April 1976, p. 553.
42 *Guardian*, 9 April 1976; *Observer*, 11 April 1976; Healey, *Time of My Life*, p. 447. Lord Callaghan to author, 7 April 1998 confirms Crosland might have gone to the Treasury later in the administration to give Healey 'a breather . . . both men would have fitted into their new tasks very well'.
43 Leonard, 'Memo on Leadership', ACP 6/4.
44 Alan Watkins, *Observer*, 11 April 1976.

Chapter 23 Foreign Secretary
1 Bill McCarthy, cited Susan Crosland, *Crosland*, p. 324.
2 TBD, 13 April 1976, pp. 557-8.
3 TBD, 9 June 1976, p. 576.

Notes

4 Susan Crosland, *Crosland*, pp. 327 and 340; TBD, 9 June 1976, p. 576.
5 Ms notes by Crosland, n/d, ACP 5/13.
6 Susan Crosland, *Crosland*, pp. 336 and 382.
7 John Killick to Crosland, 8 June 1976, ACP 5/13.
8 Susan Crosland, *Crosland*, p. 339.
9 Interview with Ted Rowlands, 9 July 1997; Susan Crosland, *Crosland*, pp. 325-6.
10 Crosland to Kissinger, 21 September 1976, ACP 5/14.
11 TBD, 23 September 1976, p. 614.
12 Susan Crosland, *Crosland*, p. 371; Kissinger to Crosland, 21 October 1976, ACP 5/14.
13 Susan Crosland, *Crosland*, pp. 337 and 375.
14 Crosland to Kissinger, 17 January 1977, ACP 5/14.
15 Susan Crosland, *Crosland*, pp. 341-2.
16 TBD, 21 July 1976, p. 598.
17 'Aug. 76', notebook, ACP 16/8.
18 Gavyn Davies of the Downing Street Policy Unit, cited Whitehead, *Writing on the Wall*, p. 187.
19 Boyle to Crosland, 20 April 1976, ACP 5/11 (Boyle's italics).
20 Reuters profile by Alan Harvey, 24 May 1976, copy in ACP 15/2.
21 *Observer*, 18 April 1976.
22 e.g. George Gale, *Daily Express*, 2 April 1976.
23 Lipsey minute to Crosland, 22 April 1976, ACP 5/12.
24 Lipsey minutes to Crosland, 16 June and 20 July 1976, ACP 5/12.
25 'Aug. 76', notebook, ACP 16/8.

Chapter 24 The IMF Crisis

1 Memorandum by David Lipsey, 1 September 1976, ACP 13/27.
2 Susan Crosland, *Crosland*, pp. 356-8.
3 'Equality in Hard Times', *Socialist Commentary*, October 1976.
4 TBD, 30 September 1976, p. 616.
5 Healey, *Time of My Life*, pp. 430-1; Barnett, *Inside the Treasury*, pp. 101-4.
6 Cole, *As It Seemed*, pp. 163-4.
7 Bernard Donoughue and Gavyn Davies: cited Morgan, *Callaghan*, p. 547.
8 Callaghan, *Time and Chance*, p. 434.
9 Edmund Dell, *A Hard Pounding. Politics and Economic Crisis 1974-76* (Oxford, 1991), pp. 257-8.
10 Susan Crosland, *Crosland*, pp. 376-7.
11 TBD, 23 November 1976, p. 654.
12 *Observer*, 5 December 1976.
13 TBD, 24 November 1976, p. 656.
14 S. Fay and H. Young, *The Day the £ Nearly Died* (London, 1978), p. 33.
15 Susan Crosland, *Crosland*, p. 380; Donoughue, *Prime Minister*, p. 97.
16 TBD, 1 December 1976, pp. 666-8.
17 Susan Crosland, *Crosland*, p. 381; Hattersley, *Who Goes Home?*, p. 176.
18 TBD, 2 December 1976, p. 674.
19 Barnett, *Inside the Treasury*, p. 105; TBD, 2 December 1976, pp. 678-9.
20 Susan Crosland, *Crosland*, p. 382; Morgan, *Callaghan*, p. 551.
21 Barnett, *Inside the Treasury*, pp. 106-9.
22 Healey, *Time of My Life*, p. 433; TBD, 16 December 1976, p. 688.
23 Cited Fay and Young, *Day £ Nearly Died*, p. 41.
24 Hattersley, *Who Goes Home?*, p. 177: David Hill made soundings towards Tony Benn's assistant, Frances Morrell.
25 *Observer*, 5 December 1976.
26 Callaghan, *Time and Chance*, p. 439.
27 Dell, *The Chancellors* (London, 1996), p. 434; Dell, *Hard Pounding*, p. 285.
28 Hattersley, *Who Goes Home?*, p. 173; interview with Roy Hattersley, 9 July 1997.
29 Healey, *Time of My Life*, p. 431; Callaghan letter to author, 7 April 1998.
30 Healey, *Time of My Life*, p. 402.
31 Hattersley, *Who Goes Home?*, p. 175; interview with Roy Hattersley, 9 July 1997.

32 Cited Fay and Young, *Day £ Nearly Died*, pp. 40-1.
33 Dell, *Hard Pounding*, p. 271.
34 Interview with Shirley Williams, 13 May 1997.
35 'Xmas 76', notebook, ACP 16/8 (Crosland's italics).
36 Jeremy Bray MP, cited M. Holmes, *The Labour Government 1974-79* (London, 1985), p. 98; Peter Hennessy, *Times Educational Supplement*, 1 May 1992.
37 Healey, *Time of My Life*, p. 433.
38 K. Burk and A. Cairncross, *'Goodbye Great Britain'. The 1976 IMF Crisis* (London and New Haven, 1992), p. 228.
39 *Observer*, 5 December 1976.
40 Susan Crosland, *Crosland*, p. 383; Barnett, *Inside the Treasury*, p. 112; telephone interview with Lord Healey, 27 April 1998. Lord Healey added that he was more content about remaining at the Treasury as the economy improved during 1977.

Chapter 25 The Final Weeks, 1976–7
1 Susan Crosland, *Crosland*, p. 383.
2 'Britain, Europe and the World', *Socialist Commentary*, November 1976. In more trenchant style, Crosland was reported as saying that he didn't share the view of pro–Marketeers that this was the most important issue in 'the last eight million years and I'm afraid I've been proved right': Reuters profile, 24 May 1976, ACP 15/2.
3 Lipsey minute to Crosland, 22 December 1976, ACP 5/13.
4 Susan Crosland, *Crosland*, pp. 384-6.
5 Transcript of 'Panorama' programme, 17 January 1977: BBC Written Archive Centre, Caversham Park, Reading.
6 Interview with Roy Hattersley, 9 July 1997.
7 Roy Hattersley, *Choose Freedom: the Future for Democratic Socialism* (London, 1986), p. xix.
8 *Observer*, 20 February 1977.
9 Susan Crosland, *Crosland*, pp. 393-4 and 399.
10 Susan Crosland, *Crosland*, p. 401.
11 Owen, *Time to Declare*, p. 252.
12 Jenkins, *European Diary 1977-81* (London, 1989), pp. 49-50.

Epilogue
1 Cited *The Times*, 22 February 1977.
2 Owen, *Time to Declare*, p. 255; Callaghan, *Time and Chance*, p. 447.
3 TBD, 19 February 1977, p. 42.
4 *Observer*, 20 February 1977.
5 *The Economist*, 19 February 1977; *Grimsby Evening Telegraph*, 19 February 1977.
6 *Daily Mail*, 21 February 1977; *Daily Telegraph*, 21 February 1977.
7 *Financial Times*, 21 February 1977.
8 TBD, 7 March 1977, pp. 57-8; Susan Crosland, *Crosland*, p. 404.
9 Lipsey and Leonard (eds), *Socialist Agenda*, pp. 15-18.
10 Susan Crosland, *Crosland*, pp. 404-5.
11 Cole, *As It Seemed*, p. 149; Falkender, *Downing Street in Perspective*, pp. 244-5.
12 Annan, *Our Age* (London, 1990), p. 416.
13 Entry for November 1980 in Jenkins, *European Diary*, p. 644; Dick Leonard to author, 21 May 1998; Lord Owen to author, 6 and 19 March 1997; Owen, *Time to Declare*, p. 255.
14 Wyatt, *Confessions*, p. 180.
15 Annan, *Our Age*, p. 416; interview with Tony Benn, 9 March 1997; interview with David Marquand, 27 May 1997.
16 *Daily Express*, 21 February 1977.
17 Lord Callaghan to author, 7 April 1998.
18 BBC Radio Programme, 'Makers of Modern Politics'; Bruce Douglas–Mann to author, 4 August 1997.
19 'Anthony Crosland: Labour's Last "Revisionist"?', *Political Quarterly*, 48 (1977), pp. 416-28.
20 'Crosland Reconsidered: The Man who Took too Much for Granted', *Encounter*, 52, 1 (1979), pp. 83-95.

Notes

21 'Inquest on a Movement', *Encounter*, 53, 1 (1979), pp. 9-18; 'Revisionism Reconsidered', in *Progressive Dilemma*, p. 221; *Times Literary Supplement*, 11 April 1997.
22 Leonard and Lipsey (eds), *Socialist Agenda*, esp. pp. 1, 21 and 42-3.
23 Brian Barry, *Political Quarterly*, 53 (1982), p. 353.
24 Roy Hattersley, 'Back to the Future', *Guardian*, 28 September 1996.
25 Raymond Plant, 'The Great Leveller', *Guardian*, 3 February 1997; C. Navari (ed.), *British Politics and the Spirit of the Age* (Keele, 1996), pp. 213-15.
26 Owen, *Time to Declare*, p. 105.
27 Reisman, *The Mixed Economy*, pp. 48-9.
28 Transcript of interview with Llew Gardiner, n/d [spring 1974], Thames Television Programme, People and Politics, copy ACP 13/20.
29 Vaizey, 'Anthony Crosland and Socialism', *Encounter*, 49, 2 (1977), p. 88.
30 Leonard and Lipsey (eds), *Socialist Agenda*, pp. 24 and 26.
31 *Royal Commission on the Distribution of Income and Wealth in Britain*, Cmnd. 6838 and 6626 (London, 1975-6).
32 Transcript of interview with George Gale, April 1974, ACP 13/20; *Social Democracy in Europe*, pp. 6-7; Vaizey, *In Breach of Promise*, p. 7.
33 C. Benn and C. Chitty, *Thirty Years On* (London, 1996); J. Pratt, *The Polytechnic Experiment* (Oxford, 1997).
34 *Guardian*, 28 July 1997.
35 Leonard and Lipsey (eds), *Socialist Agenda*, p. 31.
36 *Guardian*, 21 February 1977; Leonard and Lipsey (eds), *Socialist Agenda*, p. 24; Cole, *As It Seemed*, p. 161.
37 Hattersley, *Who Goes Home?*, p. 189; David Marquand, *Times Literary Supplement*, 11 April 1997: 'New Labour', unlike the SDP, said Marquand, could not be accused of 'offering a better yesterday'.
38 Bell, 'Anthony Crosland and Socialism', *Encounter*, 49, 2 (1977), p. 93.
39 Leonard and Lipsey (eds), *Socialist Agenda*, p. 42 (author's italics).
40 Gerald Kaufman, speaking on BBC Radio 4 Programme, 'The Week at Westminster', autumn 1997; *Sunday Mirror*, 20 February 1977.
41 *Sunday Telegraph*, 20 February 1977.

Select Bibliography

1. Private, institutional and state papers

BBC Written Archives Centre (Caversham Park, Reading)
George Brown (Bodleian Library, Oxford)
Edward Boyle (Leeds University)
G. D. H. Cole (Nuffield College, Oxford)
Conservative Party archive (Bodleian Library, Oxford)
Anthony Crosland (London School of Economics)
Hugh Dalton (London School of Economics)
Patrick Gordon-Walker (Churchill College, Cambridge)
Anthony Greenwood (Bodleian Library, Oxford)
Hansard, *House of Commons Debates*
Labour Party election manifestos, publications and minutes of
  proceedings (National Museum of Labour History, Manchester)
Oxford University Labour Club (Bodleian Library, Oxford)
Public Record Office (Kew, London):
  Cabinet minutes and conclusions
  Ministry of Education papers
  Department of Economic Affairs papers
  Prime Minister's office documents
Philip Williams (Nuffield College, Oxford)

2. Oral sources

See Preface and Acknowledgements for list of interviewees.
BBC Radio 4 programme, 'The Makers of Modern Politics:
  Anthony Crosland', presented by Anthony Howard, 1995.

3. Newspapers and periodicals

Bristol Evening Post, Daily Express, Daily Herald, Daily Mail, Daily Telegraph, The Economist, Encounter, Evening News, Financial Times, Forward, Grimsby Evening Telegraph, Guardian, The Listener, New Left Review, New Society, New Statesman, News Chronicle, Observer, Political Quarterly, Reynolds News, Socialist Commentary, The Spectator, The Times, Times Educational Supplement, Times Literary Supplement, Tribune, Sunday Times.

Select Bibliography

4. Major published works by Crosland
(hereafter books published in London, unless otherwise stated)

Books:
Britain's Economic Problem (1953)
The Future of Socialism (1956)
The Conservative Enemy. A Programme of Radical Reform for the 1960s (1962)
Socialism Now and Other Essays (1974)

Articles and pamphlets:
'The Transition from Capitalism', in Richard Crossman (ed.), *New Fabian Essays* (1952)
'The Future of the Left', *Encounter*, XIV, 3 (March 1960)
Can Labour Win?, Fabian Tract 423 (May 1960)
'Radical Reform and the Left', *Encounter*, XIV, 4 (October 1960)
'New Moods, Old Problems', *Encounter*, XVI, 2 (February 1961)
'The Future of Public Ownership', *Encounter*, XVI, 5 (May 1961)
'Some Thoughts on English Education', *Encounter*, XVII, 1 (July 1961)
Towards a Labour Housing Policy, Fabian Tract 410 (September 1971)
A Social Democratic Britain, Fabian Tract 404 (January 1971)
Social Democracy in Europe, Fabian Tract 438 (December 1975)

5. Memoirs, diaries and contemporary writing
Noel Annan, *Our Age: Portait of a Generation* (1990)
Joel Barnett, *Inside the Treasury* (1982)
Wilfred Beckerman, *Growth, the Environment and the Distribution of Incomes. Essays by a Sceptical Optimist* (1995)
Tony Benn, *Years of Hope. Diaries, Letters and Papers 1940-62* (1994)
—, *Out of the Wilderness: Diaries 1963-67* (1987)
—, *Office Without Power: Diaries 1968-72* (1988)
—, *Against the Tide: Diaries 1973-76* (1989)
—, *Conflicts of Interest: Diaries 1977-80* (1990)
George Brown, *In My Way* (Harmondsworth, 1971)
Alec Cairncross, *The Wilson Years. A Treasury Diary 1964-1969* (1997)
James Callaghan, *Time and Chance* (1987)
Barbara Castle, *The Castle Diaries 1964-76* (1990 edn)
—, *The Castle Diaries 1964-76* (1980 edn)

251

—, *Fighting All the Way* (1993)

John Cole, *As it Seemed to Me. Political Memoirs* (1995)

Hugh Dalton, *Memoirs, 1945-60: High Tide and After* (1962)

Nicholas Davenport, *Memoirs of a City Radical* (1974)

Edmund Dell, *A Hard Pounding. Politics and Economic Crisis 1974-76* (Oxford, 1991)

Bernard Donoughue, *Prime Minister. The Conduct of Policy under Harold Wilson and James Callaghan 1974-79* (1987)

Marcia Falkender, *Downing Street in Perspective* (1983)

A. H. Halsey, *No Discouragement. An Autobiography* (1996)

Roy Hattersley, *Choose Freedom: the Future for Democratic Socialism* (1986)

—, *Who Goes Home? Scenes from a Political Life* (1995)

Denis Healey, *The Time of My Life* (1989)

Denis Howell, *Made in Birmingham: the Memoirs of Denis Howell* (1990)

Douglas Jay, *Change and Fortune: A Political Record* (1980)

Roy Jenkins, *European Diary 1977-81* (1989)

—, *A Life at the Centre* (1991)

Cecil King, *The Cecil King Diary 1965-70* (1972)

M. Kogan (ed.), *The Politics of Education: Edward Boyle and Anthony Crosland in Conversation with Maurice Kogan* (Harmondsworth, 1971)

Christopher Mayhew, *Time to Explain: An Autobiography* (1987)

Ian Mikardo, *Back-Bencher* (1988)

Austin Mitchell and David Wiener (eds), *Last Time. Labour's Lessons from the Sixties* (1997)

J. Morgan (ed.), *The Backbench Diaries of Richard Crossman 1951-64* (1981)

—, *Richard Crossman: The Diaries of a Cabinet Minister*
  Vol. 1: *Ministry of Housing 1964-66* (1975)
  Vol. 2: *Lord President of the Council and Leader of the House of Commons 1966-68* (1976)
  Vol. 3: *Secretary of State for Social Services 1968-70* (1977)

David Owen, *Personally Speaking to Kenneth Harris* (1987)

—, *Time to Declare* (Harmondsworth, 1992 edn.)

R. Pearce (ed.), *Patrick Gordon Walker. Political Diaries 1932-1971* (1991)

B. Pimlott (ed.), *The Political Diary of Hugh Dalton 1918-40. 1945-60* (1986)

Edward Short, *Whip to Wilson* (1989)

Marcia Williams, *Inside Number Ten* (1972)

P. Williams (ed.), *The Diary of Hugh Gaitskell 1945-56* (1983)

Harold Wilson, *The Labour Government 1964-1970: A Personal Record* (1971)

—, *Final Term: The Labour Government 1974-76* (1979)

Woodrow Wyatt, *Confessions of an Optimist* (1985)

John Vaizey, *In Breach of Promise: Five Men who Shaped a Generation* (1983)

6. Biographical

Brian Brivati, *Hugh Gaitskell* (1996)

John Campbell, *Roy Jenkins. A Biography* (1983)

—, *Nye Bevan and the Mirage of British Socialism* (1987)

Susan Crosland, *Tony Crosland* (1982)

Ann Gold (ed.), *Edward Boyle: His Life by His Friends* (1991)

Patricia Hollis, *Jennie Lee. A Life* (Oxford, 1997)

Anthony Howard, *Crossman. The Pursuit of Power* (1990)

Mervyn Jones, *Michael Foot* (1994)

Peter Kellner and Christopher Hitchens, *Callaghan: The Road to No. 10* (1976)

Dick Leonard (ed.), *Crosland and New Labour* (1999)

David Marquand, *The Progressive Dilemma. From Lloyd George to Kinnock* (1991)

Kenneth. O. Morgan, *Labour People. Leaders and Lieutenants: Hardie to Kinnock* (Oxford, 1987)

—, *Callaghan. A Life* (Oxford, 1997)

Peter Paterson, *Tired and Emotional. The Life of Lord George-Brown* (1993)

B. Pimlott, *Hugh Dalton* (1985)

—, *Harold Wilson* (1992)

Alan Watkins, *Brief Lives* (1982)

Philip Williams, *Hugh Gaitskell. A Political Biography* (1979)

Philip Ziegler, *Harold Wilson* (1993)

7. Other secondary works

C. Benn and C. Chitty, *Thirty Years On. Is Comprehensive Education Alive and Well or Struggling to Survive?* (1996)

K. Burk and A. Cairncross, *'Goodbye. Great Britain'. The 1976 IMF Crisis* (London and New Haven, 1992)

Anthony Crosland

D. E. Butler and A. King, *The British General Election of 1964* (1965)

D. E. Butler and M. Pinto-Duschinsky, *The British General Election of 1970* (1971)

R. Coopey, S. Fielding and N. Tiratsoo (eds), *The Wilson Governments 1964-1970* (1993)

E. Dell, *The Chancellors. A History of The Chancellors of the Exchequer 1945-90* (1996)

R. Desai, *Intellectuals and Socialism. 'Social Democrats' and the British Labour Party* (1994)

H. M. Drucker, *Doctrine and Ethos in the Labour Party* (1979)

N. Ellison, *Egalitarian Thought and Labour Politics. Retreating Vision* (1994)

G. Foote, *The Labour Party's Political Thought. A History* (1985)

S. Haseler, *The Gaitskellites. Revisionism in the British Labour Party, 1951-64* (1969)

M. Hatfield, *The House the Left Built. Inside Labour Policy-Making 1970-75* (1978)

P. Hennessy and A. Seldon (eds), *Ruling Performance. British Governments from Attlee to Thatcher* (Oxford, 1987)

T. Hinde, *Highgate School. A History* (1993)

M. Holmes, *The Labour Government 1974-79. Political Aims and Economic Reality* (1985)

A. Howard and R. West, *The Making of the Prime Minister* (1965)

D. Lipsey and D. Leonard (eds), *The Socialist Agenda: Crosland's Legacy* (1981)

R. Lowe, *Education in the Post-War Years: A Social History* (1988)

D. Marquand and A. Seldon (eds), *The Ideas that Shaped Post-War Britain* (1996)

K. O. Morgan, *Labour in Power 1945-1951* (Oxford, 1984)

—, *The People's Peace. British History 1945-1989* (Oxford, 1990)

C. Ponting, *Breach of Promise. Labour in Power 1964-1970* (1989)

J. Pratt, *The Polytechnic Experiment* (Oxford, 1997)

D. Reisman, *Anthony Crosland. The Mixed Economy* (1997)

E. Shaw, *The Labour Party since 1945* (Oxford, 1996)

B. Simon, *Education and the Social Order 1940-1990* (1991)

R. Skidelsky (ed.), *The End of the Keynesian Era* (1977)

N. Thompson, *Political Economy and the Labour Party. The Economics of Democratic Socialism, 1884-1995* (1996)

P. Whitehead, *The Writing on the Wall: Britain in the Seventies* (1985)

M. Wickham-Jones, *Economic Strategy and the Labour Party. Politics and*

Policy-Making 1970-83 (1996)

R. Wicks, 'Revisionsim in the 1950s: the ideas of Anthony Crosland', in C. Navari (ed.), *British Politics and the Spirit of the Age* (Keele, 1996)

8. Journal articles

A. Arblaster, 'Anthony Crosland: Labour's Last "Revisionist"?', *Political Quarterly*, 48 (1977)

K. Burk et. al, 'Symposium: 1976 IMF Crisis', *Contemporary Record*, 3, 2 (1989)

B. Crick, 'Socialist Literature in the 1950s', *Political Quarterly*, 31 (1960)

M. Francis, 'Mr Gaitskell's Ganymede? Re-assessing Crosland's *The Future of Socialism*', *Contemporary British History*, 11, 2 (1997)

B. Harrison, 'Oxford and the Labour Movement', *Twentieth Century British History*, 2, 3 (1991)

T. Jones, 'Labour Revisionism and Public Ownership', *Contemporary Record*, 5, 3 (1991)

S. Ludlam, 'The Gnomes of Washington: Four Myths of the 1976 IMF Crisis', *Political Studies*, 40, 4 (1992)

J. Mackintosh, 'Has Social Democracy failed in Britain?', *Political Quarterly*, 49 (1978)

D. Marquand, 'Inquest on a Movement. Labour's Defeat and its Consequences', *Encounter*, 53, 1 (1979)

D. Reisman, 'Crosland's Future: the First Edition', *International Journal of Social Economics*, 23, 3 (1996)

C. Welch, 'Crosland Reconsidered. The Man who Took too Much for Granted', *Encounter*, 52, 1 (1979)

9. Unpublished theses

B. Brivati, 'The Campaign for Democratic Socialism, 1959-64', London University Ph.D (1992)

M. Donnelly, 'Labour Politics and the Affluent Society 1951-1964', Surrey University Ph.D (1994)

J. Peel-Yates, 'The Political Activities of Anthony Crosland 1950-64', Leeds University M.A. (1995)

Index

256

Index

Index

Marsh, Richard 139, 141, 143
Marx, Karl 7, 16, 28, 47
Marxism 14, 15–16, 27, 44, 45,
    57, 62, 81
Mason, Roy 141, 211
Mikardo, Ian 45, 137
miners' strike (1973) 170, 171
Mitchell, Austin 222
Mollet, Guy 37
Monte Cassino 21
Morris, William 28, 59
Morrison, Herbert 13, 56, 63,
    197
Munich agreement 7–8
Murdoch, Iris 7

National Coal Board 28
National Health Service 36, 40,
    45, 183
National Plan 98, 114, 116
nationalisation 63, 74, 76, 179,
    226, 230
NATO 202
Neale, Alan 3, 5
Neild, Robert 94, 96
New Fabian Essays (ed.
    Crossman) 44–7, 57, 77
New Labour xvi, 226, 230
New Left 62, 70, 78, 81, 84, 85
New Society 142
New Statesman 11, 13, 14, 40,
    47, 49, 76, 110
New York Review 83
News Chronicle 49, 75–6
Newsom, Sir John 107
1963 Club 119, 139, 155–6,
    157, 198
North Africa 16, 18, 19
Northern Ireland 141
Northwich, Cheshire 12

nuclear disarmament 230
Nuffield analysis 77

Oakes, Gordon 184, 190, 195,
    206
Observer 151, 168, 192, 196
Ogilvy, Angus 28
Open University 109
Orwell, George, *The Lion and
    the Unicorn* 11
Owen, David 63, 118, 119,
    158, 165, 220, 221, 223,
    227
Oxford 5–11, 50, 52, 59
    by-election (1938) 7–8
    Democratic Labour Club 219
    Democratic Socialist Club
        10, 15, 25–6, 27
    Labour Club 6, 7, 9–10, 30,
        31
    Labour Party 8
    League of Nations Society 6
    Nuffield College 91, 98
    Radcliffe Infirmary 219–20
    St John's College 219
    Trinity College 5, 6–7, 27–8,
        31, 232
    Union Society 6, 7, 8, 27, 32
Oxford Magazine 8

Pakenham, Lord *see* Longford,
    Lord
Palliser, Sir Michael 200
Pearson, Walter 71, 95
Peel, Sir Robert 181
Pickles, William 60–1
Pimlott, Ben xvi, 33, 79, 126
Plowden, William 142–3
Plymouth Brethren 2, 4
Poland 8

Index